College and University
Business Administration

College
and
University
Business
Administration

REVISED EDITION

AMERICAN COUNCIL ON EDUCATION · Washington, D.C.

Copyright © 1968 by American Council on Education
1785 Massachusetts Avenue, N.W.
Washington, D.C.

Library of Congress Catalog Card No. 68–21824

Printed in the United States of America

Foreword

FIFTEEN years ago the American Council on Education published two volumes under the title *College and University Business Administration*. As the Foreword noted, these volumes were "compiled by a distinguished national committee which over a period of seven years had diligently and effectively sought to formulate the philosophy and fundamental principles for accounting procedures which would serve the broad interests of higher education." The utility of these books is suggested by the fact that 16,530 copies have been sold. The reference, indeed, has become "required reading" for the business officers of American colleges and universities.

Writings about the business management of institutions of higher learning, however, do go out of date. The present revision of the 1952 work was begun in 1964; it is the outcome of a painstakingly achieved consensus of leading experts in the field. It sets forth the best judgments and most informed recommendations for effective practices on the part of general administrators, business officers, and professional accountants. It displays full recognition of the importance of more efficient use of institutional resources in the face of rising unit costs and rising enrollments, new demands for buildings and specialized equipment, more diverse income sources, the expanding volume of scholarship, loan, and research funds, and the wider variety of educational enterprises conducted by most colleges and universities. In short, the present work is not merely a new edition of the earlier volumes.

The present work brings under one cover the basic materials in the earlier separate volumes, updated to reflect changing needs and conditions, new management technology, and modern standards of accounting and reporting. It presents standards to help business officers establish systems and present reports that will be of improved comprehensiveness and assistance as well as more comparable among institutions.

The financial reports of many institutions of higher education cur-

[v]

11623

rently show that they have followed the recommendations of the earlier editions. It is hoped that the present volume will continue to provide the basis for setting commonly understood and widely accepted standards, both for reports and for the operations they summarize.

This volume is directed primarily to the business officer and, in a sense, defines the essentials of this position in the administration of colleges and universities. In many large or moderately large institutions, the complexity of business and financial operations exceeds that of most industrial enterprises. At one time, the business officer was often an accountant or clerk. Today, he is a highly trained professional, and those who have not recently reviewed the increased breadth and scope of his role may find this handbook useful in formulating criteria for personnel selection and evaluation.

This volume will be of interest to trustees, coordinating councils, legislators, and all those concerned with the business and financial affairs of institutions of higher education. Various parts of the book can be used with profit by anyone seriously concerned with maintaining the viability of these institutions. The previous editions have been widely used as texts in special institutes and workshops and in college and university courses in administration. The new volume should be of even greater value.

An outstanding feature of the new edition is its breadth of applicability and its topical scope. It is appropriate for, and can be adopted by, all kinds and sizes of institutions, public and private, regardless of the extent of automated processing methods used or the size of the budget.

The task of the business officer today is in most respects vastly more complex, technical, and difficult than it was when the earlier volumes were published, and it is safe to assume that his role will continue to change in the years ahead. The present edition of *College and University Business Administration* will undoubtedly be an invaluable aid to him in the effective performance of that role.

LOGAN WILSON, *President*
American Council on Education

Preface

THIS single volume, in two parts, is intended to update Volumes 1 and 2 of *College and University Business Administration,* published by the American Council on Education in 1952 and 1955. Part 1 discusses the general aspects of college and university business administration, which formerly appeared as Volume 2. Part 2 deals with principles of accounting and reporting, which formerly appeared as Volume 1.

The probable need to update and revise the earlier volumes was formally recognized by the Board of the National Federation of College and University Business Officers Associations (now the National Association of College and University Business Officers) in 1959 when a committee to consider revision was named. The committee reported the need to revise the volumes and recommended that the project be undertaken only when an adequate budget was available to finance a full-time staff and other costs. In 1960, a national committee was established under the chairmanship of Clarence Scheps and was on a stand-by basis until 1964, when financing was obtained by the American Council on Education.

In April 1964, George E. Van Dyke, who had participated in both the original committee publication in 1935 and in the 1950 revision project, was named full-time editor. He served until December 1966, when he retired. John M. Evans, vice-president for financial affairs of the University of Connecticut, served as chairman of the Editorial Committee during the period of the project and assumed the editorship role for several months after Mr. Van Dyke's retirement.

Early in 1964, a series of regional meetings with business officers and others were held in New York, Chicago, Atlanta, and Los Angeles to obtain general views on the scope of the project and to elicit comments and suggestions for specific portions of the revision. The first meeting of the National Committee to Revise Volumes I and II, *College and University Business Administration* was held in Chicago on May 11–12, 1964. Headquarters for the revision project were located on the University of Connecticut campus in space generously provided by that institution. Work on manuscripts was performed by the Editorial Subcommittee which met regularly every month on week ends in two-day sessions from May 1964 to March 1967.

Members of the National Committee to Revise Volumes I and II, *College and University Business Administration* are, as follows:

Chairman

    Clarence Scheps, Executive Vice-President, Tulane University

Representing the National Association of
College and University Business Officers

    Edward K. Cratsley, Vice-President, Swarthmore College

    Kenneth D. Creighton, Controller, Stanford University

    Kenneth R. Erfft, Vice-President for Administration, Duquesne University

    Lytle J. Freehafer, Vice-President and Treasurer, Purdue University

    W. C. Freeman, Vice-President and Comptroller, The Texas A&M University System

    Robert B. Gilmore, Vice-President for Business Affairs, California Institute of Technology

    Richard L. Helbig, Vice-President for Finance, Cazenovia College

    G. C. Henricksen, Vice-President and Treasurer, Duke University

    Paul W. Hodson, Vice-President—Business, University of Utah

    Gilbert L. Lee, Jr., Vice-President for Business and Finance, University of Chicago

    B. A. Little, Comptroller, Southern University and Agricultural and Mechanical College

    Bruce J. Partridge, Vice-President for Administration, Johns Hopkins University

    James J. Ritterskamp, Jr., Vice-President for Administration, Vassar College

    Daniel D. Robinson, Partner, Peat, Marwick, Mitchell & Co.

Designated by the American Institute of Certified Public Accountants

    Ralph S. Johns, Partner, Haskins & Sells

    Howard A. Withey, Partner, Peat, Marwick, Mitchell & Co.

Representing the U.S. Office of Education

    Paul K. Nance, Specialist for Business Administration, Higher Education Studies Branch

Representing the American Council on Education

    Fred S. Vorsanger, Treasurer and Business Manager

Special Consultants to the Committee

> J. Harvey Cain, Formerly, Chief Financial Officer, New York City Board of Higher Education
>
> R. W. Kettler, Vice-Chancellor for Finance and Management, State University of New York
>
> Lloyd Morey, Formerly, Comptroller and President Emeritus, University of Illinois (deceased)
>
> A. W. Peterson, Vice-President and Trust Officer, University of Wisconsin (deceased)

The Editorial Subcommittee

> John M. Evans, Vice-President for Financial Affairs, University of Connecticut; *Chairman*
>
> Kenneth R. Erfft, Vice-President for Administration, Duquesne University
>
> Robert B. Gilmore, Vice-President for Business Affairs, California Institute of Technology
>
> R. W. Kettler, Vice-Chancellor for Finance, State University of New York
>
> Bruce J. Partridge, Vice-President for Administration, Johns Hopkins University
>
> Clarence Scheps, Executive Vice-President, Tulane University
>
> Fred S. Vorsanger, Treasurer and Business Manager, American Council on Education

Editor

> George E. Van Dyke

This volume represents not only the work of the National Committee and the Editorial Subcommittee but also the suggestions and comments of numerous other interested and concerned members of the profession of college and university business administration. Many business officers contributed by writing drafts of chapters. Manuscripts were given wide circulation.

Financing of the project was made possible by the following educational associations, governmental agencies, and business firms:

> The American Council on Education
> The American Association of College and University
>   Business Officers
> The Central Association of College and University
>   Business Officers
> The Eastern Association of College and University
>   Business Officers

The Southern Association of College and University
    Business Officers
The Western Association of College and University
    Business Officers
The U.S. Office of Education
The Teachers Insurance and Annuity Association
The General Electric Foundation
The International Business Machines Corporation
The Shell Company Foundation
The United States Steel Foundation

Deep appreciation is expressed to the American Council on Education for the unfailing support of its staff, especially Fred S. Vorsanger, and for its financial assistance. A most highly valuable contribution to the volume was made by Price Waterhouse & Co. in preparing for the committee the financial exhibits included in Appendix B. The committee wishes to express its debt of gratitude also to the Editorial Subcommittee —which carried a substantial part of the responsibility—to the dozens of college and university business officers who contributed to this work individually, and to those educational associations, governmental agencies, and business firms that supported the project through contributions and grants. Finally, a deep sense of gratitude is expressed to George Van Dyke, whose devotion and competence served to bring a difficult and complicated job to a successful conclusion.

The Committee to Revise Volumes I and II,
College and University Business Administration
CLARENCE SCHEPS, *Chairman*

New Orleans, Louisiana
May 1968

Contents

PART 2 PRINCIPLES OF ACCOUNTING AND REPORTING

xiii

List of Illustrative Forms

STATEMENTS ILLUSTRATING "APPLIED" METHOD OF REPORTING UNRESTRICTED GIFTS

Part 1

---

*Principles of
Administration*

Principles of
College and University
Business Administration

THE administrative organization of a college or university is designed to help the institution achieve its objectives and serve the purposes for which it exists. Diversity among institutions in size, control, and programs precludes presenting and describing an organizational pattern that is equally valid for all. Within an institution, the success of the administrative plan may be measured in part by the degree to which effective coordination among the divisions and departments has been achieved. The principal areas of administration are at least four in number:

1. Instruction and research
2. Business and financial operations
3. Student services
4. Alumni and public relations

Responsibility for fund raising, frequently called "development," may be combined with alumni and public relations, or it may be recognized as a fifth area.

The organizational plan of an institution should be a description of the responsibility and authority of each principal officer and his subordinates. An organizational chart is helpful in portraying these relationships.

The Administrative Structure

The administrative organization and the scope of the authority delegated to each principal officer are determined by the governing board to the extent that they are not prescribed by the institution's charter.

THE GOVERNING BOARD

The titles most frequently given to governing boards are "board of trustees," "board of governors," and "board of regents." The powers of the body are set out in the charter or in the legislative acts establishing the institution. In publicly controlled institutions, board members are usually appointed by the governor of the state or the parent governmental body or are elected by popular ballot. In privately controlled institutions, the board of trustees is usually self-perpetuating, although some members may be elected by the alumni or by affiliated professional societies. In church-related institutions, the members are often elected by the legislative body of the religious denomination or are appointed by its executive officers.

THE PRESIDENT

A primary responsibility of the governing board is to appoint or terminate the service of the executive officer who is the principal administrator of the institution, usually with the title of "president" or "chancellor." As chief executive officer, he receives from the governing board full responsibility for the administration of all the affairs of the institution. The president in turn delegates authority to administrative officers, each responsible for one of the principal areas.

Often, in addition to the principal administrative officers, other assistants to the president are appointed to do staff work related directly to the office. These assistants may, for example, maintain the records of board meetings and committee meetings or they may be responsible for special institutional studies, projects, and programs.

The number of administrative officers reporting directly to the president should be as few as possible, at best limited to the chief academic officer, the chief business officer, the chief officer responsible for student services, the alumni secretary, and the directors of public relations and development. The president should, however, maintain a strong identification with the institution as a whole.

CENTRAL ADMINISTRATION

The functions of the principal officers should be coordinated through an administrative council or president's cabinet. This body should meet with the president at regular intervals to review and discuss all significant matters involving the administration of the institution. Policy decisions should be determined by their impact on the institution's academic program and its business and financial operations.

The officers sharing the major responsibility with the president for the central administration of an institution are usually assigned the title "vice-president." Usually there will be a vice-president for academic affairs (or provost) and a vice-president for business and financial affairs, who may also be designated as treasurer of the corporation. Because the chief business officer is, properly, responsible for many administrative functions and operations that carry beyond strictly business and financial activities of the institution, the title "vice-president for administration" may constitute a more accurate description of the areas of responsibility usually identified with this officer.

In addition to the vice-presidents, the other members of the president's cabinet usually are the officers responsible for student services, public and alumni relations, and development, when fund-raising activities are a separate area. Many times the title "vice-president" is given to all cabinet officers to indicate their responsibility for a principal area of administration.

Administrative officers are generally considered to be appointed on a continuing basis even though they serve at the pleasure of the president and the governing board. They are usually not granted tenure unless they hold concurrent academic rank or have been promoted from faculty status. Some boards re-elect these officers annually in recognition of this concept.

MULTIPLE VERSUS UNITARY ORGANIZATION

The administrative structure of an institution is determined by its governing board. If the system requires both the president and some other officer or officers to report directly to the board, it is a multiple type of organization. In this type of organization, if an officer reports directly to the board as well as to the president, he is placed in the position of reporting to two supervisors. At a greater extreme, an officer or some officers may report to the board, and not at all to the president. In either case, the arrangement denies the president full authority over all his officers even though in most instances he will be held responsible for the manner in which their duties are performed.

A plan that has proved to be administratively sound is the unitary type of organization, which requires all administrative officers to report directly to the president. The president only reports directly to the governing board. In practice, under this type of organization, the chief business officer works directly and closely with those committees of the board that are concerned with financial affairs, buildings and grounds, new construction, and long-range planning, but he does so as the representative of the president. The president may or may not choose to attend. This same practice may be followed when other senior administrative officers work with board committees.

Inasmuch as the chief business officer and the chief academic officer share with the president the major responsibility for the operation of the institution, they should be present at board meetings. In addition, the president should be permitted to invite other senior administrative officers to attend.

Some governing boards of institutions organized on the unitary plan approve the appointments of the chief academic officer and the chief business officer in addition to naming the president. In such instances, the two chief subordinates should be elected and terminated by the board only upon the recommendation of the president. All other officers should be selected and appointed by the president or by one of his designated chief officers.

Administration of Publicly Controlled Institutions

The principle of unitary organization recommended is applicable to both privately and publicly controlled institutions. Fundamental to the concept of sound administration of publicly controlled institutions is the requirement that the governing board and the administrative officers be free from interference by executive officers of the state or other government. Additional concepts—some cautionary—that apply only to publicly controlled institutions include:

1. *Autonomy*   In some states the governing boards of publicly controlled educational institutions are constitutional bodies coordinate with the executive and legislative divisions of the state or the major divisions of a city government. In other states the authority of such boards is defined by irrevocable charter. In some other states their au-

thority is determined by legislative enactments. If the authority of the board is restricted, its ability to provide the institution with an educational program of quality is substantially reduced.

2. *Coordinated Systems of Administration*   In states that have several separate institutions in a coordinated system of higher education, the patterns of business organization and control for business affairs are various. For example:

Some states have a single governing board for all publicly controlled institutions, with a chancellor (or president) as its executive officer, and with each institution having its own president (or chancellor) and chief academic and business officers. The operational responsibility for business and financial affairs may be a local concern, but everything must fall within plans, policies, and procedures prescribed by the central staff. The central staff also may review performance.

In another type of organization, also with a single governing board, the chief business officer of the coordinated system controls the business activities of the system through what are, for all practical purposes, branch offices located on member campuses. The central office determines general business policies and performs those functions requiring professional specialization on the part of the staff. The branch offices are functionally controlled and coordinated from the main office and have direct responsibility for services only of a local character.

Regardless of the arrangement, the business officer at the local level should be directly responsible to the chief administrative officer of the local campus or institution. His responsibility to the central office should be limited to observing the policies established for the administration of his area of responsibility.

In some instances, states that have established an over-all governing board for higher education have retained local boards for individual colleges or for groups of similar institutions. Several states have three governing boards—one for universities, one for state colleges, and one for junior colleges. Most states have some type of coordinating agency for public higher education in addition to a state department of education.

Institutional Research

Institutional research may include self-studies, long-range planning, studies of space utilization, financial projections, unit cost analyses, as well as a wide range of activities pertaining to the educational and instructional programs and student affairs. If the research programs concern principally business and financial operations, they may be conducted on a full-time or a part-time basis by a member of the staff of the chief business officer. If the research is essentially in the area of academic activities, it should be under the supervision of the principal academic officer. Some large institutions employ one or more full-time persons on the staff of the president to direct such programs; others establish a separate office responsible to the academic vice-president, the sole function of which is to conduct all institutional research.

Although institutional research programs may include self-studies and reports summarizing and analyzing data on finances and operations, they are intended to extend beyond the scope of these usual administrative functions. The research should seek to confirm the adequacy of current administrative policy, or to provide justification for revising policy and operating procedures on the basis of new knowledge or the interpretation of data correlated for the first time.

Staff assigned to institutional research programs must be trained in the techniques of research and have a broad understanding of the aims and objectives of the institution. Projects requiring specialized knowledge may be conducted by using faculty members on a part-time basis under the direction of a full-time coordinator.

Management Information Systems

Before proceeding to the principal areas of business management, a brief review of the growing importance of information systems techniques to institutional administration will be useful. Business officers need to understand both the current status and future possibilities: the evolution of the systems function, the growth in use of electronic computers, and the influence of management information systems concepts on administration.

In higher education, many business officers and other administrators are using punch card equipment and computers to increase efficiency and simplify the business operations. Successful uses have included payroll preparation, classification of personnel records data, accounting, inventory control and reorder notices, allocation of payments to interest and principal, and budget management. In addition, data processing systems are used for student registration class rolls, student grades and grade reports, and transcripts. (Other uses in reporting and decision making—some of them more complex than those already discussed—are cited below.)

The potential value of computer and electronic data processing systems in the decision-making function is predicated on three attributes of the equipment: (1) its ability to accumulate voluminous random information quickly and accurately; (2) its capacity to store the collected data in a central repository; and (3) its ability to analyze and report the data immediately upon request.

These three capabilities in turn call for: (1) computer equipment, commonly identified as "hardware," adequate to receive and store the range and variety of data being accumulated; (2) personnel competent to select the information to be stored; and (3) a skillful director of the system who can specify the forms in which input and output are most useful to administrators.

Whether to embark on use of computer equipment should be determined by the program of services it is expected to provide. The cost of buying or renting the equipment should be compared with the cost of obtaining similar services from manually operated equipment. As more sophisticated computer equipment has been produced, more sophisticated computer programs (which instruct the machine to perform a predetermined pattern of operation) have become available to institutions, regardless of size. Fortunately, an institution can test the potential benefits of computer capability for its own programs by looking into the communication networks—telephone lines or terminal devices —of an independent computer center designed to serve a number of institutions.

The fact that computers can manage complex masses of data in complex ways forces administrators to design each portion of the system so that it is integrated effectively with each other part. It also requires explicit statement of desired outcomes—which in turn cannot be achieved without specific inputs. The basis of any management information system is its central repository of historical and current data—often called the "data bank." It should be designed to accommodate data accumulated from each periodic operation, and its organization should take into consideration maintenance, security, inquiry response time, information retrieval, and costs.

All data collected should be stored so as to serve any required foreseeable purpose. For example, if the admissions office designs a student application form that gathers only the information it needs, without relation to the later needs of the registrar, health services, student government, and office of institutional research, then the data base probably will not satisfy the total needs of the institution. Again, the recording of names and addresses of students, alumni, faculty, and staff should be standardized for such purposes as the mailing of directories, special lists, reports, and the like.

After a central "library" of information has been established, remote terminals can be added for direct input and output of data as well as remote requests for information or analyses by administrative officers. Mechanical devices similar to typewriters, telephones, or television screens can enter data into the system almost as soon as they emerge, say, from processing an admissions application, registering a student, recording a grade, accepting a gift, hiring an employee, paying a bill, purchasing a book, or changing an address. This immediate recording of data at its source eliminates much of the clerical work associated with the conventional movement of papers from one work-station to another.

A management information system offers the significant advantage of a single, accurate, timely, and readily accessible file that can replace dozens or even hundreds of files scattered among various campus offices. As a resource for auditing and supervision, it can help assure that the entire administration is functioning effectively and efficiently.

Files should be designed to supply administrative officers promptly with any information they request. Examples are many. Most Federal programs call for detailed project reports. Legislative bodies may require governing boards to furnish extensive information and figures in support of rising budget requests. Fund-raising programs may need accurate financial or similar critical data to support appeals to alumni and other potential donors. One of the greatest contributions of computers to contemporary educational administration lies in better forecasting: through simulation techniques, alternatives can be explored even though interactions of various forces and events are complex. The effects of various combinations of increased enrollment, rising tuition, and expanded physical plant and staff can be studied as part of the decision-making process. Requests for new courses to meet the changing interests of students must be evaluated in terms of faculty and facilities required to service the demands. Multicampus institutions require skillful allocation of resources if educational objectives are to be met.

Although many institutions are adopting these concepts, some administrators regard electronic data processing equipment as a tool appropriate only for large institutions. The many options available for purchase or rental make size a secondary consideration, for most institutions can gain some of the benefits of mechanized record processing and improved management information by using a small on-premises computer system or by sharing a remotely located computer.

Inasmuch as each institution is unique, the administrator who wishes to exploit system potentials must know what is possible with any given system. He can find out about some of the possibilities by examining what similar institutions have done, and often equipment manufacturers can supply information about new techniques that have been developed by noneducational organizations.

The implementing of an effective management information system requires not only the support of all senior administrative officers, but also institution-wide cooperation. As use of the system expands, it will cross organizational lines, but it should always retain its total-institution character. One major problem is the coordination of use of computer time for administrative data processing and for teaching and research. If the scope of research activities requires extended use of computer time, it may be necessary to establish two computer centers or to rent services for research activities from off-campus computer centers.

Both efficiency and competency of institutional management may be promoted by adopting a carefully designed information system. The improved accessibility, timeliness, and quality of data on which to base decisions and action serve the purpose of helping administrators achieve the institution's educational objectives.

The Administration of the Business and Finance Functions

THE CHIEF BUSINESS OFFICER

The success of the educational programs of a college or university depends in part upon the adequacy of the administration of its business and financial operations. The magnitude of these responsibilities in the administration of budgets and the programs they support requires superior professional training, experience, management skills, and personal qualifications.

Candidates for appointment as a chief business officer should include among their qualifications one or more degrees from accredited institutions along with either special educational training or practical experience as a junior officer in the business administration of an educational institution. Intensive summer short courses and workshops in college and university business administration available at the University of Kentucky and the Municipal University of Omaha help meet the requirement for special educational training.

Business officers should have a demonstrable understanding of the general concepts of educational philosophy and of the functions which their offices must perform. They must administer the physical and financial programs in such a way as to assist in achieving the educational aims and objectives of their institutions while at the same time maintaining fiscal integrity and economy.

ORGANIZATION OF THE BUSINESS AND FINANCIAL OPERATIONS

The statutes of establishment or articles of incorporation may include a section on business organization and procedures. If they do not, the institutional bylaws should incorporate such a section. These statements are usually brief and need to be supplemented by manuals that include all operating procedures, copies of printed forms and instructions for their use, regulations governing the handling of institutional funds, and policies relating to the daily conduct of the institution's business.

Manuals relating to faculty and other staff should be developed to give information and instructions concerning terms and conditions of employment, staff benefit programs, retirement regulations, and all similar employee benefits.

The chief business officer cannot be a specialist in all the operations for which he is responsible. He must be aided by staff members with professional training and experience in the various divisions into which the business and financial operations of the institution are organized. The main divisions of such operations are characteristic of all educational institutions regardless of size and the complexity of their objectives, programs, and organization. The management and administration of the various categories of responsibility are described in detail in subsequent chapters of this volume. They include the following:

1. *Accounting and Financial Reporting* This division may be directed by an officer with the title of "controller." He and his assistants are responsible for maintaining the institutional books of accounts and for accounting, fiscal reporting, and budgetary control. A separate office or section under the controller should be responsible for the receipt

and custody of monies, frequently referred to as the "cashiering function."

2. *Investment Management*   Institutions in which the management of investments is significant assign this responsibility to an officer whose title may be "treasurer" or "investment officer."

3. *Purchasing*   The officer designated as "purchasing agent" should be responsible for all procurement required in the operation of the institution in conformity with institutional policy and established educational practice. He may also be responsible for a system of central stores.

4. *Physical Plant*   The physical plant should be under the management of an officer whose title may be "director of physical plant" or "superintendent of buildings and grounds." He is usually assisted by personnel trained in the principal areas of his responsibilities. These include custodial services; building maintenance; heating, electrical, plumbing, and air-conditioning systems; painting; grounds maintenance; campus police and security; parking and automobile services and pools; repair shops; and similar services to all departments of the institution.

5. *Personnel Services*   "Director of personnel services" is the title most frequently assigned to the officer in charge of this division. His responsibilities include recruitment of all employees except faculty and other academic personnel, and the maintenance of the personnel records for all employees of the institution. He provides information and services relating to staff benefits, training programs, salary plans, and related matters.

6. *Management of Auxiliary Enterprises*   Auxiliary enterprises operated by educational institutions include residence halls and apartment houses, dining halls and other food services, student stores, laundries, barber shops, college unions, parking facilities, recreational centers, camps, printing shops, and other similar services. The officer responsible for the business management of these activities is usually identified as "director of auxiliary enterprises."

7. *Internal Audit*   The staff member responsible for this function must work independently of all departments and divisions. He should follow a program of regular examination of all offices handling funds or accounts of financial transactions.

8. *Systems and Procedures*   The objective of this function, as noted above, should be to develop and implement methods of meeting current business requirements in the simplest way possible. This approach

will involve all aspects of work flow, rather than narrow procedural statements intended to solve particular problems. These activities lead naturally into the development of management information systems, previously discussed, and the officer in charge may have cognizance of the management information system. He should continuously coordinate the activities with the requirements of other administrative officers in order to improve the services and efficiency of the business operations.

9. *Physical Plant Planning and Architectural Services*　Institutions engaged in major expansion have found it desirable to employ a qualified person to coordinate all plans for the development of the campus and plant. Additional assignments given this officer may include: space utilization studies, utilities evaluation, and long-range planning.

Some institutions employ a registered architect to serve as a member of the business staff to coordinate the campus planning and programing preparatory to the work of architects appointed to design new buildings. He should advise the officers of the administration on all architectural matters, work closely with the project architect during the development of plans and specifications, and serve as the institutional representative on problems related to new construction.

10. *Legal Services*　Some institutions have found it advantageous to employ a legal counselor as a member of the business staff, particularly if the volume of legal work is considerable. His services should not replace those of a legal firm that serves the institution on a fee basis.

Professional Associations for Business Officers

The administration of business and financial affairs has become an important field of service in higher education. Business officers administer annual expenditures of a magnitude that place them in a position of major significance to the national as well as the local economy. Inasmuch as the training and management skills required are comparable with those in industry, commensurate compensation is also required to attract and retain persons of ability.

A number of factors have contributed to the professional development of business officers. Major among these are the professional associations of business officers, the first created in 1912 and now known as the Central Association of College and University Business Officers. Since 1920 three other regional associations have been organized—the

Eastern, the Southern, and the Western Associations of College and University Business Officers. In addition, the American Association was organized during this period. Another significant group, which began meeting on both a regional and national basis as early as 1921, is the National Association of Educational Buyers.

In September 1950 the National Federation of College and University Business Officers Associations was founded and, by 1960, had become the National Association of College and University Business Officers. In 1967 this association established an office in Washington, D.C., with a full-time director. The National Association has four basic purposes: (1) to promote the professional ideals, principles, and standards of educational business and financial administration; (2) to collect and exchange information pertaining to the business administration of higher education; (3) to cooperate with and support the regional associations; and (4) to provide the American Council on Education with information and technical assistance on fiscal affairs and to provide the means through which agencies of the Federal Government may be informed on the points of view of colleges and universities on matters involving fiscal and business affairs. Its Committee on Governmental Relations, a standing committee originally constituted in 1948, is principally concerned with research administration and agreements between institutions and Federal agencies.

In addition, there are a number of other organizations that deal with specialized areas of business administration. All the organizations have supported short courses and workshops for training college and university business officers. Together they have made a significant contribution to the profession.

As early as 1910, a few publications in educational business administration were prepared, principally through foundation sponsorship. The first volume that sought to standardize reporting and financial accounting among colleges and universities appeared in 1935 through the cooperative efforts of the regional associations, with financial support from the General Education Board. A series of twenty studies, published during the period 1935–42 by the Financial Advisory Service of the American Council on Education, materially assisted institutions in following the principles of the 1935 volume. Other volumes appeared which were soon recognized as authoritative in accounting for colleges and universities.

In 1949 a National Committee on the Preparation of a Manual on

College and University Business Administration was formed by representatives from the regional associations, the American Council on Education, and the United States Office of Education. This committee prepared *College and University Business Administration,* the first authoritative publication to cover all areas of business administration. Volume 1 appeared in 1952 and Volume 2 in 1955. Representatives of the regional associations meeting as members of the National Association Board voted in 1963 to revise and update the two volumes, and this present single volume constitutes that revision.

2

Legal Problems

THE chief business officer of a college or university needs to know enough of the principles of business law to avoid creating legal problems, to recognize potentially serious problems, and to be able to seek and use legal assistance effectively. Inasmuch as the general principles of business law are available in a number of standard reference works, this chapter will concentrate only on their special applicability to college and university administration.

Court decisions and interpretations of the law vary from jurisdiction to jurisdiction so that decisions made in one state, while having persuasive effect, are not binding in another state. Some principles, however, are virtually universal, and decisions in one state may forecast those to be made in another.

Organization and Arrangements for Legal Counsel

Every transaction entered into by an institution has legal implications; yet it is clearly impractical to seek formal legal advice for every decision. What is imperative is for the administrator to be able to recognize situations that require advice or action by an attorney and to have competent legal counsel available when needed.

A senior official, frequently the chief business officer, should be responsible for coordinating all aspects of legal problems involving the institution. This responsibility should include developing appropriate working relationships with counsel, providing periodic review of the legal implications of corporate action, coordinating inquiries to counsel, and maintaining records and files pertaining to legal action.

Some institutions employ attorneys as members of the administrative staff; others maintain, on retainer basis, a continuous relationship with one or more law firms; still others employ counsel only as specific problems arise. Only large institutions need full-time staff counsel. If an institution depends upon sporadic employment of attorneys in private practice, one drawback is the lack of opportunity for the frequent contact that may prevent small matters from growing into serious problems. Many institutions favor the retainer relationship because it offers not only continuity but also flexibility and freedom of access to the specialties of the firm's members. In any event, the staff counsel or a legal firm on retainer will suggest that specialists be employed to handle important or unusual matters such as patent cases, relationships with a state or municipality, and, perhaps, unusual investment matters or cases involving liability.

Whatever the type of relationship, the institution should not accept legal services as a donation. Almost always such an arrangement makes institutional administrators reluctant to seek counsel and tends to negate the advantages of close and frequent contact with counsel.

Often, tax-supported institutions seeking legal advice are required by statute to use the services of the attorney general of the state, the municipal staff, or other public officials responsible for legal services. In such circumstances an institution should endeavor to have a qualified deputy assigned continuously to its affairs so that he will be familiar with its problems. Even such a relationship usually lacks continuity and restricts familiarity with the institution and its officers. Furthermore, in certain legal situations, the institution may have interests in conflict with those of governmental officials. Therefore, whenever possible, legal counsel should be sought from sources other than governmental officials.

Corporate Organization

Generally, a university or college is a corporation, the powers of which are limited by the terms of its charter or of the statute under which it was created. The authority of the institution includes, by implication, the acts that are necessary to carry out the stated objectives. Courts have usually held that this implied authority extends to operation of residence halls, food services, student stores, and, if appropriate, dairy farms, printing shops, and similar activities related to the basic purposes of the institution. An institution considering the establishment of an unrelated business should seek the advice of counsel to ascertain possible limitations in corporate authority and to identify and evaluate tax implications.

The ultimate authority of an institution usually rests with the trustees as a body; individual trustees seldom have authority to bind the institution except as the governing board may have delegated specific authority for a special purpose. The governing board delegates portions of its authority to administrative officers and to the faculty. Each individual or group has only the authority so delegated, coupled with such incidental authority as may be necessary to accomplish the specified responsibilities. The bylaws of the institution should describe the general powers of the major officers, of standing committees of the governing board, and of faculty bodies such as the senate and the general faculty. A distinction should be clearly drawn, especially in regard to committees and representative assemblies, between advisory responsibility on the one hand and, on the other, legislative or executive authority.

The relationships of an institution and its administrators with public officials may lead to misunderstandings. Although problems are more likely to arise in publicly controlled institutions, privately controlled institutions are also affected through the applicability of general statutes and regulations. Powers of an institution and of its officers are established by the terms of its charter and, in some instances, by the state constitution. These powers may be extended or limited by statutes that are not inconsistent with the charter or the constitution. Each institution should designate one person who is informed in the law and conversant with the affairs of the institution to be responsible for keeping current with proposed legislation and administrative regulations. This person should make sure that they are evaluated by appropriate staff members to determine the effect on the institution. Such review is most likely to be effective when a bill or regulation is in the formative stage, since change is usually easier to achieve before, rather than after, it takes effect when modification requires formal amendment.

If a statute, regulation, or act of a public official appears to usurp the prerogatives or encroach upon the authority of the institutional administration, advice of counsel should be sought and corrective action instituted promptly. Permitting an invasion of authority to continue unquestioned may result in an abdication of a right otherwise reserved to the institution.

Relationships with Students

In general, attendance at an institution of higher education is a privilege, not a right. However, especially in publicly controlled institutions, students who have been admitted may not be suspended or disciplined capriciously. There is no recognized right to representation by counsel or to confrontation of witnesses in disciplinary cases, but the institution's regulations must be administered uniformly and equitably, and due attention must be given the right of a student to a fair hearing before dismissal. Most courts have held that, by the act of matriculating, students accept the authority and regulations of the institution as they exist and are reasonably administered.

There is disagreement among court decisions whether student personnel and disciplinary records are privileged or whether the information they contain must be furnished to investigating officials and the courts. In each instance where the question arises, advice of counsel should be sought. Under no circumstances should confidential or derogatory information about a student be released without careful consideration of the possible exposure to suit for libel or slander. In this connection, administrative officers and faculty members should be reminded of the need for care in preparing letters of personal recommendation, especially if damaging opinions are expressed in such a way that a malicious motive might be imputed to the writer.

It has generally been held that an institution may withhold the transcript of the record of a student who has not fulfilled his financial obligations to the institution. In order to make this right clear, it is desirable to announce such a policy in the catalogue or other suitable publication.

Racial discrimination is prohibited in most situations by Federal law and by decisions of the United States Supreme Court. Other types of discriminations such as by reason of religion, sex, or geographic origin may be prohibited, but if they are related to the fundamental purposes of an institution, they may be permissible.

Most undergraduate students are minors and, consequently, may escape responsibility for certain types of contractual obligations they may incur. In order to enforce commitments against such minors, an institution should protect itself by requiring cosignature of a parent or other responsible adult, especially in documents relating to student loans and to deferred payment of fees.

Institutions are liable for many of the acts of their faculty and staff members. Consequently, situations involving personal hazard to students—for example, in chemistry laboratories, psychological experiments, and athletic events—should be reviewed periodically to ensure that students are adequately supervised, that proper safety procedures are followed, and that appropriate insurance is carried.

Relationships with Faculty and Other Staff

Institutions are subject to governmental regulations concerning hours of employment, working conditions, and terms of payment to staff members. It is generally agreed that institutions are intrastate in character and so are not subject to Federal regulations in labor disputes. Conditions of employment should be drafted with the assistance of counsel and reviewed periodically to ensure compliance with regulations.

The contract of employment is enforceable against an institution. Discharge may result in claims for severance pay or even for damages if the action is such that it injures the professional reputation of the staff or faculty member. The published rules of an institution regarding tenure are part of the employment contract. For this reason, as well as to avoid misunderstanding, the tenure regulations should include specific reservation to the institution of the right to discharge for incompetence or moral turpitude, and because of budget exigencies. These limitations upon tenure should also be included in the statement of regulations.

Discharge for failure to comply with established institutional policies has usually been upheld. In any personnel problem that may lead to discharge, advice of counsel is necessary at an early stage. Throughout any disciplinary or discharge action, administrative officers should adhere precisely to established institutional policies that provide the staff or faculty member with adequate means of appeal and review.

Questions also may arise when a faculty member is serving as a consultant to two parties with possible conflicting interests. Such situations should be the subject of carefully considered and formally adopted and published policy.

No individual should deal both for his employer and for himself in the same transaction. If he attempts to do so, his employer may recover any profit he made in the transaction, and usually may discharge him for breach of faith. Under most circumstances, an institution should not deal with its faculty or staff members or with firms in which they have major interests. Such a prohibition is even more essential if senior adminstrators or members of the governing board are involved. If such a relationship is unavoidable, as might occur if a staff member owns a parcel of real estate needed by the institution, all the facts surrounding the matter should be reported to the individual's superiors and, in most cases, to the governing board. Special care should be taken to ensure that the interests of the institution and of the individual are protected and that values are established by competent and disinterested appraisers.

Institutions receive gifts and grants designed to support the research or other activities of individual faculty members. Despite the identification of the grant with the individual, the institution is responsible for prudent and effective management of the funds. Policies and procedures should be established to safeguard the interests of the institution and the grantor, as well as of the individual.

Interpretations of the rights of faculty members to patentable inventions and to copyrights often lead to confusion. Responsibilities and authority in such matters should be defined in published policy and incorporated by reference in contracts of employment. Further information concerning the administration of patent rights appears in chapter 5, "Administration of Research and Other Sponsored Programs."

Federal acts and many state and municipal regulations prohibit discrimination in employment and in employer-employee relationships. Advertising for positions, personnel policies and records, and personnel practices, all should be reviewed periodically by someone familiar with the laws to ensure compliance.

The authority of any employee is limited to that which is delegated to him by his superiors and to other implied powers that he needs to discharge the delegated duties. However, if he acts outside his authority and if the institution fails to repudiate his actions, the public is entitled to assume that he has full authority for similar actions in the future. Thus, if a faculty member orders equipment that should have been ordered through its purchasing department, and the institution honors the commitment, in the absence of notice to the contrary, the supplier can assume that the faculty member may continue to commit the institution for other purchases. To avoid liability, any misuse of authority should be dealt with promptly and notice given to those who were aware of the action that similar actions are not authorized in the future.

Responsibilities to Donors

By accepting a gift, an institution accepts responsibility for adhering to any restrictions the donor may have imposed on its use. Such restrictions must be observed for as long as the fund is held by the institution and may be changed only by application to a court in an action of cy pres. A more complete discussion of this question occurs in chapter 4, "Management of Endowment and Similar Funds."

If the donor does not impose specific restrictions on the investment of donated funds, in most states the institution is required only to invest them with reasonable prudence. Colleges and universities are not required to limit their investments to securities legally approved for savings banks or insurance companies. One or more investment pools may be established, commingling assets, as long as the equity of each fund is retained and identified.

Many times donors ask advice concerning the tax status of contemplated gifts to institutions. It is permissible, and often desirable, to inform donors of actions planned by an institution, such as the means to be used for evaluation of the gift, if in kind, the plan for application of the funds, or the classification of the gift. However, neither the institution's counsel nor any officer of the institution should give or appear to give legal or tax advice. In every instance the potential donor should be urged to seek the advice of his own counsel or tax adviser, with the explanation that it is improper for representatives of the institution to advise him.

Institutions may receive gifts in kind, such as works of art and rare books. Institutional policy should require that donors have such gifts evaluated by qualified and disinterested appraisers to establish a defensible value on the date of consummation of the gift. In order to protect both the donor and the institution, such appraisal information and values should be recorded in the permanent records of the institution.

Gifts subject to life income sometimes create tax problems, especially for donors. Capital gains on a donated security may be taxable to the donor under some circumstances, especially when the security is sold and the proceeds are reinvested in tax exempt securities. If tax exempt securities are purchased at a premium for a life income agreement, the premium should be amortized to avoid converting principal to income. As a matter of policy, many institutions prefer gifts subject to life income rather than those subject to annuity because of the legal requirements involved in the latter. Each gift subject to life income should be reviewed by counsel before acceptance by the institution.

Relationships with the Public

Institutions are responsible for the actions or failures to act of their officers and employees while performing their duties. Liability insurance should be purchased to protect the institution from claims for negligence. A more complete discussion of such coverage occurs in chapter 7, "Insurance."

Some privately controlled institutions have relied on the historical immunity of charitable institutions from responsibility for negligence. This immunity is being eroded by court decisions and, in some states, by statute, and therefore it should be evaluated periodically by counsel. Publicly controlled institutions may share the sovereign immunity of the state but this, too, should be evaluated by counsel and institutional policy should be formally adopted.

Many contractual commitments are made by issuance of purchase orders. These forms, as well as contract documents for such projects as construction and remodeling, should be designed with the advice of counsel, to make sure their acceptance creates a valid legal obligation, and that they incorporate necessary references to minimum wages, antidiscriminatory practices, and other applicable Federal and state regulations.

Most publicly controlled and some privately controlled institutions have the power of eminent domain. Under this power, an institution may condemn land owned by private individuals or corporations when it is needed for the corporate purposes of the institution. Such condemnation must follow prescribed legal procedures, and entails payment of a sum which is determined by the court to be reasonable for the property in question.

Any continuous use of real property that is adverse to the rights of the owner may, in time, give to the user rights which he did not formerly have. Therefore, with the advice of counsel, institutions should take appropriate action to make sure that any casual but regular use by the public or by specific individuals of paths or roads, or other similar adverse uses of property, are controlled in such manner as to prevent the loss of institutional rights in the property. Similar attention should be given to any encroachment on institutional property of buildings, fences, parking lots, or other facilities.

Problems Relating to Taxation and Regulatory Bodies

Most institutional real property used for corporate purposes is exempt from taxation. In some jurisdictions this exemption applies only to property used for instruction and research and for the housing and care of students; more commonly the exemption applies to all institutional property, including housing rented to faculty members. Real property used for commercial enterprises or held solely as the investment of endowment or other funds generally is not exempted from taxation.

Private institutions are subject to zoning regulations unless they are specifically exempted either by regulations or by general statutes or charter. Publicly controlled institutions are often specifically exempted from the need to comply with local zoning regulations. Reference should be made to institutional charters, statutes, and administrative regulations to determine the extent to which zoning regulations apply.

Revenues, except those from "unrelated business" as defined by the Internal Revenue Code, are exempt from Federal and usually from state income taxes. Revenues from unrelated businesses are taxable and require the filing of income tax returns. Therefore, consideration should be given to forming separate corporations to operate any business enterprises which might be defined as "unrelated" so as to avoid reporting all institutional revenues.

The applicability of sales and use taxes depends upon the statutes which establish the taxes. Institutions are required to deduct Federal income and social security taxes from payments of salaries and wages, and must file with appropriate governmental agencies information forms reporting compensation payments to individuals which exceed specified minimums.

There are frequent changes in regulations concerning the taxability of prizes and of stipends paid to graduate students and postdoctoral fellows. Advice of counsel should be requested to determine appropriate institutional policies and practices.

Compliance with Laws and Regulations

Because of its eleemosynary character, an institution of higher education is accorded certain privileges under the law. In addition, by custom and as a result of the respect accorded such institutions, other privileges often have been granted. In order not to jeopardize these privileges and in order to continue to warrant the esteem of society, colleges and universities should seek to comply in every respect with the spirit as well as the letter of the law.

3

Investment
Management

Oʙᴊᴇᴄᴛɪᴠᴇs and policies of investment management vary markedly among investors. The principles that guide the typical institution of higher education differ in important respects from those of a bank, insurance company, foundation, pension fund, or mutual fund. The differences stem principally from four characteristics of a college or university: (1) its perpetual nature and, therefore, its minimum requirements for liquidity of assets; (2) its exemption from income and capital gains taxation; (3) its need both for current income and for protection of its purchasing power into the indefinite future; and (4) its general freedom from most governmental regulations (this last characteristic does not hold in all cases for publicly controlled colleges and universities).

Investment management for an educational institution involves principally endowment, term endowment, and quasi-endowment funds (the last is also referred to as "funds functioning as endowment"). In the main these types of funds are invested for relatively long periods to provide recurring income for institutional operating purposes. Life income and annuity funds may also be administered on a similar basis.

In addition, an educational institution may have current funds that are not needed immediately for operating purposes and funds that are earmarked for use in due course for plant construction or capital needs. Normally, these funds are invested for relatively short periods, with maturities spaced to coincide with anticipated needs.

A few institutions manage the investment of employee pension funds. These funds require investment policies that differ from those applicable to other institutional funds.

Responsibility for Investment Management

The ultimate responsibility for managing an institution's investments rests with the governing board. This responsibility is usually discharged through an investment committee which sets the over-all policies and reviews recommendations and actions of its investment counselors. The establishment of a committee and the selection of its members should both be considered with care. It is advantageous for all committee members to meet regularly so as to maintain continuity of objectives and policy. Thus, selection should take into account where members live and the ease with which they can attend meetings.

ORGANIZATION

The investment committee may draw upon one or more of the following sources for advice: (1) the institution's chief business officer; (2) a full-time investment officer employed by the institution; and (3) an independent investment adviser such as a bank, trust company, or investment counsel firm.

Whatever the form of organization for managing investments, the president and the chief business officer should be closely involved to ensure that the policies are related to both present and long-term needs of the institution in light of current operations, capital expenditures, and other calls on funds. Otherwise, the portfolio may be managed with too narrow an objective and with inappropriate emphasis, for example, on safety of principal or production of current income. Moreover, the chief business officer should make the investment committee aware in all discussions of the nature of, and distinction between, endowment funds, quasi-endowment funds, and unexpended plant and current funds. The principal of endowment funds is maintained in perpetuity and invested for the purpose of producing present and future income. Term endowment funds may be transferred to other fund groups only at the expiration of the specified period or upon the happening of a specified event. Quasi-endowment funds may be transferred to other fund groups at the discretion of the governing board. Capital gains realized on transactions involving funds other than endowment funds may be expended as the principal is expended.

The size of the portfolio has a direct bearing on the form of management organization. A large portfolio should have continuous supervision by a full-time investment officer with supporting professional staff, or by an independent investment adviser, or by a combination of the two. If an independent investment adviser is retained, the institution should ascertain what other kinds of clients he has and what priority he will accord the problems of the institution.

An institution that has a small portfolio should also provide continuous investment supervision, even though maintenance of an institutional professional staff is precluded by reason of cost. One possible arrangement is to organize a small, closely knit investment committee of the board, all of whose members are to some extent professionals involved with investments in their daily occupations. A second possibility is to retain an independent investment adviser. If this is done, the same inquiries should be made of the adviser as in the case of a large portfolio. The cost of this arrangement will be relatively greater for a small portfolio than for a large one.

An institution that depends on a member of the institution's investment committee for its professional needs runs two risks: If the committee member is active in the investment banking or brokerage business, there may be a conflict of interest. And such an arrangement may become difficult and embarrassing to escape, either if it is not in fact working satisfactorily or if other board members come to believe it is not a good arrangement.

The critical consideration in establishing an investment management organization, regardless of the size of the portfolio, is that the professional nature of the task be recognized by the governing board and officers. Once this is recognized, various forms of organization are possible, and each institution should select the form that best suits its circumstances.

PORTFOLIO SUPERVISION

The procedures for supervision of the portfolio vary among institutions. Sometimes an investment committee of the board may define policy in broad terms and then delegate responsibility for decisions to others, for example, to the institution's treasurer or to an independent investment advisory firm. A more usual arrangement is for the institution's full-time investment officer or an independent investment adviser to operate within the limits of a comprehensive policy established by the investment committee, but with the reservation that the committee continue to control specific decisions. The committee may, for example, exercise its control by approving a recommended list of securities which the investment officer is authorized to purchase at his discretion. The adviser's responsibilities for supervising the portfolio include keeping himself informed on the investments in the portfolio through information developed internally and from other sources such as investment bankers, brokers, and advisory services; preparing recommendations for changes or modifications in investment policy; and preparing recommendations for the investment of new funds received by the institution and for changes in investments. The investment adviser, whether an officer of the institution or an independent counsel, should meet with the investment committee regularly.

Frequency of meetings of the investment committee should be determined by the institution. Quarterly meetings should be considered the minimum. Holding meetings too frequently may lead to undue activity at the expense of long-range objectives; holding meetings too infrequently may inhibit flexibility. Between meetings, especially if they are held infrequently, the adviser should provide committee members with investment information in written form. Procedures must be established to permit prompt action between meetings and may call for frequent contact between the adviser and the chairman of the committee and in some circumstances other committee members as well. Often, when no change in over-all policy is involved, the policy for interim action will include authority to change investments between meetings provided the change is approved by a specified number of committee members.

An investment committee should confine its meetings to matters of policy and to making decisions growing out of recommendations for investments prepared in advance by the adviser. In addition, it should evaluate the degree to which prescribed policy is being followed and the effectiveness of that policy. The committee should rely primarily upon its adviser for the selection of individual investments for purchase or sale.

In establishing policy and in making specific investment decisions, an investment committee should operate on the basis of a consensus of its members. If action can be taken only after unanimous agreement, there is a tendency to minority rule, which often leads to inaction.

CUSTODIAL ARRANGEMENTS

A custodial arrangement with a bank or trust company can be advantageous, especially in facilitating preparation of up-to-date portfolio appraisals and for ensuring the timely exercise or sale of stock rights, presentation of called bonds for payment, and conversion or sale of called convertible securities. It also can be extended to include use of the custodian's nominee name, a device that reduces the complications of transfers and places on the corporate custodian the responsibility for transactions. Further, such an arrangement, especially if securities are held in the name of the custodian's nominee, facilitates the prompt investment and reinvestment of cash, with the resulting benefit of additional income for the institution.

Arrangements for custodian services should be specified by written agreement. They may include safekeeping, receipt and delivery of securities as authorized, collection of coupons and dividends, voting of proxies, notification of calls and maturities of bonds and preferred stocks, information about issuance of subscription rights and of stock dividends, interest defaults, plans for recapitalization, reorganizations, formation of protection committees, and other information requiring institutional action. Also, the bank or trust company reports of custodianship may include listings of security holdings by classes and types and by industries, amounts of interest and dividends received, and amortization schedules.

Under custodian arrangements, receipts and deliveries of securities may be from or to brokers against payments that are charged or credited to a designated bank account or are received or remitted by check.

Regardless of the form or philosophy of an institution's investment management, it is of primary importance that responsibility for investment of funds be defined clearly and that such responsibility be backed by governing board authority.

EXECUTION OF TRANSACTIONS

The arrangement for buying and selling investments will vary with the nature of the portfolio and the form of management organization. The chief business officer or a full-time investment officer employed by the institution should be responsible for executions. This task may involve frequent contacts with investment bankers and brokers. The volume of contacts, however, should be carefully controlled and should be confined to those persons and firms that can provide valuable investment information, opportunities to buy or sell in blocks of securities, and other services of value.

An independent adviser—whether a bank, a trust company, or an investment counsel firm—may have its own trading department with personnel whose principal responsibilities are executions, checking markets, and identifying prospective sellers or purchasers of particular securities. This arrangement affords the services of professional traders with broad contacts in securities markets and knowledge of where to buy or sell most advantageously. Even though the investment counsel executes transactions, the allocation of the institution's business should be determined by the institution in consultation with its investment committee. Most institutions, in determining which investment banking and brokerage firms they will do business with, draw from a relatively small list. The list should include firms that: (1) have the ability to execute orders promptly and efficiently; (2) have good research divisions that can provide a flow of valuable investment information; (3) are active in underwriting new issues or in managing private placements; and (4) make a market for, or deal in, certain securities.

COSTS OF INVESTMENT MANAGEMENT

Costs of investment management include: direct costs of supervision of securities, of investments in real estate, and of other types of investments; cost of custodial arrangements; and other items directly identifiable as expense of investment management. In addition, indirect costs —for accounting and auditing investment transactions—may be included.

Expenses for investment management should be deducted from income before the income is distributed to its appropriate uses so that each fund bears its proportionate share. Otherwise, a fund which, by its terms, requires income to be added to principal, one whose income is severely restricted so that it is usable only infrequently, or one whose income is paid out to a life income beneficiary, will not bear its fair share of the cost of management.

Investment Objectives

The investment objective of an educational institution has traditionally been stated to be the preservation of principal and the production of dependable income. Yet, an educational institution also must consider carefully its needs for future as well as present investment income. Current income is essential to help keep the institution operating, and to this end most institutions invest their portfolios as balanced funds, with both equity holdings and fixed income investments. Future income needs also have important implications for investment policy because of the necessity to offset rising operating costs caused by inflation and other factors. Hence, an institution's investment objectives should be viewed as present income and future income, as well as safety of principal.

If an institution is successful in achieving these objectives, its investment income will grow, over time, through increasing dividends from the growth sector of its equities and also through realization of capital gains and reinvestment of these gains. This objective is not inconsistent with protection of principal.

Investment Policy

After an institution's investment objectives have been determined, the investment committee must translate the objectives into policy. Policy ordinarily will not be developed at one sitting but, rather, will be evolved over a period of time, often as a result of a series of decisions on specific investments. Changes will, of course, be made from time to time in light of the institution's need for current income, the availability of various kinds of investments, the general level of interest rates and of the stock market, the outlook for business and profits, and many other factors. Some changes will be basic; others may be little more than shifts in emphasis.

An investment portfolio will usually include marketable bonds and stocks. However, determinations must be made on the extent to which an institution will include in its portfolio other types of investments, such as convertibles, mortgages, ownership of real estate, private placements, and so on.

EMPHASIS IN FIXED INCOME INVESTMENTS

The investment committee must determine policy for the degree of emphasis to be placed on bond quality ratings, types of debentures, mortgages, leasebacks and other special investments, and the extent to which the fixed income segment should be readily marketable. In addition, consideration should be given to the distribution of maturities of investments, including the role of commercial paper and other short-term securities.

Emphasis in equities investments

With respect to equities investments, the basic decision is the emphasis to be placed on present and on future income, and the balance to be struck between the two. This decision involves the important question of the proportions of the portfolio to be invested in fixed income and in equities investments. Equally significant are the questions of kinds of investments to be included in both the fixed income and the equities segments. In the common stock section of the equities segment, striking the proper balance between present and future income calls for close attention to the proportions of income stocks and growth stocks.

Size and number of individual investment holdings

The size and number of individual commitments depend on the size of the portfolio, its diversification between fixed income and equities, and between industries and companies, the availability at a given time of particular investments, and, in some circumstances, marketability.

It is desirable to establish a figure for a normal commitment and also figures for maximum and minimum amounts, subject to some exceptions. All limits should be in terms of market value. Setting an amount below which the institution will not invest acts as a safeguard against a tendency to hold too many different issues or to make some investments that would not be acceptable for really substantial commitments. In establishing commitment limits for fixed income investments, different issues of the same debtor may properly be classified together.

The list of investments should be kept under constant review. The tendency toward too many different holdings is encouraged both by the volume of gifts and bequests received in the form of securities and by the desire of some donors to have their gifts of securities retained. A useful rule is to require that all securities received by gift or bequest be disposed of as promptly as possible unless prohibited by provisions or terms of the gift or bequest and unless a particular security is already held in the portfolio or is under consideration as an addition to the portfolio in the near future. An unusually large appreciation in the value of a particular holding should not, of itself, require automatic reduction. Size of company, nature of its business, and quality of its management are other relevant factors.

DIVERSIFICATION OF INVESTMENT

Diversification of investments is essential for protection against: (1) unforeseeable trends in the economy; (2) unwise selection or retention of industries or companies; and (3) participation in enterprises involving substantial risk.

Diversification relates to the allocation both between fixed income and equities investments and among various types of securities within each of these categories. Decisions on both aspects will depend upon the investment objectives. The proportions in the debt and equity segments should not be defined rigidly but, rather, stated more generally as a range within which the investment officer or adviser may operate. A leeway of 10 percent from a norm is often selected to provide this latitude. Special factors that affect decisions on proportions are: type and quality of the holdings in the fixed income sector, and emphasis on future, as opposed to present, income in the equities area. These will be discussed in the next section.

Types of Investments

The types of investments commonly held by educational institutions include bonds, debentures, notes, preferred stocks, convertibles, common stocks, mutual fund shares, real estate, leasebacks, and mortgages. In addition, other types may be found, such as ownership of a business and oil and gas production payments.

BONDS, DEBENTURES, AND NOTES

Bonds, debentures, and notes all represent obligations of borrowers to lenders. The principal difference is that a bond ordinarily is secured by a mortgage or pledge of specific property, whereas a debenture or note usually represents simply the promise of the borrower to pay interest and to repay principal.

Various maturities on bonds, debentures, and notes are available, and an institution must determine what proportion of long-term, medium-term, and short-term obligations best meets its need. Bonds and debentures may be in either coupon or registered form, each of which has advantages in special circumstances.

PREFERRED STOCKS

Preferred stocks have a prior claim to dividend payments and other preferences over common stocks, but the company has no obligation to pay preferred dividends. Preferred stocks are not usually considered a desirable form of investment for educational institutions unless they are convertible or have some other special feature.

CONVERTIBLES AND SIMILAR SECURITIES

A convertible security may be in the form of a bond, debenture, note, or preferred stock. All permit the holder to convert them into another class of securities, usually common stock, at a specified ratio, which is made adjustable so as to protect against dilution by reason of stock splits, stock dividends, or other increases in the common stock capitalization.

Other securities which have equity characteristics but are less frequently issued by business enterprises are nonconvertible debentures with warrants for the purchase of common stock or some other provision for participation, with the common stock, in the income of the enterprise, over and above the fixed interest rate of the debenture.

COMMON STOCKS

Common stocks represent shares of ownership in the issuing corporation. Dividends may be paid periodically, usually on a quarterly basis. Ownership of common stocks, as indicated above, is an important means through which an educational institution can obtain present income and also have an opportunity for increased income in the future.

MUTUAL FUND SHARES

Mutual fund or investment company shares may be suitable investments for colleges and universities in two kinds of situation. First, an educational institution with a small portfolio may find open-end mutual fund or investment company shares a useful way to afford more diversification than it could achieve by holding individual corporate stocks. Common stock mutual funds, especially, provide a means of equity diversification. Second, an institution with a large portfolio may have a number of funds that must be invested separately; for these, diversification may be achieved through investment in mutual fund shares.

REAL ESTATE OWNERSHIP

Many institutions invest in real estate that may involve property management. Real estate ownership and operations usually are highly specialized matters requiring talent and close attention in their handling. The cost of managing real estate, as well as depreciation allowances, should be identified and charged against the income from the property to prevent overstating the income realized from such investments.

LEASEBACKS

Under a leaseback arrangement, an institution purchases commercial real property, such as a manufacturing plant, a department store, or a group of gasoline stations, and leases it back to the user. The lease rental covers interest and amortization of principal, so that at the expiration of the lease the institution has recovered its investment. A leaseback is a fixed income investment, the security of which depends upon the credit rating of the lessee rather than on the intrinsic value of the property subject to lease.

MORTGAGES

It is possible for an institution to purchase groups of residential mortgages insured or guaranteed by governmental agencies. Often a management firm is employed, for a negotiated portion of the income, to service the mortgages and to inspect mortgaged properties periodically. These and other direct costs of mortgage investments should be charged against gross income received, so that the revenues to the institution will not be overstated. Occasionally an institution will invest in conventional mortgages, but this type of investment calls for special knowledge on the part of the investment staff.

Institutions with sophisticated investment staffs may also hold sizable commercial or industrial mortgages or mortgages secured by ground rents. Such investments demand careful and expert management, and can provide attractive yields.

OPERATION OF A BUSINESS

An institution may acquire or attain control of a business, through either direct ownership or ownership of enough stock to give effective voting control. Few institutional business officers have sufficient time or staff to assume the active management of a business operation or even to supervise such management. Even after competent management has been retained, the business may consume an inordinate amount of time of the business officer and also of the governing board.

Direct ownership of a business by a college or university involves additional serious problems under the provisions of the Federal income tax law relating to operation of businesses unrelated to the educational purposes of an institution. If such an investment is considered, the institution should consult its legal counsel. Usually if an educational institution must own and operate a business, it is preferable to incorporate the business and control it by the means of stock ownership, with the separate corporation being fully subject to income taxes.

OTHER TYPES OF INVESTMENT

Oil and gas production payments, patents and other royalty-producing investments, leases and leasebacks, ownership and leasing of tankers, and many other unusual types of investments have been held in various institutional portfolios. Purchase or retention of such investments should not be considered unless the institution has on its staff specially qualified persons who are thoroughly conversant with the particular investment medium under consideration.

INSTITUTIONAL PROPERTY

An institution may transfer quasi-endowment funds that are wholly unrestricted as to use of principal and income to plant funds for the acquisition or construction of revenue-producing properties such as dormitories and dining halls. However, if the transaction is a loan to plant funds for the purpose of acquiring or constructing self-liquidating or revenue-producing properties, the investment should be accounted for and managed in the same manner as if commercial borrowers were involved.

4

Management of Endowment and Similar Funds

T HE preceding chapter dealt with principles of managing the investment of endowment and other funds; the present chapter deals with principles of managing the principal of such funds. It will present definitions and characteristics of the funds, and distinguish between endowment funds and other funds that do not possess the same characteristics and qualifications as endowment funds but that, for investment purposes, can be conveniently classified and reported with endowment funds.

Definitions

The first category of funds in this group includes those given by a donor who stipulates, as a condition of his gift, that the principal of the fund is to be maintained inviolate and in perpetuity, and that only the income from the investments of the fund may be expanded. They are designated by the title *endowment funds*.

Another category includes funds whose donor or other outside agency, by the terms of the instrument of gift, provides for the eventual release from the inviolability of the fund, and permits all or part of it to be expended upon the happening of a particular event or the passage of a stated period of time. Such funds are identified as *term endowment funds*.

A third category of funds includes those that the governing board, rather than donors or other outside agencies, has determined are to be retained and invested. The governing board also has the right to decide at any time to expend the principal of the fund. Such funds are identified as *quasi-endowment funds* (they are also referred to as *funds functioning as endowment*).

All three types of funds should be reported in the Endowment and Similar Funds section of the Balance Sheet, the identity of the groups being clearly differentiated in the equity section of the Balance Sheet.

In the accounting records and in some financial reports, the funds in this group may be classified according to limitations, if any, placed on the use of their income. When no limitations are imposed by donors, the funds are described as "income unrestricted"; if donors impose limitations, the term "income restricted" should be used. If the governing board, rather than a donor, establishes limitations on the use of income from any funds in this group, the term "designated" should be applied to such funds.

Thus, each fund in this group should be identified in two ways: (1) according to limitations on the expenditure of principal; (2) according to limitations on the use of income from the investment of the funds. For example, a gift whose donor specifies only that the principal must be retained but which bears no stipulations concerning use of the income is an "unrestricted endowment" fund. If the donor specifies that the income from the fund is to be used for a certain instructional department or other identified purpose, the gift is a "restricted endowment" fund. If the governing board decides to use the income from an unrestricted endowment fund for a specific purpose, that fund becomes a "designated endowment" fund. The same situations regarding use of income from term endowment funds may also exist, and this category of funds may be identified as "unrestricted term endowment funds," "restricted term endowment funds," and "designated term endowment funds."

If a donor makes a gift to an institution and specifies only that it is to be used for a certain instructional department, no stipulation being made that the principal be maintained in perpetuity or for a period of time, and if the governing board elects to invest the principal and expend only the income for the purpose stipulated by the donor, the fund becomes a "restricted quasi-endowment fund." Other funds in this category may be identified as "unrestricted," or as "designated quasi-endowment funds," depending upon board action on the use of the income from the investments of such funds.

Characteristics of Endowment and Similar Funds

Educational institutions are charitable corporations and, as such, endowment funds donated to them are their property, subject to the terms and conditions established by donors. Colleges and universities seldom function as trustees in the strictly legal sense.

Bequests and instruments of gift sometimes use such language as: "I give, devise, and bequeath the sum of $——— *upon and subject to the trust, uses and conditions* that the principal shall be maintained . . . ." The italicized words are technical trust language, and when used in a gift or bequest may be held to force the institution to function in a legal sense as a trustee. The language is not necessary in donations to charitable corporations, and even when used, frequently is not held by the courts to be binding on such institutions. However, if an institution is made a trustee, it must render annual reports of accounting to cognizant courts or public officials, as well as filing Federal fiduciary returns. If it does appear that an institution may be forced to serve as a trustee in the technical sense, the problem should be resolved in the courts as promptly as possible, by applying for relief from the formal requirements of trusteeships.

Fortunately, bequests and gifts to colleges and universities usually are made without the use of technical trust language. This practice should be encouraged by financial and business officers and by those responsible for fund-raising activities.

Institutions may receive gifts or bequests subject to the payment of income to one or more beneficiaries for life. All fiduciary tax returns required under tax laws and regulations should be complied with by the institution. The agreement should provide that, upon the death of the last beneficiary, the fund becomes the unencumbered property of the institution.

Whenever possible, colleges and universities should avoid the role of executor or testamentary trustee. The naming of trust companies and trust departments of banks for this purpose reduces the likelihood of disputes between the institution and beneficiaries.

Cy Pres

In some instances, a donor may, by severely restricting the possible uses of endowment funds, limit their value to the institution. Sometimes the originally specified purpose of the endowment fund becomes impractical. In order to gain relief from impractical restrictions, a cy pres action can be brought in the courts to permit the institution to use the income from the endowment fund in some manner similar to, but somewhat different from, that originally specified. Without such action, however, the chief business officer is responsible for ensuring that all funds are used in compliance with any applicable restrictions.

Donor Relationships

Potential donors and their advisers should be encouraged to discuss terms of proposed gifts and bequests with institutional representatives. Conferences will help donors to recognize the wisdom of making wholly unrestricted gifts—some of which may be treated as quasi-endowment funds—or of establishing term endowment funds, rather than giving funds that must be retained in perpetuity. Frequently, it is possible to encourage the granting of broad latitude not only in the use of the funds and their income, but also in the manner in which they are invested, rather than the establishing of restrictions, which may become impractical or even impossible to fulfill with the passage of time.

Finally, whenever possible, a representative of the institution should review gift instruments in draft form, to suggest any changes in terms or wording that will help the institution comply with the wishes of the donor. In such relationships, however, it is essential that representatives of the institution avoid any acts or statements which might be construed as offering tax or legal advice. For such matters, a donor should be referred to his own counsel or financial adviser.

Policies for Management of Endowment and Similar Funds

A college and university should establish policies for the administration and management of endowment and similar funds that will ensure compliance with all conditions, restrictions, and designations imposed by donors and by the governing board on the use of the funds and their income. Management policies and prevailing practices should be examined periodically, possibly as a part of the audit performed by independent auditors. Such examination should be supplemented from time to time with a review by legal counsel.

The principal of endowment funds must not be hypothecated, and the investments of such funds must not be pledged, for any purpose.

Endowment funds should not be invested in institutional property whether income-producing or not. This principle does not apply to quasi-endowment funds, since such funds may be put to any use designated by the governing board.

Adequate management of endowment and similar funds requires the maintenance of a register of all such funds. The register should include such information as: (1) name and brief biographical comments about the donor; (2) amount and date of donation; (3) identification of the type of fund; (4) designations of or restrictions on the use of the fund or of the income; (5) identification of the source of such limitations, that is, donor or grantor or the governing board; (6) limitations on investments; and (7) reference to formal acceptance and other actions by the governing board.

Organizational units of the institution designated as the recipients of income from restricted endowment, term endowment, and quasi-endowment funds should be informed by the business office of the amount of expendable income that will be available for their use.

Management of the Assets of Endowment and Similar Funds

To the extent legally possible, colleges and universities should pool the investment of endowment and similar funds. An investment pool permits broad diversification with attendant protection of principal and relative stability of income. In addition, it permits economies in administration and accounting. Even though assets are invested as a pool, the identity of the separate funds must be maintained. Individual accounts must be kept, usually in subsidiary records, for the principal of each fund in the investment pool. This does not mean, however, that specific investments will be identified with any particular fund.

A consolidated pool is desirable for the investment of endowment, term endowment, and quasi-endowment funds. However, it is preferable to have separate investment pools for funds such as annuity and life income funds that have objectives and characteristics different from endowment and similar funds. The terms of some funds may prohibit pooling or commingling of assets. In the absence of such restrictions, new funds should be admitted routinely to the investment pool. Legal interpretation of complex language in the instruments of gift may be necessary.

In general, the requirement that a fund "be held separate" is not construed as requiring that the assets of the fund be separately invested, but rather that the principal of the fund be separately identified at all times. However, language to the effect that the fund be "invested separately" or that "its assets shall not be commingled" clearly requires that the fund have its own separate investments. Separate investment may be necessary because of special investment provisions in the terms of gifts or bequests. Examples are restrictions requiring retention of a particular investment and limitations on the types of securities in which the fund may be invested. The requirement that a fund be held in "income-producing investments" usually does not prohibit its investment in a diversified pool, whereas limiting terms such as "investments in interest-bearing securities" probably would exclude it from a pool that includes equities. When it is possible to guide a donor in drafting a gift document, the benefits to the fund and to the institution of pooling investments should be explained and the donor's consent sought for participation in the pool.

Operating Investment Pools

The operation of an investment pool necessitates procedures that will permit equitable distribution of income and assignment of capital appreciation or shrinkage to the various funds.

Under the preferred method, known as the "market-value" method, investment income is distributed to the various funds on the basis of the assignment to each fund of a number of shares that is calculated on the market value of the assets of the pool at the time of the entry of the fund into the pool. When an investment pool is inaugurated, or when a change is made from the book-value to the market-value method, an arbitrary value, perhaps $10, is assigned to a share or unit. Each fund is then considered to have the number of shares or units that is in direct proportion to its book value at the time the market-value method is inaugurated. For example, if $10 is assigned for each share, a fund of $10,000 will have 1,000 shares.

Thereafter, the pooled assets are valued at specific intervals, usually monthly or quarterly, and a new unit share value is determined by dividing the new total market value by the total number of shares. This new share value is used to determine the number of shares assigned to, or "purchased" by, a new fund as it enters the pool. The new share value is also used in calculating the value of a fund which may be withdrawn from the pool. For example, the market value of the assets of an investment pool having a total of 100,000 shares may be $1.5 million at a given monthly or quarterly valuation date; the value of each share, therefore, would be $15 ($1.5 million divided by 100,000). A new fund of $30,000 entering the pool on that date would be assigned 2,000 shares ($30,000 divided by $15). Also, a fund holding 3,000 shares being withdrawn from the pool would have a value of $45,000 (3,000 multiplied by $15). An alternative basis for handling withdrawals is described below in the discussion of realized gains and losses.

In distributing income from the pool, the total investment income is divided by the total number of shares held by all the funds participating in the pool, to determine the "dividend," or rate of income per share. Income is distributed at this rate on the basis of the number of shares held by each fund, suitable adjustments being made for shares held less than a full year.

Under the second method, known as the "book-value method," income from the pool and realized gains or losses are allocated among the funds on the ratio of the historic fund balances of all funds in the pool. The book-value method is unfair to funds which entered the pool when its asset value was relatively low, as compared with those which entered at higher asset values. The market-value method is preferable since it is more equitable to the participating funds. As a collateral advantage, the fluctuations in share value of the pool provide a useful measure of the market action of the investment pool, undistorted by additions or withdrawals of funds.

Either of two procedures may be followed in admitting funds to, or withdrawing funds from, the pool. In one, funds enter or leave the pool only on valuation dates. Under the other method they may enter or leave the pool at any time, the valuation of shares being that of the latest valuation date. If the latter method is employed, share values should be determined with sufficient frequency to avoid inequities which would result from undue variations in share market value. Thus, new funds, in effect, buy shares in the investment pool at the average price as determined on the valuation dates, and funds withdrawn from the pool do so at the price similarly established.

An account for realized gains and losses on investment transactions should be established for investment pools. This account is charged, or credited, for share valuation adjustments upon withdrawal of participating funds from the pool. Upon withdrawal at market value per share, the difference between book value upon entry and withdrawal value represents a portion of the aggregate of realized gains and unrealized appreciation of the portfolio. Accordingly, upon withdrawal of a fund, the distribution of unrealized appreciation is shared ratably by the surviving pooled funds; a charge to the realized gain account is an equitable and appropriate disposition of the adjustment. If the aggregate of share adjustments is material in relation to undistributed realized gains and losses, appropriate disclosure should be made in the Balance Sheet.

The realized gains and losses, and share adjustment, account is usually accumulated, but may, if desired, be distributed on the books of account to the principal of each of the participating funds, following the same method used for distribution of investment income. In the event an institution handles withdrawals on an alternative basis, that of valuing at book value plus only realized gains, then annual distribution of realized gains and losses is mandatory; on this withdrawal basis, there is no share adjustment to be made.

The account for realized gains and losses is not assigned shares in the investment pool, and no income is distributed to it. Thus, the income that would otherwise have been allocated to the account is distributed to each of the funds participating in the pool in proportion to the number of shares held by each fund.

Realized gains and losses on separately invested funds should be distributed directly to the funds; thus, the fund balance changes each time an investment is sold and a gain or loss is realized.

Income Stabilization Reserve

To stabilize the amount available for annual use from the income of pooled investments, an income stabilization reserve may be established. The size of the reserve must be decided by each institution, but should be reasonable, depending upon the needs of the institutions.

Either of two methods may be followed in establishing the reserve. In one, a portion of the total income from the investment pool is not allocated to the participating funds, the portion withheld being set aside for the stabilization reserve before the balance of investment pool income is distributed to the participating funds as described. When this method is followed, it must be recognized that income is being withheld from all funds participating in the pool. Some of these may be restricted endowment funds; others may be those of fund groups other than endowment and similar funds. The Income Stabilization Reserve established under this method should appear on the Balance Sheet as a separately listed equity of the Restricted Current Funds. If, under this method, the income flow is materially affected in any one year; that is, if the total amount earned by the investment pool is significantly different from the amount distributed to the participating funds, this fact should be appropriately footnoted in the financial reports.

Under the second method, all income from the pool is distributed to the participating funds as described. The amount applicable to the unrestricted endowment funds is reported in full as unrestricted current funds revenue under the title "Endowment Income," and the amount set aside for the stabilization reserve is shown in the same statement as a Transfer to Unrestricted Current Funds Balance—Allocated. Under this method, the reserve relates only to income from the unrestricted endowment funds, and is reflected in the Balance Sheet as a separately listed equity of Unrestricted Current Funds Balance—Allocated.

5

Administration of Research and Other Sponsored Programs

Awards for research and other sponsored projects accepted by institutions of higher education carry with them responsibilities that have significant implications in the internal adminstration of the institutions. Colleges and universities must accept responsibilities for contract negotiations, management of inventions, the maintenance of accounts and records, the preparation and submission of reports, and compliance with property and security regulations imposed by agencies outside the institution. Both academic and business administrators are involved in developing policies and procedures to meet these responsibilities and to deal effectively with other related problems.

Research grants and contracts are awarded to institutions, not to faculty members. Faculty members are under the direction of regular academic authority in carrying on the research; but the agreement is with, and the award is to, the institution, and the institution, not the faculty member, assumes full responsibility for it.

Types of Agreements

There are several types of research agreements, and the sponsoring agency usually will determine the type of agreement when awards are made. As a practical matter, there are few real distinctions between the obligations assumed by an institution under grants as opposed to contracts.

COST-REIMBURSEMENT CONTRACTS

Under a cost-reimbursement contract, the sponsor agrees to reimburse the institution, up to a predetermined total figure, for the cost incurred in a project. This type of agreement recognizes the difficulty of accurately estimating the costs of a project in advance; and it limits the sponsor's payment to actual costs incurred, both direct and indirect. Often the agreement contains an escape clause specifying that an institution is not required to incur costs in excess of the amount set forth in the document.

Cost-reimbursement contracts prescribe a definite period of time for the work. They are sometimes amended to provide supplemental funds or additional time for completion of the program. Arrangements for such extensions should be initiated well in advance of the expiration date. These contracts may permit payments in advance; otherwise, payments are made upon the periodic submission of invoices.

FIXED-PRICE CONTRACTS

A fixed-price contract provides for payment to an institution of a specific sum for performing a project or program. The payment may be made in a lump sum, either in advance or upon completion of the project, or it may be made in installments as the work progresses.

A statement of costs incurred for the work must be submitted by the institution, following, in general, the form of the budget submitted with the original proposal. If the costs exceed the amount of the contract, renegotiation—not easy under a fixed-price contract—is necessary to recover any part of the excess. Amounts not expended on the project during the term of the agreement may, however, be refundable to the sponsor.

Fixed-price contracts are undesirable for projects for which the costs are difficult to estimate. They should be limited to use for projects where the level of effort can be accurately estimated in advance, where the cost of performing the work can be predicted with reasonable accuracy, and where costs are not subject to significant change.

GRANTS

The grant is a type of agreement preferred over contracts by some sponsors of basic research. Sponsoring agencies using this form of agreement provide regulations and statements of management policies relating to the terms and conditions of their grants. These publications have the same force and effect as contractual terms, and require careful attention by the chief business officer and his staff.

BASIC CONTRACTS AND TASK ORDERS

This type of agreement conserves the time of negotiators, since a single basic agreement is negotiated covering all the general terms and conditions under which research work sponsored by an agency is to be undertaken by an institution. Task orders then are issued for separate research projects, and these specify the character of the research work, the duration of the project, financial arrangements, and reporting requirements. This system obviates negotiating separate agreements for each research project and avoids possible confusion arising from a single agency incorporating differing general provisions among its contracts.

Administrative Organization and Responsibilities

Both academic and business office personnel have responsibilities for the proper execution of sponsored research agreements. For example, a proposal is initiated by a member or members of the academic staff and approved by department chairman and other appropriate academic officers. The budget, space, and equipment requirements and other provisions of the proposal should be reviewed for approval by the chief business officer or his appointed representative. Final approval of applications should be the responsibility of a designated academic officer or faculty committee.

The business office should have primary responsibility for contractual negotiations, for accounting and preparation of financial reports, and for the collection of payments from sponsoring agencies. Prosecution of the research work, disclosure of inventions, and the submission of technical reports are the responsibility of the principal investigator.

The form of administrative organization depends upon the extent to which an institution deems it desirable and necessary to have centralized responsibility for the administrative and managerial functions of the research program. Regardless of the organizational pattern, the responsibilities and duties of those concerned with the program should be defined and made known. An individual or an office should be assigned the responsibility for maintaining a complete and up-to-date file on the legislation concerning sponsoring agencies and their administrative rulings, policy developments, regulations, and instructions. The information should be made known to faculty members, and the file should be available for faculty use at all times.

Whatever the type of organization, responsibility for the academic and scientific aspects of the sponsored research program should always remain with the deans and academic officers, while responsibility for all business and financial matters should rest with the business office.

In one organizational plan, an officer for sponsored research, usually having the title "director of research," acts under the authority of the chief academic officer. His primary responsibility is the administration of the academic and scientific aspects of the research program. All business and financial operations of the program are the responsibility of the chief business officer. In another type of organization, the officer for sponsored research, under the direction of the chief business officer, has primary responsibility for the business and financial aspects of the program. He is responsible for the preparation of proposals and negotiation of agreements; for coordinating and expediting patent and invention matters; property accountability and security; accounting, reporting, and billing functions; and all other management and administrative functions of the sponsored research and other sponsored programs. Under this plan, responsibility for the scientific and academic aspects of the research work is retained by the deans and other academic officers.

Proposals

A proposal represents an offer by an institution to engage in a research project or a program under certain conditions. A proposal should not be initiated unless the institution is prepared to undertake the work. Nor should the same project be submitted to different sponsoring agencies concurrently unless this circumstance is made clear to each prospective sponsor. The sponsor should be notified immediately if an institution, after submitting a proposal, finds itself unable to conduct the research under the conditions originally proposed.

Negotiation and Acceptance

The terms and conditions governing work under research agreements generally are established in negotiations between the sponsoring agency and the institution. The business officer must take the initiative in requesting the sponsor to modify the provisions to accommodate the policy needs of his institution. Requests for such modifications should be made a condition for acceptance of the award or agreement.

Although variations exist among the agencies, familiarity with their manuals, circulars, letters of instructions, and other publications will be helpful in negotiating agreements. Institutional officers should become thoroughly familiar with such documents. Business officers should maintain close liaison with neighboring institutions having similar sponsored research activities in order to benefit from the experience of other institutions.

Both when a proposal has been accepted and when negotiations have been completed, notifications should be given to the principal investigator, to the departmental chairman, dean, or other academic officer, and to the divisions of the business office responsible for the accounting, reporting, billing, and other financial and business functions. In addition, a check list enumerating the obligations required to fulfill the agreement should be furnished to the principal investigator, the director of sponsored research, and the business office.

Indirect Costs

The total costs of a research project include both direct and indirect expenditures. Direct costs include the salaries and wages of those working on the project, expenditures for equipment and materials used, and other expenses specifically identified with the project. Indirect costs are those incurred by an institution in implementing and supporting the entire research program. They include an allotted share of such items as operation and maintenance of the plant; costs of departmental, college, and institutional administration; costs of library operations; use charges for equipment and facilities; and certain other expenses of a general nature that are to some degree attributable to sponsored research.

Indirect costs are difficult to establish with precision, even though they are no less real than the direct costs of research work. Unless institutions are reimbursed by sponsoring agencies for such costs, they must use their own funds to meet them, and, in that way, divert support from other educational objectives.

It is impracticable to determine indirect costs separately for each research project. An indirect cost rate, usually expressed as a percentage of salaries and wages, should be computed annually for the total research program of an institution, in accordance with pertinent governmental regulations, where applicable.

Indirect cost rates are applicable to research agreements with sponsoring agencies of the government. They may be established either on a provisional basis, subject to later negotiation, or on a predetermined fixed basis. When rates have been changed as a result of negotiation, research agreements which specify provisional rates should be reviewed to ensure the incorporation of the new rates.

Prior Approvals

Many agreements require prior approval on specified management and administrative matters. Some of the most important of these relate to salaries and wages, travel, certain types of purchases, and subcontracts. Institutional procedures applying to these matters should be developed with care. It is particularly important to determine the degree of centralization of responsibility for compliance with, and for maintenance of records relating to, these requirements.

Compensation of staff members participating in sponsored research and other sponsored programs should be in accordance with regularly established salary policies of the institution. A sponsor may examine and approve the program of compensation in the proposal as a condition of the award of the agreement, but this review should not be extended to modification of basic salary policies of the institution or to approval of any specific salaries.

Research agreements may stipulate provisions that must be included in purchase orders and subcontracts, such as patent rights, copyright ownership, and assurances of compliance with various current laws and regulations.

Property Ownership and Accountability

Government agencies have discretionary authority to vest in colleges and universities title to property acquired with governmental funds for research. The title to such property may be vested in the institution when the agreement is negotiated or at any time during the period of the sponsored program. Government-owned property used in research projects and held in the custody of the educational institution must be accounted for to the cognizant government agency.

Inventions and Patents

Most research agreements contain provisions governing the reporting of inventions and the disposition of patent rights. Government policy regarding inventions developed in federally sponsored programs usually requires the granting of a nonexclusive, royalty-free license for use for public purposes. Some governmental agencies retain the right to determine the disposition of inventions and patents, but may accord this right to a grantee institution if the patent policy of the institution is approved as being in the public interest, and if certain other criteria are met. Some private sponsoring organizations have fixed policies on the disposition of patents and inventions, although there may be latitude for negotiation of patent rights in many of these cases.

Patent matters are especially important in connection with sponsored research activities, but they also have significance to educational institutions in other areas and may arise outside the sponsored research program. In keeping with the public service function of colleges and universities, there is a strong obligation to permit inventions to be brought into public use. This requires disclosure by the inventor and arrangements to secure the patent, followed by efforts to license the patent for commercial development and marketing. Financial arrangements regarding inventions should provide a share of the institution's royalties to the inventor as an incentive to disclose the invention and assist in its development.

If an institution's patent policy does not require every employee to execute an agreement to report all inventions and to dispose of them as determined by the institution, special employee agreements are necessary and often are required under research agreements. Such agreements should require employees and consultants to comply with the invention provisions of the research agreement under which they work. Employee agreements usually are necessary whether or not any of the employee's compensation is paid out of contract or grant funds, to protect the respective interests of the employee and the institution.

Government agreements relating to inventions apply whether or not patent applications are to be filed. Therefore, it is necessary to establish procedures for the periodic review of research activities and for reports of sponsored research work to ensure compliance with agreement provisions. Institutions not having a patent officer on the staff should employ patent counsel, since research workers themselves may not be adequately informed about what constitutes an invention.

Publication and Copyrights

Educational institutions should protect their right to publish the results of research. Some institutions decline to undertake research programs in which information must be classified for security reasons or is otherwise restricted. Federal agencies generally require that the government be given a royalty-free license to use, reproduce, and disclose any information developed under a contract, and agreements of all research employees to comply with this requirement are desirable. Compliance with the requirement means that any materials published in a copyrighted journal or other publication must contain an acknowledgment of government sponsorship.

Accounting Records and Audits

Generally accepted accounting and reporting procedures for colleges and universities as described in this volume should be followed in the management and administration of research activities. However, requirements of sponsors may force some modifications in billing and reporting procedures. Separate accounts for each research project should be established, and these records should be retained as required by regulations and made available for government or other special audits.

Where the volume of sponsored research is relatively large, probably special financial reports will have to be provided to those concerned with the various projects and for internal control purposes.

Institutions should be aware that an audit by the sponsoring agency of the Federal Government does not necessarily constitute a final audit of the records. The U.S. General Accounting Office reserves the right to audit, within the legal retention period, any records pertaining to disbursements by any Federal agency.

Security

To assure compliance with governmental security regulations, an administrative officer or a reliable staff member should be designated as security officer in order to supervise compliance. He should be responsible for keeping himself and others within the institution informed of all security regulations of sponsoring agencies. He should ensure that safeguards for mail and storage facilities are available on the campus; arrange for internal security procedures; aid in acquiring facility clearance so that classified information may be obtained by faculty members from the Federal Government; arrange visit clearances for staff members attending meetings for which clearance is necessary; and perform all other duties necessary to comply with security regulations.

Educational institutions have the right to terminate an agreement if an unclassified program is given a classified status or if a project is moved from a lower to a higher security classification. However, every reasonable effort compatible with the institution's established policies should be made to continue performance of the work under the existing contract. Institutions also have the right to terminate an agreement in the event changes in security regulations impose more restrictive area controls.

Termination

Research agreements should contain specific statements regarding termination. When work under a program has been ended for the convenience of the sponsor, the most satisfactory means of settling termination claims is by negotiation of a termination agreement.

Disputes

Every agreement for sponsored research should contain a disputes article that provides for access to appeal procedures in cases where decisions of individual contracting officers may be unacceptable to an institution. Reference to binding arbitration also may be appropriate in some instances.

Other Sponsored Programs

Other types of programs that are subject to agreements with sponsoring agencies include institutes, workshops, training projects, and the like. It is important that responsibility for the administration and operation of sponsored programs be clearly defined and that their operations be related to the administrative organization of the institution. The directors of the programs should be responsible to the departmental chairmen, deans, or other academic officers of the areas in which the respective programs fall. All those responsible for sponsored programs need to be aware of and use the established channels and organization for academic administration.

6

Student
Financial Assistance

THE usual forms of financial assistance to college and university students are scholarships, fellowships, grants-in-aid, loans, part-time employment, and special arrangements for the payment of tuition and other charges. This segment of the financial affairs of the institution, affecting the welfare of individual students, must obviously be administered as judiciously and effectively as possible.

Administration

The administration of the student financial assistance program is a dual responsibility of academic and financial administrative officers. Broad policies and procedures may be adopted by the institution based upon recommendations of a committee composed of representatives from the academic departments, the admissions office, the student personnel office, and the business office. The student financial aid committee should determine the standards and requirements relating to academic and other qualifications of applicants and the methods used to appraise their financial needs.

An officer should be appointed to implement the financial aid policies, to coordinate the work of the program, and to centralize in one office all information relating to the entire program of financial assistance. In small institutions this responsibility may be a part-time assignment; in large institutions, a full-time administrator is usually required.

Within the framework of the approved policies, the financial aid officer should be responsible for administering the program, including

[58]

such procedures as the receipt of applications for all forms of financial assistance, evaluation of financial need and qualifications of applicants, and decisions concerning the amounts and kinds of financial aid to be granted. The aid officer should comply with all restrictions pertaining to financial assistance funds.

The business officer should be responsible for the custody and disbursement of all funds for student financial assistance and for all aspects of their accounting and reporting. It is his responsibility to inform the financial aid officer, and others concerned in the student aid program, about restrictions and limitations which may exist on the use of such funds and to ensure their observance.

Information describing the total program of student financial assistance should be published in a convenient and easily understood form. The publication should include the amounts of aid available from all sources, general rules and regulations of the institution in granting financial assistance, qualifications and eligibility requirements applicable to special funds and types of aid, methods of applying for financial assistance, and procedures to be followed in arranging for deferred payments of fees and charges. Information on loan funds should include rates of interest, repayment schedules, and obligations of borrowers to keep the institution informed of changes of address and occupation.

Such a publication will also be of value to prospective donors. It should include a recommendation that any restrictions imposed by the donors be in accordance with the established policies of the institution. Donors should be encouraged to avoid extensive restrictions that prevent making the best possible use of their gifts.

Selection, Criteria, and Methods of Making Awards

Academic achievement, character, economic need, and vocational objectives are some of the factors usually considered in granting financial assistance. All students seeking aid should be required to complete the application form, which will reveal information on these factors.

Professional services are available to evaluate applications for financial assistance and relate them to costs of attending colleges and universities. The results of these comparisons are sent on a confidential basis to institutions to use in determining the amounts of financial assistance to be awarded.

In order to make the most effective use of their student aid funds, institutions often grant assistance to students through a combination of scholarships and other forms of aid. Frequently, freshman students are awarded full scholarships for the first year but with the understanding that the assistance, if it is continued, may be reduced in amount in later years, when they can supplement scholarship aid with part-time employment and loans.

When students are granted aid through a combination of scholarship awards and loans, it should be made clear to them that the loan portion of the award is an obligation which must eventually be repaid.

Scholarships and Fellowships

Scholarships generally are awarded to both undergraduates and graduates on the basis of their scholastic achievement and financial need, and may cover their total educational expenses or only a part of them. Certain scholarships are awarded regardless of financial need. Fellowships generally are in larger amounts and are awarded to graduate or postgraduate students, who are not required to demonstrate economic need but must show scholastic excellence.

Recipients of scholarships and fellowships are not required to render service to the institution as a consideration of their awards, nor are they expected to repay them. Awards to be repaid are "loans," and should be handled through the student loan funds accounts. Awards that require the performance of services should be charged as expense of the departments in which the work is performed, regardless of the basis on which the recipients are selected.

Financial aid officers and appropriate staff in the business office should review periodically, and become fully acquainted with, the provisions of tax laws and Internal Revenue Service regulations as they relate to all forms of payments to students.

Foundations, fraternal orders, religious groups, and similar agencies often grant scholarships directly to students of their own selection, relying in many cases on information supplied by the institution in selecting the students to receive their awards. Financial aid officers should cooperate with such organizations, but should suggest that, whenever possible, the standards, qualifications of students, and other regulations of their own institutions be followed.

Institutions are sometimes asked to accept gifts to which the term "scholarship" is applied, but with the donor reserving the right to designate the person to receive the award. Such receipts cannot be treated as scholarship funds, and donors should be informed that their funds are being accepted as "agency" funds for the use of the designated students.

Loan Funds

Student loan funds become available from gifts, endowment income, other institutional funds, and appropriations of governmental agencies. In addition, there are Federal, state, and private programs of low-interest, insured loans, and certain programs in which a governmental agency pays a portion of the interest on the loans. Some loans are made directly to students by agencies outside the institution. As with scholarship awards from outside sources, colleges and universities should cooperate with the organizations to encourage them to observe the institution's standards, policies, and regulations in administering loan funds.

The usual type of loan fund is the revolving fund, which is loaned to students and, when repaid, is again made available for lending. Interest on the loans, if any, is added to the loan fund, and this helps to cover occasional losses and to ensure the perpetuity of the loan fund.

In the case of loan funds created by the income from restricted endowment funds, a variety of methods are available for handling both interest and principal payments. The income from such restricted endowment funds becomes the student loan fund and is so recorded. In some cases, when a loan is repaid, the interest must be added to the principal of the restricted endowment fund. In other cases the loan fund and all principal repayments and interest charges may remain with the student loan funds. It is the responsibility of the chief business officer to see that loan funds deriving from restricted endowments are administered and accounted for in accordance with prescribed regulations.

A student should be granted a loan only after review of his application form, a personal interview by the financial aid officer, and the execution of a loan note. In addition to other information about the student, the application form should disclose all sources and amounts of income of the applicant for the coming year, estimates of expenses during the year, and amount of the loan requested. Names and addresses of references and of a co-signer, if there is one, may be required. (This information is valuable later in locating borrowers who fail to keep the institution informed of changes of address.) On a loan made to a minor, a co-signer may be necessary to enforce the legal right to collect the note.

In interviewing the student prior to granting a loan, the financial aid officer should emphasize that when the loan is obtained, the borrower is entering upon a business transaction with the institution and all terms and conditions of the agreement must be fulfilled. The interview should include a discussion of such matters as: the rate of interest, if any, on the loan; the necessity to pay interest and principal promptly on the dates established; and the responsibility for informing the institution of changes of address.

The administration of loans approved by the student financial aid officer is a responsibility of the business office. This office should review the authorizations, verify the terms of loans, prepare the notes, and issue checks payable to students for the amount of the loans. Checks should be endorsed by the students, even though the proceeds from the loans are to be applied immediately to the student's account. The issuance of checks to the students borrowing funds and their endorsement emphasizes the business nature of the loan.

Before a student to whom a loan has been made leaves the institution, he should be interviewed to stress his obligation to pay any interest stipulated, to repay the loan, and to keep the institution advised of his correct address. At this interview, a written agreement should confirm interest payments and the schedule, preferably on a monthly basis, for repaying the loan note.

The chief business officer is responsible for developing an efficient system for collecting student loans. Advance notices of interest and principal payments due should be sent regularly by the business office to all borrowers. Notices of payments made, which should also show the balance of principal still unpaid, and reminder letters should originate in the business office. Data processing equipment is effective in preparing bills and statements, notices and requests for payment, analyses and reports on student loan fund activities, the aging of loan notes, and other phases of accounting and reporting for student loan funds.

An institution that accepts funds to be loaned to students, regardless of the source, accepts the responsibility for administering the funds in the most effective manner possible.

Part-time Employment

Part-time student employment should be incorporated in the student financial assistance program, and students seeking financial aid should be offered the opportunity of accepting part-time employment as part of their financial assistance plan.

After being interviewed by the financial aid officer, students seeking part-time employment should be referred to the personnel office for job assignment. Final selection of students to be employed should be the responsibility of those in the areas where the students will work. Supervisors of student employees should insist on prompt, efficient, and conscientious performance. Failure to require satisfactory performance will be a disservice to the students as well as to the institution.

Deferred Payment Plans

Many colleges and universities will arrange for students and parents to pay tuition, fees, board and room charges, and other expenses, on a deferred payment plan. Deferments usually extend over short periods of time, not beyond the end of the semester or term, or, at most, beyond the end of the academic year. If financial assistance is necessary for longer periods of time, the student or parents should be advised to consider a loan. A charge should be assessed against those using a deferred payment plan, such as interest on the unpaid balance of the bill or a flat fee for each deferred payment.

Although deferred payment plans are a part of the total student financial assistance program, they should be handled through the business office since academic factors generally are not involved. If the program of deferred payments is understood by students and well administered by the institution, collection problems are minimized.

Arrangements for deferred payments should be in writing. The payment agreement form should be signed by the student and in some instances by his parents. The agreement should indicate the amounts to be paid, the dates on which payments are due, and the penalties to be incurred in case of failure to meet payments on the dates specified.

Many commercial agencies and banks offer loans, described as deferred payment plans, under which parents may spread the cost of tuition, board and room, and other charges, in monthly payments over a period of years. These plans may include insurance on the lives of the parents for the full amount of the contract.

7

Insurance

T HE chief business officer is responsible for seeing that the institution is properly protected by insurance and that the insurance program is effectively managed. One person designated by, and on the staff of, the chief business officer should select the coverages and place all insurance for the institution, regardless of the area to which it applies. Because of the complexities involved, the insurance officer must have acquired a sound background in the principles of insurance, the hazards to which the institution is exposed, and types of protection available. The sources of technical information are several: basic information can be obtained from textbooks and from manuals used to prepare for agents examinations; descriptive and analytical materials pertinent to the institution's needs can be had from brokers and insurance company representatives.

Principles of Insurance

Insurance consists of sharing the risks of possible catastrophic losses from specified hazards by a group of "individuals." Each member, or policyholder, within the group agrees to pay a portion of the losses suffered by any other member of the group. In this way, the annual cost to each policyholder of such contingencies is predictable with reasonable accuracy and removes uncertainty about whether the member would face larger costs by assuming individually the results of a catastrophe to his property. The larger and more widespread the risk-sharing group, the more mathematically predictable will be the anticipated losses in any given period of time.

In exchange for the benefits gained by spreading the risk among many individuals, the policyholder must pay not only his share of the estimated cost of catastrophes predicted to occur to members of the group during a future period of time but also his share of the operating costs of the organization.

THE ECONOMIC BASIS FOR PREMIUMS

Several factors enter into the size of insurance premiums. The total amount collected in premiums must cover: (1) anticipated claims for losses of policyholders during the coming year, determined on mathematical and statistical bases; (2) the operating expenses of the company; (3) agents' commissions; and (4) any amounts to be retained by the company or paid to the stockholders. The total of these costs is reduced by earnings on the investment of reserves and other funds of the insurance company.

No insurance company can escape the economics of this formula. Lower costs to educational institutions can be realized only by purchasing insurance from companies that have operated economically. Companies that have selected risks wisely, that hold down operating expenses and commissions, and that reduce or eliminate dividends to stockholders may offer satisfactory protection to colleges and universities at minimum costs. Insurance should be purchased on the basis of these factors—not on the basis of friendship, patronage, or reciprocity.

TYPES OF INSURERS

There are four types of organizations from which an institution may purchase insurance coverage. The simplest is typified by Lloyd's of London. Lloyd's is not an insurance company in the usual sense: it is a group of underwriters who are willing to insure an individual or corporation against various hazards for rates which they develop to fit the circumstances. Although this corporation might be a good source of insurance protection for unusual risks, such as the hazard of a torrential downpour on Homecoming Day, most colleges and universities would find it inconvenient to deal with Lloyd's for their ordinary insurance needs.

The simplest of the insurance companies is exemplified by the so-called farmers mutuals. In these organizations, many neighboring farmers agree to apportion among themselves the losses which any of their members suffer in the course of a year. Expenses, or "loading" costs, are low since no elaborate corporate structure is required and usually no commissions are paid. Anticipated losses are not determined in advance and apportioned among the members in the form of prepaid premiums. When a fire or other catastrophe occurs, assessments are levied against the policyholders, who contribute their shares to reimburse the policyholder who suffered the loss. This kind of insurance works to the advantage of the policyholders when catastrophes are infrequent. However, it proves costly if a number of disasters occur in a single year. Colleges and universities generally should avoid insuring in assessable mutual insurance companies.

The other two types of insurers are: the stock company, and the *nonassessable* mutual company, or, as it may be called with equal accuracy, the dividend-paying stock company. From the standpoint of protection afforded the policyholder, there is no difference between the two. Both types are prohibited by their charters from assessing additional premiums after the close of a policy year to pay losses, regardless of any adverse loss experience which may have occurred. The only fundamental difference between the two types is that the stock company pays dividends to its stockholders when earned and declared, while the nonassessable mutual company pays them to its policyholders. From this fact, it might be assumed that, for comparable coverage, the nonassessable mutual company would offer lower net premium cost than the stock companies. However, this is not always the case.

The buyer of institutional insurance should insist that the policy be nonassessable. Otherwise, he should ignore the form of corporate structure and place insurance on the basis of net premiums, after any allowable policyholder dividends, for comparable coverage, protection, and service.

Selection of insurers

In selecting insurers, the institutional insurance officer should compare the services provided by various insurance companies. Since generally he cannot have firsthand knowledge of the practices of all insurance companies doing business in his state, he should consult objective evaluations of insurance companies such as those published by the Alfred M. Best Company of New York. These evaluate financial size, security, and strength (called "financial rating") and the service and claims practices (called "policyholders' ratings"). Use of the ratings will assist the institutional buyer of insurance in selecting insurance carriers.

In exchange for commissions earned on the insurance policies he services, the broker should routinely advise the institution about possible improvements in coverage, reductions in premiums, and opportunities for more favorable classification or rate reduction. In addition, he should cooperate with the insurer in providing safety engineering and fire prevention services, and should assist with prosecution of claims.

In placing insurance, the purchaser should give consideration to the caliber of the brokers, agents, or the insurance company officials who will service the policy. Since brokers and agents usually cannot bind the company nor speak for it, institutional insurance officers should require written confirmation, signed by an officer of the insurance company itself, of all important interpretations and conditions of the coverage.

PREMIUM DETERMINATION

Premium rates are closely related to the level of claims anticipated for the particular type of coverage. From this standpoint, it is desirable for the insurance buyer to select carriers that will group his institution with other risks having relatively low loss ratios, rather than with groups exhibiting less favorable experience. Such selective grouping of low-hazard insureds enables insurance companies to offer institutions both special concessions in rates and broader coverage.

Most companies base their premium charges on rates promulgated by state rating bureaus or by similar bureaus representing groups of insurance companies. The rates are of two types: those for general classes, such as "schools, colleges, and universities"; and those for specific buildings. Using these promulgated rates as a base, some companies offer lower rates, either by initial discount or by subsequent dividends, subject to limitations imposed by the laws of the states and the agreements they have with other insurance companies. After the rate is determined, premiums on large policies are usually adjusted to reflect the actual loss experience of the policyholder. In most states such experience ratings are required on all large policies of certain types. Credits are allowed for favorable records, and debits are charged for unfavorable experience.

Policy premiums for certain types of coverage are based on unit costs, for example, customer attendance at public functions, such as football games. At the end of the policy period, an audit is made to determined the actual attendance, and the premium is adjusted accordingly.

On some types of policies, especially for fire and allied lines, premium reductions are granted for terms longer than one year. The longer terms have the advantage of giving the policyholder extended protection against general rate increases, yet they do not deny him the benefit of any intervening rate decreases.

For an additional charge, it is possible to have the total premium of a multiyear policy spread in installments over the years covered. However, the same result can be obtained without additional cost for such coverages as fire insurance by having one-third of the coverage expire in each of the three years of the term.

PREMIUM SAVINGS

An institution can effect substantial savings by reducing its record of losses. An important service offered by insurance companies furnishing liability and compensation coverages is periodic inspection of the campus to detect potential hazards, some of which can, perhaps, be corrected with little expense. Corrective and preventive measures can reduce claims, and thus improve experience ratings which, in turn, are reflected in lower premiums.

More immediate savings often can be effected by reviewing the premium credits available under the terms of the policy. Safety devices such as elevator door interlocks, panic hardware on exit doors, guards on mechanical equipment, fire extinguishers of approved types, and sprinkler systems often will pay for themselves in a few years through reduction in insurance premiums. The institution may earn premium credits that more than recompense the additional costs for labor by such changes as providing a clerk to serve as a guard to accompany a cashier to the bank, or by adjusting watchmen's schedules.

Another possible source of savings in insurance costs is to be found in increased deductibles. Since the policyholder must ultimately pay the insurance company's operating expenses, any reduction in these costs should redound to the policyholder's benefit. The cost of processing a small claim is nearly as great as that for a large claim. Therefore, elimination of small claims reduces the ratio of costs to claims, and permits the insurance company to charge a lower premium per thousand dollars of coverage. The institutional insurance buyer should be willing to relieve the insurance company of the obligation to pay for small losses, in exchange for a reduction in premium that reflects the savings in administrative costs.

To evaluate savings as compared with possible losses to the institution, separate bids should be taken on coverages with varying levels of deductibles.

Self-insurance

Closely allied to the use of high deductibles is the question of self-insurance. Every institution is a self-insurer to some extent because no college or university can purchase complete coverage for all possible hazards. Any part of any hazard that is left uninsured is technically self-insured. However, when the term "self-insurance" is used, it generally refers to the assumption by the institution of the total risk of loss from fire and similar hazards.

If insurance is thought of as a device to spread risks, a small college with one main building or with a closely connected complex of buildings should not self-insure, because a single serious fire could wipe out a major portion of the physical plant facilities. At the other extreme, a multi-campus university with hundreds of buildings, each of which constitutes only a fraction of the total assets of the institution, might constitute a broad risk group in itself, and thus be appropriate for self-insurance.

Self-insurance plans must be funded adequately. In establishing the funded reserve initially, the amount should be equal to the insurable value of the greatest loss that reasonably could be expected to occur in any one year. As new buildings are added to the campus, and as the values of existing buildings increase from year to year, small amounts should be added to the reserve from current funds or other sources. Another method of maintaining an adequate reserve is to add to it each year the premium savings resulting from a phased reduction in insurance coverage. Publicly controlled institutions in some states achieve effective self-insurance through a continuing statutory provision that when a loss occurs, the responsible agency may start reconstruction with the assurance that an automatic appropriation will be made for the replacement costs.

In other states where all physical properties of state agencies are covered by state self-insurance plans, an annual charge is made to the agencies for contributions or deposits into a funded self-insurance plan. Usually these annual charges are much less than standard fire insurance premiums. Institutions that are part of state systems should explore various methods of self-insurance; but few privately controlled institutions are sufficiently large and decentralized to find reasonable safety in self-insurance plans.

Purchasing Insurance

Opinions vary markedly even among experts about the amounts and kinds of protection an institution should purchase under any given circumstances. Furthermore, there are few services for which price is so little related to value.

Insurance is a service, and although the quality of the services supplied is one of the important factors in the selection of a carrier, the techniques for purchasing insurance more closely resemble those for purchasing a commodity. The insurance officer of an institution should prepare a set of basic specifications covering general terms such as the corporate name of the institution, the minimum standards for the insurer and the broker, and the requirements for reporting claims and settlements. For each type of coverage, he should prepare a set of individual specifications setting forth the exact protection desired, a description of the property, any unit measurements required for premium determination, the terms and effective dates, and the record of claims experience.

Oftentimes it is helpful to ask the present carrier of each type of insurance and at least one other potential bidder to review the specifications in draft form. The review will help ensure that all essential information is provided, that no areas of premium reduction are overlooked, and that the bids as ultimately submitted will be comparable. Suggestions from competitors at this stage will disclose any specifications that inadvertently may have been drawn to favor one potential bidder over others. Bids that are based on deviations from the specifications should usually be rejected. However, if the proposed change constitutes an appreciable improvement in the specifications, all carriers should be asked to rebid accordingly. Only after rebidding can proposals be compared, since it is difficult for anyone but an actuary to estimate the effect the variation in coverage will have on the premiums.

Some institutions permit only a few insurers to bid. Others open bidding to all who can meet the specifications. In either case, the insurance should be awarded to the qualified bidder who offers the lowest premium while meeting the detailed specifications.

Collection of Claims

Responsibility for the collection of all insurance claims should be assigned to the institutional officer responsible for purchasing insurance. Prosecution of claims calls for a thorough knowledge of all coverages and provisions, and the institutional insurance officer is usually the person best qualified in these respects.

Fire and Allied Coverages

General Provisions The standard fire policy insures against all direct loss by fire or lightning. Except in prescribed circumstances, it excludes losses from other causes, such as theft, even though they may occur during a fire. Loss must be from a "hostile fire," which is defined as one which escapes from its normal confines and ignites some other object. If a hostile fire occurs, coverage is also afforded for smoke damage and other directly related hazards, including damage from water and chemicals used in extinguishing the fire.

In most states ordinary policies are not valued contracts that fix in advance the amount of recovery in the event of total loss. Instead, reimbursement is limited to the current cash value of the property lost or damaged, up to the maximum specified in the policy. Because of required allowances for depreciation, the recovery may be substantially less than the replacement cost. For an additional premium, an institution can buy depreciation insurance which provides funds to replace a destroyed building with another of similar size and quality on the same site. Institutions having several old buildings should consider this coverage to avoid serious losses on buildings for which depreciation, as determined by insurance companies, has reduced the recovery value to a fraction of the replacement cost.

Extended Coverage Attached to fire policies and made a part of them is usually an extended coverage endorsement which provides against loss from windstorm, hail, explosion, riot, smoke damage, and other hazards. In addition, protection may be obtained against vandalism and malicious mischief. In areas of high earthquake incidence, protection against damage from this hazard, although expensive, may also be desirable. Like the fire policy itself, the extended coverage endorsements contain specific exclusions that should be carefully read and understood.

Policy Forms Designed for Institutions Most states now permit insurance carriers to use the Public and Institutional Property Form, which is designed especially for educational institutions, public buildings, churches, and hospitals. It combines many separate coverages in such a way as to maximize protection while often minimizing premium cost. It should be borne in mind that use of the Public and Institutional Property Form may require self-inspection of each building. Another form of policy available to educational institutions is the multiple location rating plan, under which credits may be offered when a large risk is spread out geographically. Other variations in policy form including combinations with other classes of insurance, sometimes called a "package" policy, are available in some states, offering comparable benefits in coverage and premium reduction.

Coinsurance If an institution were to carry fire insurance for only a fraction of its building value, most losses would still be covered, yet the premium would be insufficient to support the total protection afforded. To avoid this inequity, insurance companies require the application of a coinsurance clause, in which the insured agrees to carry insurance at a stated percentage of total value. If this provision is misunderstood, an institution may experience a serious loss.

In any loss, each insurance company contributes to the settlement in the same proportion that its policies bear to the total coverage. A 90 percent coinsurance clause requires the institution to self-insure any difference between the total insurance carried and 90 percent of the actual value at the time of a loss. Then, if the institution is actually carrying less insurance than the 90 percent of value, it must itself assume the uncovered proportion in the settlement of loss. This contingent obligation makes it imperative that the institution review values annually to make sure that insurance protection is maintained at the level agreed upon in the coinsurance clause.

In a few states it is permissible to have insurance policies with agreed-upon stated values—a fixed sum which will be paid in case of total loss, and some states require the use of stated values. Agreement on a stated value eliminates the requirement for coinsurance.

Concurrence Usually an institution's fire insurance coverage is divided among several policies. If any one policy omits a clause that is included in others covering the same property, there is said to be "nonconcurrence." In the event of loss, settlement will be assigned proportionately to each policy as if all other policies concurred exactly with it. For example, if one-third of the protection is provided by policies which accidentally omit a given coverage, the remaining policies may deny coverage entirely or may settle for only two-thirds of the total amount that would otherwise be recoverable. Because nonconcurrence can result in limited recovery of loss, it is important that the institution's insurance officer check all policies carefully to ensure their concurrence in every detail.

Boiler and Pressure Vessels   Most fire policies exclude losses caused by failure of boilers or pressure vessels. However, other kinds of insurance coverages are available to cover the institution's liability for bodily injury and for damage to the property of others, as well as damage to institutional property arising from such failures. Whatever coverage is arranged should be coordinated with institutional fire and liability insurance policies.

Buildings under Construction   Protection for a building under construction may be purchased as a separate policy, but it is usually covered by endorsement to the fire insurance policies of the institution. The insured value may be equal to the estimated completed value of the building or addition, or it may be increased periodically as construction progresses. If the latter method is used, reports must be filed periodically as required, so that the stated coverage does not fall below the specified coinsurance value. Procedures should be developed to keep the institutional insurance officer informed of the current status of work.

Damage to Property of Others   If an institution leases buildings owned by others, it may become liable for fire damage caused by negligence of the institution or its employees. Protection against this exposure may be obtained under a *fire legal liability policy,* available in conjunction with other standard coverages.

When a fire occurs in a residence hall, damage to student property often creates a problem in public relations. Insurance protection for such losses is both difficult to purchase and expensive. Problems can be reduced by calling to the attention of each student whose property has been damaged that most family fire insurance policies include protection for personal property located away from the home. In this way, a good many students may recover within the specified limits of their family's fire insurance policies, without reference to the insurance of the institution.

When damage occurs to the property of members of the faculty, staff, and general public, the institution should be ready to assist with recovery under their individual policies. Such recovery may be limited by exclusions in the policies relating to use of personal property in business or professional activities.

Miscellaneous Coverages

Institutions that are heavily dependent for revenues upon one or more buildings, or which are required to do so by terms of bond indentures, can purchase *business interruption* insurance which reimburses for loss of tuition or other student fees resulting from damage to the buildings by any of the covered hazards. Institutions may also wish to obtain, through endorsement, coverages known as *demolition and increased cost of construction, rental income, extra expense,* or any of scores of other types of protection. In each instance, the decision should be based on a firm estimate of cost, the degree of exposure, and the ability of the institution to self-insure itself against the particular type of loss under consideration.

General Liability

Many institutions carry a comprehensive general liability policy to protect them from suits for damages brought by individuals who have suffered injury or loss as a result of the negligence of the institution or its employees. Some institutions still rely upon the ancient immunity of charitable or state-supported institutions from liability for such negligence. Those institutions still depending upon immunity rather than insurance should seek competent legal advice periodically to reassess the probability and extent of liability on the basis of recent court decisions.

An important feature of comprehensive general liability coverage is the automatic assumption of protection on newly acquired property and new operations. The automatic coverage applies, however, only to additional exposures within classes for which coverage already is specifically provided. The insurance contract should be studied carefully in all its details to ascertain the extent of automatic coverage and to establish procedures so that the insurance company will be notified within the required periods of time.

Public liability insurance coverage assumes the obligation of the insurance company to defend the institution from legal actions, regardless of the merits of the suits. The experience of insurance company lawyers in negligence actions can be of great value to the institution. Because the obligation of the company to defend may be nullified by any assumption of responsibility by the institution, no commitments should be made without written authority from the company.

The limits of liability insurance coverage should be reconsidered periodically in light of recent experience. The cost of increased insurance limits is relatively insignificant when compared with the problems that could arise if a judgment exceeded the amount of the protection.

Special Hazards

Even a comprehensive general liability policy has certain specified exclusions. The most common are related to outside bleachers, transportation hazards, elevators, structural alterations, contingent liability for contractual obligations, aircraft and watercraft ownership or operation, and products coverage. Each hazard in these classes must be specifically listed in the policy for protection to be afforded, and any additional exposures during a policy period require prompt written notice to the insurance company.

Institutions responsible for activities in other countries will need special coverage, since most casualty policies are applicable only in the United States and Canada.

Colleges and universities are exposed to suits for actions or omissions of physicians and nurses in their health services and in medical schools. Although *malpractice insurance* is expensive, it is desirable.

Suits may be brought against teachers for alleged negligence in supervision of student activities in the classroom and in extracurricular activities. Actions have arisen not only for bodily injury but also for libel, slander, malicious prosecution, invasion of privacy, and undue familiarity. Some institutions have met this problem by purchasing *teachers liability insurance*. Others have urged faculty members and administrators to attach to their individual liability policies such endorsements as the *business pursuits endorsement,* extending coverage to professional activities. Whichever solution is selected, the question is serious enough to warrant institutional concern and the establishment of an institutional policy.

Any two or more of these types of protection may be obtained through a single manuscript policy, thereby reducing the dangers of nonconcurrence and inadvertent gaps in coverage.

It usually costs nothing to add specific protection for officers and trustees as a class. Although in some states the unqualified term "insured" includes officers and trustees, they should be referred to specifically in the insuring clause to make sure they are protected from any personal loss because of performing their professional activities on behalf of the institution.

Nuclear Exposures

Standard fire and liability insurance policies exclude most nuclear hazards; consequently, specific insurance must be purchased to fill this gap in coverage. Because of the absence of experience on which to predicate premiums and policy terms, insurance companies have banded together into two groups—one of stock companies, and one of nonassessable mutual companies—to provide insurance protection from nuclear hazards. In addition, the Atomic Energy Commission, in its contracts with colleges and universities, often agrees to furnish insurance above that available from commercial insurers. The insurance officer should familiarize himself with the requirements of research agreements relating to the handling, storage, use, and transportation of radioactive materials and should work closely with the institutional committees involved to select appropriate insurance protection.

Automobile Insurance

Automobile Liability Insurance This insurance provides the same type of protection as comprehensive general liability insurance, but is limited to accidents resulting from the ownership or operation of motor vehicles. Limits for such insurance should be comparable to those for comprehensive general liability insurance.

Certain hazards are excluded unless specifically covered: vehicles furnished in a rental service, any assumption of liability by the insured, and the use of vehicles in countries other than the United States and

Canada. If an insured vehicle is used to pull a trailer, the liability coverage on the hauling vehicle is voided unless the trailer is also insured in the same company and for the same limits.

Special fleet discounts are applicable if several vehicles are owned by an institution, the amount of the discount increasing as the size of the fleet increases. Such discounts may be applied even if the vehicles are insured in more than one company, although administration is made more difficult by a division of coverage. Automatic coverage is available, however, only if all vehicles of an institution are insured by one company.

Another important area of exposure to liability arises when vehicles not owned by the institution are used for institutional business. Insurance against this hazard is available through *non-owned automobile liability insurance*, with premiums based on the number of employees using their own vehicles for institutional business. Some policy forms also provide protection when students use their own vehicles on behalf of the institution; if the basic form does not include this coverage, an appropriate endorsement should be requested.

Automobile Physical Damage   The maximum loss by damage to a vehicle is limited to its total destruction. Therefore, an institution should consider self-insurance, thereby assuming the risk of losses from collision, fire, and theft. Collision insurance is expensive, even with the application of substantial deductibles. On the other hand, the premium cost of fire and theft coverage is relatively small and may be warranted, especially if a number of institutional vehicles are used frequently in areas where the incidence of theft is high, or if many are garaged in an area that might be subject to a single catastrophic loss.

Surety and Fidelity Coverages

Performance Payment Bonds   Although technically bonds are not insurance, for purposes of administration they may be grouped with insurance against loss through larceny. Among the several hundred kinds of bonds, all share the basic principle that the surety (the insuring company) promises to recompense the beneficiary (the college or university) if the principal (the employee or a contractor) fails to perform his obligations.

Institutions frequently require performance bonds as part of construction contracts. These are purchased by the contractor, at a cost of about 1 percent of the total contract, but the premiums are passed along ultimately to the institution. Some institutions waive the bonding requirement for certain contractors if they deem the risk worth the appreciable savings at stake. On the other hand, if the contractor fails to perform satisfactorily, the possibility of appeal to a bonding company is a strong incentive to the contractor to improve his performance, rather than risk future inability to secure bonds. The decision whether to require performance bond should be made independently for each contract.

Fidelity Bonds   The other type of bond most often encountered in institutional administration is the fidelity bond. In its simplest form the fidelity bond reimburses the institution for losses resulting from the dishonesty of a given employee. Recovery is limited to losses that occur within the term of the bond and are discovered within that term or a stated period thereafter.

The *name schedule bond* lists each person and the amount of coverage applying to him. The *position schedule bond* enumerates positions rather than individuals and eliminates the necessity of amending the schedule with every change of personnel and assignments.

The *blanket bond* provides a much broader coverage that protects the institution against peculations by all employees regardless of their position. It automatically covers additions and transfers, without notice to the surety. Most important, in the event of a loss other than an inventory shortage, the specific employees who caused the loss need not be identified as long as there is evidence that at least one covered employee was involved. There are two basic types of blanket bonds: the *blanket position bond* provides a face amount of coverage for each employee; the *primary commercial blanket bond* provides up to the face amount of protection for each loss. Each type has its advantages, and the institution's insurance officer should select the type appropriate to the circumstance.

In all fidelity bonds, requests should be made for premium reductions in exchange for agreements to have annual audits by public accounting firms and to continue specified methods of internal audit, control, and similar protective measures.

Larceny   Most institutions need protection against losses from burglary and robbery. An analysis of office procedures may indicate that different limits are required for different exposures, such as inside and outside robbery, burglary, forgery, and securities protection. Bids should be requested independently for each type of coverage so that decisions can be made as to which costs are warranted. Limits should be reviewed annually with a view to modifying them to reflect changes in operations. Since unnecessarily high limits are an extravagance, the possibility of revising procedures in order to reduce cash on hand, and hence the exposure to larceny, should be investigated. As an example: for a small additional premium, on certain days of the year when cash receipts are unusually high, such as during registration, the limits may be increased. Short-term increases are much less expensive than maintaining higher limits throughout the year.

Fidelity bonds and larceny insurance coverages can be merged into a combination policy that offers protection against loss from dishonesty, destruction, and disappearance. These so-called *"3-D" policies* eliminate gaps between separate policies and provide additional protection which usually is worth the additional cost. Other combinations of coverages can be obtained through purchase of a *scheduled crime policy,* which permits an institution to tailor coverage to its specific needs.

Inland Marine Coverages

Special inland marine policies are available to cover musical instruments, art objects, rare books, audio-visual equipment, and similar items. These are called *floaters* because they insure irrespective of the location of the property. Competitive policy forms should be evaluated carefully because coverages vary widely. The most desirable coverage is that which includes all hazards except those specifically excluded, rather than that which includes only named hazards. Unlike most other types of insurance, floaters should be valued policies to obviate disagreements about value when losses occur. Insured items must be carefully inventoried, and losses must be reported promptly.

Travel and Personal Injury Insurance

Some colleges and universities have adopted the policy that insurance coverage for travel by employees or students is a personal expense of the individual. Others assume the cost of providing such protection.

Where the latter practice is in effect, the insurance officer should investigate a group travel policy which provides the desired uniform coverage at substantial savings compared to the cost of individual policies.

Similarly, many institutions provide group coverage for injuries to students participating in intercollegiate or intramural athletics. Since this coverage often includes travel protection, if both travel and athletics policies are purchased, care should be taken to avoid wasteful duplication of coverage.

Workmen's Compensation

Although workmen's compensation is not insurance, it has many of the characteristics of insurance. Laws vary considerably among the states regarding the provisions institutions must make for coverage. Some states allow institutions to choose between a state fund, a private carrier, and direct institutional assumption of the obligation. In any event, the award to an employee who has suffered an injury or illness as a result of his work is determined by state laws and regulations.

Workmen's compensation coverage may be restricted to operations within the state. Therefore, institutions assigning employees even temporarily to work outside the state or the country should request appropriate endorsements. Special arrangements must be made with the appropriate agencies by institutions having employees classified as longshoremen, railroad crews and work gangs, crews of vessels and aircraft, and certain other classes of employees covered by Federal compensation statutes.

Experience ratings play a large part in determining premium costs. Therefore, at least annually the institutional insurance officer should review the loss record. An analysis of accidents may reveal areas of exposure which can be corrected, to reduce the number of injuries and lower premium costs. The claims-handling procedures of the carrier and policies for the establishment of reserves should also be reviewed.

The premium is adjusted at the end of each policy year on the basis of a payroll audit. At that time, the institutional insurance officer should insist upon receiving a copy of the audit work sheets from the insurance company auditors. If a review of these papers reveals that some employees have been classified in more expensive rate classes than are justified, adjustments can produce substantial premium savings.

Insurance Records and Management

The insurance officer of a college or university must maintain detailed records of all insurance coverages. Each policy should be summarized on a separate card or ledger sheet that shows the term, premium, company and brokerage, and the coverage provided. As a device to avoid lapses in coverages, the cards or ledger sheets may be filed by expiration dates.

Although insurance may, of course, be purchased at any time, renewals can profitably be scheduled to coincide with the beginning of the institution's fiscal year: the institution can then invite bids on its entire insurance program and be able to attract the interest of even the largest insurance carriers; and the uniform expiration date reduces clerical work and facilitates the combining of policies and coverages.

Detailed records of loss reimbursements from policies should be maintained. Companies furnishing student accident and health insurance, liability insurance, and other types of coverage in which payments are made directly to individuals, should be required to furnish annual statements of all claims made against the policies, details of claims paid and denied, and reports of contingent claim reserves established and closed out. The reports will help the institution to assess the effectiveness of each coverage and to furnish information to other bidders for the contracts.

Annually, all claims should be analyzed to assess the levels of deductibles and to consider possible changes in coverage. Records of accidents and other losses may reveal physical changes that could eliminate hazards. The review should also expose possibilities for credits or reclassifications that would reduce premiums.

8

Personnel

Administration

Pᴇʀsᴏɴɴᴇʟ administration is a systematic approach to manpower re-cruitment, use, and development. Its role in business organizations has grown from primarily that of record keeping to more encompassing concepts of employment, provisions for employees' welfare, and, finally, a comprehensive approach to the allocation and utilization of human resources. The chief business officer of a college or university should have an understanding of the objectives of personnel adminis-tration and of the policies and programs that will be most effective in achieving those objectives.

The administration of the personnel program should be the responsi-bility of the chief business officer. The immediate responsibility for car-rying out the program should be assigned to a single administrative of-ficer. In small institutions this person may be the chief business officer; in large institutions the personnel program may be carried out by a professionally trained staff under a director who is responsible to the chief business officer.

Personnel administration in colleges and universities is primarily concerned with technical, clerical, and service personnel, with the re-sponsibility for faculty selection, remuneration, and promotion lying with the chief academic officer. It does include, however, the adminis-tration of both the academic and nonacademic staff benefit programs and the maintenance of certain personnel records and information for all employees. Personnel administration should serve in a staff capacity and should not have line authority over employees. Although personnel policies should apply to all organizational units of the institution, the operating departments will have the final responsibility for employee relations. A primary objective of personnel management is to assist supervisors and directors of all departments in performing their functions effectively.

A statement of policies regarding the selection, remuneration, and promotion of technical, clerical, and service personnel should be prepared. It should be approved by the administrative officers and circulated to the governing board and to the members of the faculty and staff. Within the policies thus established and approved, the personnel department should be responsible for the following activities:

1. Recruiting and screening applicants;
2. Establishing training and supervisory programs;
3. Establishing a classification system;
4. Developing salary and wage plans;
5. Establishing and administering policies governing relationships between the institution and its staff members;
6. Maintaining complete personnel records and information on all technical, clerical, and service personnel, and maintaining such records on the faculty and other professional staff members as are needed for administering the program of staff benefits; and
7. Administering the program of staff benefits, both for faculty and other professional staff members and for the technical, clerical, and service personnel.

Frequently, the personnel department is also responsible for helping to develop and for administering the institutional program of safety among employees.

Recruitment

As an aid to recruitment, it is desirable to have a central employment office, with branch offices as dictated by size of the campus and geographical location of divisions. The central office should have precise information from all organizational units about the requirements for jobs to be filled. Only with comprehensive information on the skills and abilities needed can suitable candidates be recruited.

Applicants should be interviewed in private and in surroundings that will put them at ease. The person conducting the interview should be realistic in evaluating the qualifications of applicants in relation to the requirements of the job. During the interview, applicants should be given complete information about pay periods, vacations, sick leave, insurance, retirement benefits, recreational and educational privileges, and other staff benefits.

Pre-employment tests of aptitude, intelligence, and skills may be desirable in selecting technical, clerical, and service personnel. Information about suitable tests and their administration and evaluation can be obtained from members of the academic staff and from professional testing services. Testing represents only one facet of the recruiting function; results on tests should not be the sole criterion in selecting new employees.

Physical examinations are desirable to determine the physical fitness of applicants to perform the duties expected of them without undue risk of injury to themselves or their co-workers. Further, they serve to record the physical condition of workers at the time of employment, as a safeguard against unjustified claims for occupational disability. In most states such examinations are mandatory for food service employees.

After screening and examination by the personnel department, an applicant should be referred to the department chairman or supervisor where he will work. Whenever possible, two or more applicants should be referred for any given position. Final selection is the responsibility of the supervisor of the employing department.

The personnel procedures for nonprofessional positions should call for a reasonable probationary or trial period of employment. The employee's work should be reviewed during this period, and at its close a definite decision should be reached whether to continue his employment, terminate his connection with the institution, transfer him to a department or area more suited to his interests and abilities, or extend his probationary period.

Personnel administrators should be aware of, and comply with, both Federal and state legislation and regulations concerning wages, hours, and working conditions as well as discrimination in employment because of race, religion, sex, and age.

Training and Supervision of Staff Members

An effective personnel program should provide for orientation and training of all new technical, clerical, and service personnel. The extent of the training program will vary among institutions and among departments, depending on the job requirements and the abilities of the new appointees. In general, training activities should be the responsibility of the department chairman or supervisor with the assistance and advice of the personnel department.

The personnel department should develop training programs for supervisors in such areas as:

1. Functions of, and effective procedures in, administration, delegation, and supervision of duties;
2. Procedures in work analysis for training purposes;
3. Work simplification methods and procedures; and
4. Techniques for on-the-job training.

In addition, the personnel department should arrange for programs in which both supervisors and key clerical workers will be instructed in the business procedures of the institution.

Personnel policies should encourage employees to upgrade themselves. Academic courses and outside reading can broaden the range of abilities of technical workers and help supervisors and administrators gain perspective. The personnel department should encourage nonacademic staff to take advantage of courses offered in academic departments by offering tuition remissions, special enrollment privileges, or time-off arrangements, with the personnel department acting as clearinghouse for applications and approvals. In similar fashion, the staff can be given library privileges and encouragement to use them.

Classification Procedures

A sound classification plan is based on job descriptions enumerating the skills and responsibilities of all jobs. After job descriptions are prepared, like positions should be grouped into a logical system. In developing the classification plan, the requirements of a position must be carefully differentiated from the qualifications of the person who fills the position. The place of a position in the classification scheme should be determined by the duties assigned to it and the skills required to perform those duties, rather than by qualifications of the incumbent.

Wage and Salary Administration

The compensation plan should be institutionwide, although differences in requirements, qualifications, and even locations may dictate some variations among divisions or departments.

The compensation levels should, to the extent feasible, be comparable to those for positions of a similar nature in the local community and consistent within the organizational units of the institution. The compensation plan should be reviewed and adjusted periodically to reflect changes in local and national trends and changes in job requirements.

The plan should establish a minimum and a maximum salary for each position. Performance and length of service, or a combination of these two factors, usually are the bases for advancement within the position classification. Major emphasis should be placed on performance, although length of service should be given some consideration. Length of service should be less important in highly skilled or professional positions than in those which are unskilled or semiskilled.

In addition to rates of compensation, the plan should specify working hours and staff benefits.

Employee Relationships

Employee morale is improved by the development in each staff member of a sense of participation and a recognition of his part in the educational and research program of the institution. As a first step, staff members should be informed about personnel policies and procedures.

Authority and responsibility for supervising and directing the work of employees rests with departmental supervisors, not with the personnel department. Nothing in policy statements or in practices should suggest that this authority and responsibility are subject to removal from the departmental supervisors, with whom they properly rest. Staff members should have available to them a procedure for review of problems and grievances. The review should start at an administrative level above that where the grievance originates, and the procedure should provide for appeal and consideration through successive levels of supervision and administration.

Interviews with departing staff members often will reveal problems that can be corrected. Useful information is more likely to be gained if the interviews are conducted by members of the personnel department rather than by the employee's supervisor.

Personnel Records

The personnel department should maintain not only the personnel records of technical, clerical, and service employees but also such statistical information about members of the faculty and professional staff as may be required to administer the program of staff benefits. Other information of a statistical nature relating to faculty and professional staff members may be maintained by the central personnel office or by an academic administrative office or by the individual deans. Information on professional accomplishments, publications, and other academic credentials normally is maintained in the appropriate academic office, rather than in the central personnel office.

Regardless of where the records are maintained, information should be disclosed only to those who are authorized to have it.

Administering the Program of Staff Benefits

The personnel department should be responsible for administering the staff benefit program for all employees—faculty and professional staff as well as the technical, clerical, and service personnel.

Safety

The personnel department may be responsible for administering the personnel safety program and for providing training in safety measures. Sometimes the safety program and training are assigned to the director of the physical plant. Adherence to safety principles will reduce accidents, improve quality of service, and often reduce cost of operations. The elements of a sound safety program include active executive supervision, constant search for and correction of physical defects and unsafe practices, and training of workmen in safety measures.

Claims under workmen's compensation and disability laws should be processed through the personnel department.

9

Staff Benefits

A<small>N</small> important factor in attracting and retaining persons of outstanding talent and ability in colleges and universities is a staff benefits program designed to meet the special needs of those who serve higher education. Such programs in educational institutions usually include plans for retirement benefits, life insurance, medical expense insurance, and disability insurance. Other benefits offered by some institutions include provisions for the remission of tuition and fee charges for faculty and other staff members and for their dependents, housing programs, periodic health examinations, travel and personal accident insurance, recreational and cultural programs, plans for leaves of absence, and credit unions.

Since wide variation exists among institutions in regard to philosophies for staff benefits programs and in financial ability to meet their costs, only the four plans found most frequently in the programs of colleges and universities are described in this chapter.

Full communication to participants regarding the benefits available to them and on proposed changes and new features of the program is essential for successful staff benefits programs.

The Retirement Plan

The retirement plan is basic in the staff benefits program and usually represents the largest single financial commitment of an institution in such a program. In developing an adequate retirement program, consideration must be given to such factors as (1) classes of personnel to be included in the plan; (2) waiting periods; (3) retirement age; (4)

sharing of costs; (5) amount of retirement income to be provided; and (6) ownership of retirement contracts.

Participants in the retirement plan

A comprehensive retirement plan should include all personnel for whom an institution will have some responsibility at the time of retirement. As a rule, part-time and temporary appointees are not included. Retirement programs usually recognize differences among professional, technical, clerical, and service personnel by variations in the provisions of a single retirement plan or by separate plans for the different groups.

Time of participation

Some retirement plans require waiting periods before technical, clerical, and service staff members are eligible, or required, to participate. Waiting periods are less frequently required for members of the faculty and administrative officers. Waiting periods may be based on age, on length of service, or on a combination of the two factors.

Participation in the retirement plan should be mandatory during the major portion of an individual's working years. However, participation may be optional for those in service at the time a new plan is first established, and it may not be required of those appointed within a short period of time before reaching retirement age. Immediate participation should be permitted for new faculty and other staff members who bring with them retirement contracts with the same organization carrying the retirement contracts for the employing institution or who bring contracts with other carriers approved by the institution.

Age of retirement

Retirement plans should specify an age for retirement. Provision may be made for extension of service in individual cases at the option of the institution. Unless controlled, extensions may become the rule rather than the exception. Therefore, extensions should be made subject to special vote of the governing board, making clear that they are not automatic and that retirement is not postponed indefinitely but will occur on a certain date.

Sharing the costs

Arrangements for meeting the costs of retirement plans vary widely among institutions. The costs may be divided evenly between the institution and participants; the total cost may be assumed by the institution; or, varying ratios of sharing may be employed.

LEVELS OF RETIREMENT BENEFITS

The level of retirement income to be provided should be decided by institutional policy and should be reviewed periodically. Social security benefits should be considered as partial funding for this level. The retirement plan should reflect changes in the compensation of faculty and other staff members. It should also provide suitable arrangements for the payment of premiums when leaves of absence are granted, so that the steady accumulation of benefits will not be interrupted.

If the objectives of the plan are to be realized for both the early and the later years of retirement, the retirement income should be protected against the effects of inflation during the retirement years. One method of achieving this is through the use of the variable annuity contract. Such retirement contracts provide periodic payments to retired persons in amounts which reflect the changing value of the purchasing power of the dollar. Premium payments under such contracts are invested in common stocks on the assumption that the cost of living and yields from common stock investments follow similar trends.

OWNERSHIP OF BENEFITS

All staff members should have full vesting rights to their retirement contracts. "Full vesting" means that if an individual leaves his employer at any time before retirement, he takes with him all the benefits purchased by his own and his employer's contributions. Retirement contributions of the employer are a part of compensation, and if a person is deprived of immediate vesting rights, he is in effect being deprived of a portion of his compensation. The retirement plan should not allow a retiring or terminating faculty or other staff member to receive a cash settlement in lieu of a retirement annuity. The accumulated funds should be kept intact to be used solely for their intended purpose, that is, to provide retirement or death benefits.

PRIOR SERVICE BENEFITS

When a retirement plan is first established, provisions should be made for faculty and other staff members who have served the institution for many years but who will not be employed for a sufficient number of years before reaching retirement age to achieve an adequate retirement income under the regular provisions of the new plan. In establishing benefits for prior service, a method must be developed for determining the amount of retirement income applicable to the years of service before the plan becomes effective in order to ensure that benefits are made available uniformly to all.

A plan must be adopted for the payment of the cost of prior service benefits. Either of two methods may be followed. One way is to meet the payments out of current revenue. This might involve large expenditures from operating funds for many years. Another method is to fund the benefit payments through the purchase of annuity contracts. This may be done by the payment of a single premium for each eligible person when the plan is initiated or when the staff member retires. As an alternative, a series of periodic premium payments may be made, the amount of the payments being calculated to provide the desired benefits at the time of retirement. This plan spreads the cost of financing prior service benefits over the individual's remaining years of service.

OPTIONAL RETIREMENT BENEFIT PAYMENTS

Retirement plans should provide options among methods of paying the retirement benefits, so that the retiring faculty or other staff member can select an annuity applying only to himself or one applying to himself and his spouse or other beneficiary. The plan should not require selection of the option prior to the retirement date.

Retirement benefits should be explained clearly to those participating in the program, and individual conferences should be held with those to be retired perhaps two years before scheduled retirement, and again a few months before retirement date.

SALARY-OR-ANNUITY OPTION

Present regulations of the Internal Revenue Service make it possible, under a formula, for a faculty or other staff member of a college or university to reduce his salary or to forego an increase in salary, in return for the purchase by the institution of a fully vested, nonassignable annuity contract for him. This option may prove helpful to institutions in meeting the needs of older staff members who are able to give up part of current income in order to build greater security for their retirement years. Each institution should review its own needs, and obtain competent advice before adopting the salary-or-annuity option as part of its retirement program.

Life Insurance

Life insurance programs in colleges and universities usually consist of term insurance, rather than other types of coverage which accumulate cash reserves. The insurance is written on a group basis, and is issued without medical examination provided a minimum percentage of the group participates in the plan. In establishing a new life insurance plan, or in reviewing an existing plan, consideration should be given to such factors as classes of personnel to be included, waiting periods, amounts of insurance, sharing premium costs, and continuing insurance after retirement.

Life insurance plans should include all permanent, full-time personnel, either as a single group or in selected classifications. Participation should be available at the time of employment.

Amounts of insurance may be determined by one of a number of methods. Two of the principal methods are: (1) the same level of insurance is carried by the individual, regardless of age, either at a fixed amount or at a stated multiple of his basic salary or wage; and (2) the amount of insurance decreases as the age of the individual increases. This latter method is especially effective when the insurance plan is coordinated with a retirement plan in which death benefits to beneficiaries increase from year to year. Under either plan, variations in amounts of insurance may be made according to rank or job classification. Some plans permit participants to elect to take additional insurance above that provided in the basic schedules.

The cost of life insurance plans may be shared by the institution and the participants, or it may be assumed in full by the institution. If group life insurance is term insurance, coverage ceases a short time after a faculty or staff member leaves the institution. The departing individual usually has the right to convert his insurance to a permanent, individual policy without medical examination during a prescribed period of time and at the premium rate established for his age at the time of conversion. Some institutions provide continued life insurance protection after an employee retires. Such coverage will substantially increase the cost of the life insurance program.

A group life insurance plan enables a college or university to provide some life insurance protection at relatively low cost for the families of its faculty and other staff members. The plan should not be considered a substitute for personal insurance programs of individuals; instead, it should supplement such programs.

Medical Expense Insurance

The medical expense insurance plans of colleges and universities usually fall into two categories: basic hospital-surgical-medical insurance, and major medical insurance. Basic plans are designed to cover the initial expenses of hospitalization and surgical treatment. Certain hospital expenses and charges as well as surgical fees are covered by this insurance up to scheduled amounts. Major medical insurance is designed to meet the costs of catastrophic or extraordinary medical expenses. Both insurance plans provide coverage for the employee as well as for his dependents within specified classifications.

All full-time, permanent faculty and other staff members should be eligible for participation in the medical expense insurance plan at, or soon after, the time of employment. The cost of the insurance may be paid entirely by the institution, or by the individual, or it may be shared. One method of sharing the cost is payment by the institution of the premiums for the faculty or other staff member, and payment by the individual of the premiums for his dependents.

Disability Income Insurance

Most periods of disability of college and university personnel because of sickness and injury are of short duration and are not a threat to a faculty or other staff member's financial security. In contrast, disability of long duration almost invariably has a severe economic impact on the individual and his family. Protection against loss of earnings during a short-term disability usually is provided by colleges and universities through salary continuation programs, either formal or informal. In addition, workmen's compensation laws provide income benefits for injuries arising in the course of employment or for occupational illness.

Long-term disability insurance provides an income to the totally disabled person beginning after a specified period of disability and continuing during disability to the age of retirement. The plan may also continue regular contributions to the retirement annuity contract so that retirement income will not be reduced by disability.

Federal Social Security Provisions

The Federal social security program provides substantial retirement, disability, and survivor benefits, based on prescribed earnings schedules. It also provides medical expense benefits. Benefits available through Federal programs should be taken into consideration in designing retirement and insurance programs in colleges and universities.

Review of the Staff Benefits Program

Every college and university should review its program of staff benefits periodically to determine its effectiveness and to adjust the program to changing conditions.

10

Physical Plant

The operation and maintenance of buildings, grounds, and other physical facilities of an educational institution are the responsibility of the chief business officer. These functions are usually coordinated by a professionally trained person who reports to the chief business officer and is designated "director of physical plant" or "superintendent of buildings and grounds."

For administrative purposes, the physical plant division should be organized according to functions. The head of the division should appoint a supervisor for each function that he does not personally direct. Generally there are six basic areas of responsibility in the physical plant division: custodial services; maintenance of buildings; maintenance of grounds; heating, air conditioning, and utility systems; physical plant shops and stores; physical plant services. In addition, various other responsibilities frequently are assigned to the physical plant organization.

Custodial Services

Custodial care includes sweeping, mopping, waxing, dusting, refuse disposal, and similar daily routines required to keep buildings in a clean, orderly, and comfortable condition. There is an identifiable correlation between the level of maintenance in college buildings and the respect shown the physical plant facilities by students and faculty.

The area assigned to each custodian may vary from an entire building, including adjacent walkways and grounds, to one part of one floor in a large, complex structure. There are no fixed rules for correlating square feet, number of student stations, number of rooms, or nature of the facilities, with man-hours or number of personnel required to perform the work. The controlling factors in assigning custodians are the skill, training, and experience of the worker, the adequacy of supervision, the age and type of building, and the standard of performance required. In addition, the extent to which mechanized equipment is provided and used properly will have a direct bearing on the efficiency of the custodian.

Local fire prevention and safety ordinances, institutional policies regarding smoking, the presence of eating areas in addition to the regular dining halls, cafeterias, and lunchrooms, and the housekeeping standards set and maintained—all will affect the amount of time custodial work will take and, therefore, how many people will be required and how much it will cost. The only confirmed ways of determining the number of custodians needed are: regular review of work assignments by experienced supervisors, and adjustments of work loads so that they are consistent with desired results. Adequate training of custodial personnel (an administrative responsibility of supervisors) influences both quality and efficiency of service.

Maintenance of Buildings

The maintenance of buildings, as distinguished from custodial services, includes minor repairs, replacements, painting, other preventive maintenance, and changes that can be handled by full-time skilled or semiskilled physical plant personnel. This group of workers may include electricians, plumbers, painters, carpenters, and skilled mechanics. The work of these men should be planned and organized on the basis of regularly required servicing, emergency requests, and an annual schedule for painting, repairs, and other preventive maintenance activities. In small institutions the maintenance crew may be limited to one or two men, including the director himself. In large universities each one of the skills may be represented by a separate staff of several men.

When extensive repair or renovation projects must be completed during brief periods, such as between school sessions and during vacation periods, additional help may be employed on a temporary basis, or the projects may be performed under contract with outside concerns. If a particular project requires skills or costly equipment not available at the institution, the services and equipment should be obtained from outside sources on the basis of competitive bids.

Maintenance of Grounds

Maintenance of an attractively landscaped campus will enhance the respect shown the institution by students, staff, and the general public. This responsibility of the physical plant division requires personnel to maintain lawns, shrubbery, flower beds, walkways, and parking areas, and to remove snow and perform other similar services. In addition, professional service is needed for both landscape design and supervision of the groundskeepers. In large institutions, the responsibilities may require the attention of a full-time staff member; in institutions with limited needs, the services may be obtained on a contract basis. Some institutions use local nurseries for all grounds maintenance work.

A master plan for campus landscape development should be prepared by a landscape architect engaged especially for the purpose or by the institution's supervising architect, if one has been appointed. The master plan should include projections of the location of future buildings, roads, parking lots, walkways and playing fields and should deal comprehensively with the location of subsurface utilities, service roads, maintenance buildings, and the practical aspects of maintaining lawns with sprinkler systems and mechanical equipment. For practical reasons, the supervisory personnel concerned with campus maintenance should be asked to study and approve any master plan and modifications of it before they are adopted. After a master plan has been adopted, all plantings of lawns, trees, and shrubbery should proceed according to the plan in order to ensure consistent development of landscape treatment.

Heating, Air Conditioning, and Utility Systems

The cost of operating the heating system is a major item in the physical plant budget. The director of the physical plant should determine whether the system in use is both efficient and economical in view of the services to be provided. The cost and availability of gas, electricity, oil, and coal may decide which fuel is best used.

Choice of a central heating plant or of individual heating units in each building, or a combination of the two, is a matter that will be governed by such factors as age of existing buildings and cost and availability of different types of fuels. Recommendations and decisions regarding changes in existing heating services or in services to be provided in new buildings should be predicated on professional engineering studies that set forth both the probable cost of original installation and of operation. Institutions located in urban centers should explore the potential advantage of buying steam from municipal sources, if it is available.

The inclusion of air-conditioning systems in new buildings and structures requires evaluations similar to those considered in judging heating systems. The costs of systems serving individual buildings should be compared with those for central systems, for example, a system that circulates chilled water to many buildings. In considering the installation of air-conditioning systems in older buildings, the costs of initial installation and of operating individual room package-units should be compared with the costs of a central air-conditioning system.

The operation of the utilities systems requires technical competence and constant supervision. Proposals for utilities systems should be reviewed by the insurance carriers' engineering and inspection divisions since the safety and risk features of systems have a direct bearing on premium rates. The use of automatic electronic controls for routine operations usually reduces the number of service personnel needed, and, often, the extra initial cost of the devices is offset by savings in salaries. Any plan for modification or expansion of utility systems should be required to include consideration of the latest engineering developments.

Physical Plant Shops and Stores

The physical plant division must be provided with a shop equipped with the basic tools and machines that the maintenance personnel will need. Its size and the variety and sophistication of the equipment will be governed by number of buildings and size of campus. Most institutions have found it advantageous to construct or assign a separate building, usually on the periphery of the campus, exclusively to this purpose.

If practical, the service building should house the offices of the director of the physical plant and his staff, and should also serve as the headquarters for the maintenance staff. With the exception of custodial personnel, who go directly to and depart from their duty stations, all plant employees should report at a central point in the service building at both the beginning and the end of their working hours. On very large campuses there may be several reporting stations. If work schedules are planned in advance and are assigned at the beginning of working days, this reporting system promotes efficient use of the time of physical plant staff members. Supervisors should prepare work assignments based on daily progress. Variations from the total time estimated for each assignment should be reviewed and explained as part of the supervisory responsibility.

An essential adjunct of the physical plant shop is a storeroom or warehouse for supplies used in plant operation and maintenance. If possible, the storage area should be in the service building, and all shipments of custodial and shop supplies should be delivered there. A receiving clerk should verify shipments with purchase orders and place the goods on shelves according to a predetermined system for inventory control and for efficient service to the physical plant personnel.

Withdrawals from the stores should be by requisitions that identify the buildings and work orders involved. This procedure provides data essential for cost accounting and for control of materials. The variety and volume of supplies stocked will be determined by the size and complexity of the institution. The chief business officer should review the annual inventory of the stores to determine that stock and proposed purchases are limited to essential and regularly used items.

The physical plant stores may be a part of a central stores system operated by the purchasing department.

Other Physical Plant Services

In addition to the responsibilities and functions described above, the physical plant division frequently is assigned responsibility for other services and activities.

MAJOR PLANT PROJECTS

Academic departments and administrative offices may request unusual repairs, replacements, building or room modifications, or new construction which are beyond the scope of routine maintenance, for which funds normally are provided in the budget of the physical plant division. Three principal methods are used by colleges and universities for budgeting, accounting, and reporting the cost of such projects.

In one method, a schedule of requests is reviewed and costs are estimated at the time of budget preparation. To the extent that funds are available, amounts are allocated to the physical plant division, identified under a separate budget category such as Major Plant Projects.

Another method is to allocate funds for the projects to the departments and organizational units requesting work. This method has the disadvantage of distorting the operating budgets and financial reports of the departments and organizational units for the year in which the major projects are performed. Furthermore, departmental chairmen and directors of organizational units may feel entitled to use the budget allocation for other purposes if, for some reason, it is not used for its approved purpose.

A third plan is to budget all major plant projects in the Funds for Renewals and Replacement in the plant funds accounts.

An institution should select the method, or perhaps a combination of methods, that best suits its situation.

If a project cannot be performed by the physical plant staff, for any reason, the work may be assigned to an outside contractor selected on the basis of the lowest acceptable bid. This procedure assigns responsibility for building modifications and repairs to the director of the physical plant, with whom such responsibility should reside.

Communications services

Responsibility for the supervision of the telephone system, intracampus communications systems, and campus mail service may be assigned to the physical plant division. Requests for additional services by departments, offices, and other organizational units should be evaluated according to the established need for them and with recognition of the costs involved.

Campus security control

Administration of security systems and programs usually is the responsibility of the physical plant division. Institutional security includes the campus police and watchman service; supervision and control of campus traffic, parking, and parking lots; and maintenance of order and control of crowds attending events on the campus. In some large institutions, security services are complex organizations under the direction of a trained specialist. In such cases, the director may report to the chief business officer rather than to the director of the physical plant division. Many urban institutions find it economically advantageous to contract on an annual basis with private agencies that provide complete security services, including personnel and alarm and similar safety protective devices.

Responsibility for the development and administration of safety programs, including the identification of safety hazards to students, faculty, and staff members as well as to the general public, may be assigned to the physical plant division, or it may be under the direction of other offices or divisions (such as the personnel department) responsible to the chief business officer.

The problem of law violation on institutional property by students, staff, or the public should be resolved in cooperation with public agencies. This sensitive area of administration involves the responsibility and authority of both institutional and public police personnel. Consideration should be given to having at least some of the institutionally employed police become deputized officers of the law, so that their scope of authority is enlarged in dealing with violations of the law. The chief business officer and his representatives should avoid assuming responsibility of a disciplinary or law enforcement character, which properly belongs to other administrative officers of the institution or to the public police authorities.

TRANSPORTATION

Responsibility for the administrative control, maintenance, service, and repair of all institutionally owned motor vehicles may be assigned to the physical plant division or it may be assigned to the supervisor of a motor pool operated as a service department. Automobiles usually are assigned for use by faculty and staff on the basis of approved requisitions. The extent to which an institution maintains repair facilities for its motor pool depends on the number of units. If buses or large numbers of vehicles are involved, campus-based repair shops usually are economically feasible. Some institutions use vehicle-rental agencies that supply cars, trucks, buses, and all other types of motor units on an annual contract basis.

Campus Planning

Institutions concerned with the expansion of enrollments or with the extensive improvement and rehabilitation of plant facilities should establish a formal long-range campus plan. This plan must be based on detailed institutional plans and objectives as determined by the responsible academic and administrative officers and committees.

The physical facilities plan should be developed and maintained under the direction of a permanent campus planning committee that is appointed by the president, and functions under the direction of a coordinating officer. Its membership should include the chief academic officer, the chief business officer, the director of the physical plant division, and representatives of the faculty. It should have the assistance of professional architects, engineers, and landscape architects.

The plan should identify the location of new buildings, utilities and service connections, road systems, walkways, parking, playing fields, and all aspects of lawns and landscaping, taking into account both function and aesthetics. It should be the responsibility of the committee to select and recommend to the president the sites for new buildings, with the recommendations being appropriate to the use of the buildings and consistent with the master plan.

The first step in developing a master plan should be an analysis to determine the capacity of existing facilities. The determination of adequacy should be based on studies of current space utilization and also of requirements previously established for classrooms, lecture rooms, laboratories, offices, and communication and other special-purpose facilities. The analysis should then proceed to projected requirements for increased numbers of students and faculty and for new educational, research, and service programs. Based on these projections, the number of additional or replacement structures required can be anticipated. The comparative urgency of needs should be translated into some rating of priorities which, in turn, must be related to over-all institutional needs and resources.

New Construction

A small *ad hoc* committee should be appointed to oversee the planning of each building project. Committee members should include representatives of the business office and of the departments and organizational units that are to use the new structure.

An architect should be appointed for each building project. In selecting the architect, the following steps should be observed:

1. Several interested architects, or architectural firms, should be invited to submit their credentials for consideration.

2. Of the firms submitting credentials, the selection should be made from among those having experience in designing buildings comparable to the one proposed.

3. Each of the firms selected for further consideration should be invited to meet with the governing board or a committee of the board to describe the size of their staff, their philosophy of design, and their method of translating building programs into design. They should also be asked to submit visual presentations of some of their designs already constructed.

4. The chief business officer should talk personally with clients named by the architect as references and with several other clients the architect is known to have served. He should inquire into the following:

a) The architect's ability to establish and maintain good working relationships with programing committees and administrative personnel during the design period;

b) The extent to which bids on construction came within projected budgets;

c) The number and nature of change orders required during construction;

d) The degree of supervision exercised by the architect during construction;

e) The degree to which the completed building served the program for which it was planned;

f) Defects in the building traceable to defective architectural design.

In addition, the chief business officer and committee members or officers directly concerned with the proposed project should visit comparable buildings designed by the candidates. During the visits, officers at the host institution may be asked about the points listed above.

A written summary of the composite views of the visitors should be submitted to the president in supporting nominations for appointments.

5. Final appointment of an architect should be by action of the governing board, upon recommendation of the president.

Each new building project requires at least the following steps from the planning stage through acceptance of the job as completed:

1. Cooperative preparation, by the architect and the *ad hoc* commit-

tee for the project, of a detailed program of the functions or purposes for which the new building is to be planned.

2. Preparation by the architect and review by the committee of schematic drawings that suggest room arrangements and broad features of design of the project.

3. Preparation by the architect of preliminary drawings which present in semifinal form the design and plan of the project, together with preliminary cost estimates. These plans may include a model or an artist's drawing of the final appearance of the building. The preliminary plans should be approved by the governing board before the architect is authorized to proceed further with his work.

4. Preparation of final working drawings and specifications for contractors to bid on and to follow during construction.

5. Preparation of invitations to bid on the project. A group of selected contractors may be invited to bid, or the project may be offered to all contractors wishing to submit bids. Bids may be taken from a single contractor for the total project. Or, depending on the complexity of the project, separate bids may be taken for basic construction; plumbing, heating, ventilation, and air conditioning; electrical work; elevators; special installations, and other areas of construction or installation.

When public funds are involved, the chief business officer must ensure that regulations and statutes applicable to the advertising and receipt of bids and the awarding of contracts are followed. Guidance, if needed, should be sought from the architect and from legal counsel.

6. During construction, the architect is expected to make regular inspections of the project and to guard against defects and deficiencies in the work of the contractor. To minimize the possibility of mistakes by construction workers, a project inspector, or clerk-of-the-works, acceptable to both the architect and the institution, should be employed. The salary is paid by the institution and is accounted for as part of the project cost.

7. Before buildings are accepted from contractors as completed, the architect, the director of the physical plant, the clerk-of-the-works, and the chief business officer should conduct a thorough inspection in company with the contractor. A final list of all uncompleted or unsatisfactory items should be made. Before final payment is made, all items on the "punch list" should have been completed to the satisfaction of the institution and architect.

Building Records

A record file of each building should be maintained in the office of the director of the physical plant. The records should include, among the items, the date of construction; original cost; date, nature, and cost of major renovations; electrical and plumbing systems; floor plans; a record of painting and routine maintenance; and the original architectural drawings and construction specifications. For accurate information and future use, the file should also include "as built plans" and the working drawings and plans of subcontractors and each of the mechanical trades. The drawings should be on cloth of a type that permits making additional copies.

11

Inventory of Plant Assets

T‍HE value of all permanent property of a college or university should be recorded in the general accounting records by means of control accounts for each major class or category of property. These values should be substantiated by inventory records that also reflect the value of property on loan or lease or otherwise in the custody of the institution. Because the establishment and maintenance of inventory records can be costly in time and money, the complexity of an inventory system should be limited to that information needed for the management of the institution.

Inventory records can be regarded as adequate if they serve such management purposes as:

1. Identifying equipment in the case of loss by fire, theft, or disappearance;
2. Identifying property acquired under sponsored research projects, including buildings as well as equipment, whether such property is owned by the institution, by the government, or by another sponsoring organization;
3. Aiding in the computation of indirect costs for research and other sponsored projects;
4. Providing information to determine departmental custody and responsibility;
5. Providing historical information on location, age, quantity, source of funds for the purchase of plant assets, and similar data; and
6. Aiding in the maximum utilization of plant assets, especially

equipment, and expediting the transfer of such items from department to department.

Each institution must decide how extensive its inventory records need be and then adopt policies and procedures that will yield information effectively and economically. Governmental regulations may also influence inventory procedures.

The work of establishing and maintaining inventory records can be simplified by using data processing, tabulating, and other mechanical equipment. Sophisticated equipment, with its various types of memory banks, frequently obviates the need to set up ledger sheets, inventory lists, and card files, and reduces the work of updating records. If such equipment is available, many of the procedures described in this chapter can be omitted. Otherwise, the procedures and inventory record forms described will be found essential for an adequate inventory system.

Classification and Valuation of Plant Assets

Plant assets of educational institutions are classified as: land, buildings, improvements other than buildings, and equipment. Additional classifications found in some institutions are livestock, leasehold improvements, and equities in properties held by others. Real properties held as investments of endowment funds should be separately identified in the inventory records.

Plant assets may be acquired by purchase, gift, construction, or exchange. Those acquired by purchase or construction should be valued at cost; those acquired by gift, at appraised value as of date of gift; and those received in exchange for other property of the institution may be carried either at the value of the property given in exchange, or at appraised value on date of exchange. Plant assets should be carried at these values in the inventory records and in the plant accounts as long as they remain in the possession of the institution. If the valuation is based on an appraisal, this should be disclosed in the financial reports.

Equipment not owned by an institution but in its custody (for example, laboratory equipment loaned by an outside agency) should be reflected in the inventory records at reasonable valuations, even though such equipment is not carried in the accounting records.

Land

Separate ledger sheets for all tracts of land or campus areas should be set up in a subsidiary ledger to support the general ledger account for land. The valuation of the land should be the cost or, in the case of gifts, appraised value. In addition, other records should be established in the inventory system, and kept up to date, to record the following information: complete legal description of each tract; zoning and other legal restrictions; area in acres or square feet; use; date and source of acquisition; deed, abstract, and title reference; reference to vouchers, orders, contracts, and accounts or appropriations to which the cost of each tract was charged; and reference to minutes of the governing board relating to the acquisition of the land.

In addition to the actual purchase price, the valuation of land should include commissions and fees to attorneys, brokers, agents, appraisers, and others; costs of search, examination, registration, and guaranty or insurance of titles; conveyance and recording fees; taxes assumed at date of purchase; costs of grading, building demolition, or other conditioning of the land for use when such expenses are not in connection with the construction or improvement of buildings; and other similar special items of expense.

Buildings and Improvements Other than Buildings

A separate ledger sheet for each building and facility should be set up in a subsidiary ledger to support the general ledger accounts for buildings and for improvements other than buildings.

Buildings includes all structures and the permanently affixed furniture, machinery, appurtenances, and appliances, such as: laboratory tables, lockers, bookcases, and dressers; boilers, furnaces, fixtures, and machinery for heating, lighting, plumbing, air conditioning, and other power plant equipment; elevators and auxiliary elevator equipment; vaults and conduits constructed as part of the buildings; signal and clock systems; utility systems; and compressed air systems.

Improvements Other than Buildings includes streets, roads, sidewalks, bridges, and viaducts; tunnels and conduit systems outside buildings; central air conditioning, lighting, water, and sewer systems; trees, plantings, and landscaping; and retaining walls when not a part of buildings. Costs of surfacing, fencing, lighting, and similar improvements to athletic fields, other recreational areas, and parking lots should be included in this classification, the value of the land itself being carried in the account for land.

The valuation of buildings and other structures should include payments to contractors or, if no contractor is employed, payments by the institution for the purchase of materials and for labor; legal, architectural, and engineering fees; and costs of surveys, permits, test drillings, and performance bonds. Insurance paid by the institution and interest costs during construction should also be included.

Other identifiable direct expenses of the institution during construction, such as salaries and wages of physical plant staff involved in construction projects and the costs of utilities furnished for construction projects, should be included in the valuation of the structures.

When a building is purchased, a fair apportionment of the value of the land included in the purchase price should be made to the inventory records for land and to the account for land.

When major improvements add substantially to the value of buildings, the cost should be reflected in the appropriate ledger sheets. Expenditures for the installation of such improvements as laboratory tables, hoods, air-conditioning equipment and systems, elevator systems, and similar facilities should be recorded in the building inventory records. If attached equipment or facilities are removed from buildings, as frequently is done during programs of remodeling, renovation, and rehabilitation, the building inventory records should be adjusted accordingly. Unless the original cost of the facilities being removed can be determined, it may be desirable to establish their value through appraisal.

Building programs sometimes involve the removal of landscaping, sidewalks, curbs, streets, and other similar improvements from the site of new structures. When this is done, the property records should reflect appropriate reductions in the recorded value of these items.

In addition, other records should be maintained in the inventory system, to record the following information: a complete description of each structure, including reduced scale plans; number of floors; area and volume; construction materials; date of construction or acquisition; cost; location; use; source of the acquisition; in the case of buildings or structures purchased from others; notation of the location of deed and abstracts; references to vouchers, orders, contracts, and accounts or appropriations to which the purchase or construction costs were charged;

and citation to minutes of the governing board relating to the acquisition or construction of the property.

Equipment

This category includes all movable property of a permanent nature. Because a large number of items are involved, an equipment inventory system is expensive. Therefore, the estimated cost of any proposed system should be weighed carefully against the benefits anticipated from it. Decisions about inclusion or exclusion of equipment items in the inventory records should be based on such factors as probable useful life, established minimum cost per unit, or a combination of these factors. Determining factors will vary among institutions, and frequently publicly controlled institutions are directed by statutory or other regulations which items of equipment are to be inventoried. In general, considerable unjustifiable expense and work can be avoided by excluding from the inventory records many low-cost items that are normally classified as equipment but that fall below the minimum standards set for inclusion in the inventory records.

A standardized terminology should be developed and used to ensure that identical items are described, classified, and recorded alike.

Equipment in use on sponsored research projects should be included in inventory records as required by contract or grant terms, but those items to which the institution does not hold title should be excluded from plant funds accounts (see section on "Property Ownership and Accountability" in chapter 5, "Administration of Research and Other Sponsored Programs," pages 53–54).

Inventory records should indicate the extent to which government funds have been used in the acquisition of equipment and the construction of buildings, in order to help to determine the rate of reimbursement for indirect costs on federally sponsored programs.

A SIMPLIFIED EQUIPMENT INVENTORY SYSTEM

The objectives of an adequate equipment inventory system may be achieved without complex and expensive procedures. The system should provide a listing of all equipment items purchased or acquired by the institution, together with concise information about date of acquisition, cost, description, and other data deemed necessary by management. The system should provide for periodic verification that the

equipment items still are in existence on the campus, except that re-
movable equipment items highly susceptible to theft should be subject
to more frequent and special verification.

Some institutions have developed equipment inventory systems that
are adequate, yet modest in cost of maintenance. One technique is the
periodic use of a camera with a wide-angle lens to photograph the contents of a room or an equipment cupboard. Identification is provided
by including in each picture a small chalk board or sign showing the
name of the building, the room number, and the date of the record. In
the event of fire, the appropriate pictures are enlarged, and accounting
records are examined to ascertain the cost of each piece of equipment
or furniture in the damaged area. From this information, claims lists
are prepared. In view of the infrequency of total-loss fires, this system
is more economical than a complex inventory system.

No inventory system will prevent thefts; it will only indicate when
they have occurred. Items of high theft incidence, such as projectors,
adding machines, microscopes, fans, cameras, tape recorders, typewriters, audio-visual equipment, calculators, and similar easily portable
items should be stenciled with the name of the institution in large
print. Generally it is considered unnecessary to affix institutional identification tags or numbers to desks, tables, bookcases, and other items
which are less susceptible to theft.

For institutions that need to substantiate values of equipment for use
in computing indirect cost rates, simple lists of items originally on hand
plus lists of equipment subsequently purchased usually suffice. When
these are accompanied by periodic photographic records of equipment
actually in place, audits can determine the validity of values claimed.

A DETAILED EQUIPMENT INVENTORY SYSTEM

A more complete system of equipment inventory may be developed
by institutions that are required to maintain fuller records and by those
desiring to do so. Although the information to be entered in the inventory records will depend on the needs of the institution, the following
items should be considered: a complete description of each item, including size, material, type and color of finish, model or serial number,
and perhaps the vendor's catalogue number; date of acquisition; cost;
source of acquisition; citation of vouchers, orders, and accounts or appropriations to which the purchase was charged; location of the equipment by building and room; and the institution's identifying number.

The ultimate disposition of the items of equipment also should be a part of the inventory records. The inventory records for motor vehicles and motorized equipment may call for more detailed information, such as the complete data needed for state and municipal registration.

A separate card may be prepared for each item of equipment, a device that facilitates periodic physical inventory verification. Groups of identical items, such as classroom chairs and tables, in which the unit cost figure is less than the minimum established for equipment to be inventoried but which involve large expenditures of funds and many individual items, may be recorded in the inventory records in total figures only. Items in different buildings should not be grouped in one inventory record; nor should items be grouped if the essential information does not apply uniformly.

Tabulating and data processing equipment is especially effective in inventory records and reports for movable equipment. Information can be sorted and reproduced in a variety of ways quickly so that duplicate files of cards and other information become unnecessary.

Consumable items purchased for installation in new buildings, such as linens and dishes, may be inventoried in total and included at cost in the account for equipment. Complete details need not be included in the inventory records. Replacements should be charged to operating expense accounts or to the renewal and replacement reserves.

Since the costs shown on the equipment inventory records substantiate the value shown in the account for equipment in the plant funds accounts, procedures must provide for accumulating the value of new equipment acquired during a fiscal period. One way is to prepare new inventory cards promptly from either the original purchase orders or vouchers and keep them as a separate file during the year. Then, before they are transferred to the permanent files, the total cost of equipment purchased during the year is determined from the cards and the value added to the equipment account in the plant funds account.

New equipment which is to be labeled with a code number should be marked promptly upon delivery to the campus and acceptance by the institution. If this is not possible, each item should be marked when the physical inventory is verified against the inventory cards for new equipment purchased during the year, before they are placed in the permanent files.

Inventory cards usually are filed by location (that is, by building and room) or by department. If tabulating or data processing equipment is not available, it may be desirable to maintain a duplicate file by class of equipment, such as microscopes, typewriters, chairs, and tables. A third file arranged by departments, may be useful.

A form should be developed to report items that become unserviceable or obsolete and items that are no longer needed by departments and offices. The business office should arrange for the physical removal of the equipment. This same form should be used to report equipment that has disappeared or that has been destroyed or otherwise disposed of by a department or office. The inventory cards should note the final disposition of items so reported and the cards should be retained in a separate file during the fiscal year. At the end of the year the plant funds accounts should be adjusted by the book value of the items involved. The inventory cards should then be placed in the permanent file for equipment items no longer in the possession of the institution.

Books and Collections

Although books and collections are items of movable equipment, their inventory records call for procedures different in some respects from those for other equipment.

The general library should maintain records of all books and other library items regardless of the source of funds used in acquiring them and regardless of their location within the institution. These records will suffice as detailed inventory records and should not be duplicated in the inventory records of the business office.

Books, periodicals, microfilms, and the binding of periodicals should be included in the inventory records at cost. Adjustments should be made in the records for volumes and materials discarded, lost, or for other reasons removed from the library, according to information provided by the library personnel. Such adjustments may be made at the rate—annually revised—of "average cost per volume acquired."

In the case of art and scientific collections, including slide collections, the department or office having custody of the collection may establish its own record of each item; frequently it employs specialist personnel to maintain the inventory records as well as the collection. In such cases the inventory records in the business office should include only the official name of the collection, a general description, and the total estimated value.

Responsibility for Inventory

Ownership of items of equipment rests with the institution rather than with a department or office, regardless of whether the equipment may have been purchased from departmental budget allocations or from special appropriations or allocations for equipment.

The business office should be responsible for custody and transfer of equipment items and for maintenance of inventory records. Loans of equipment, either to or by an institution, should be under the control of the business office, rather than departments or other units. The obligations of both the borrower and the lender during the period of the loan should be clearly defined. Such loans should be recorded in the central inventory records if an appreciable length of time is involved.

The business office should also have responsibility for all records and reports of equipment in the custody of, but not owned by, the institution. Such equipment may be on loan or it may have been purchased with research funds but with title remaining with the granting agency. Any special treatment related to custody, insurance obligations, and inventory reports should be handled by the business office.

Within the departments, chairmen should be responsible for the proper use and protection of equipment. They should submit scheduled, periodic reports to the business office and cooperate with that office in taking physical inventories. They should also notify the business office promptly of the acquisition of equipment through gifts and loans; of lost, damaged, obsolete, and worn-out items; of thefts and other disappearances of equipment; and of items no longer needed.

Personal books and equipment of professors and other employees brought to the campus should be so identified by the owners in order to avoid misunderstanding about ownership.

Physical Inventory Verification

Equipment inventory cards constitute the subsidiary ledger supporting the total value in the general ledger account for equipment. Depending on the amount of detail recorded and the uses of the records, periodic verifications and reconciliations should be made of the inventory cards, the general ledger account, and the equipment items.

Institutional policy should determine the frequency of physical verification. In some institutions this may be annually. In others, only selected items, chosen because they are subject to frequent loss, are physically verified each year. A third means is to verify the equipment in only a portion of the campus—buildings and locations—each year, the entire institution to be covered in a period of, say, five years.

Establishing Inventory Records

In setting up a physical plant inventory records system where there has been none, first, work sheets should be developed to list the information to be included in the permanent inventory records. Different types of sheets should be developed for land, for buildings, for improvements other than buildings, and for equipment.

Historical information on acquisition and cost may not still exist if purchase orders, vouchers, contracts, and minutes of the governing board are not available. If it is impractical to devote the time, effort, and funds necessary to locate them, appraisal firms may be employed to establish valuations. If complete and accurate descriptions of land holdings are not readily at hand, the services of surveying and title-examining firms may be used to obtain them.

Field work will be necessary to record descriptions and locations of equipment items. Separate work sheets should be used for each room in each building, and the institution's identifying number should be affixed to the items as the field work is being done.

Work papers may serve as the inventory records for a year or two until the complete physical verification of equipment and the review of land and buildings can be completed. This interim form will obviate extensive corrections and changes in permanent records, which might be required were the information transferred immediately to permanent inventory records.

Purchasing

C OLLEGES and universities require a wide variety of supplies, equipment, and services. An effective organization for purchasing is essential to promote the basic objectives of an educational institution by freeing faculty and staff members from the necessity of procuring their own supplies and equipment. The purchasing function can be performed more effectively and economically by specialists than by those for whom purchasing is not a primary responsibility.

The objective of purchasing is to procure products and services with due consideration to quality, quantity, delivery date, and price. To the fullest extent possible, the purchasing department should group the requirements of all departments and offices in the institution to obtain the benefits of quantity buying. Standardization of materials and equipment is desirable. An effective stores system will reduce expensive emergency buying. The use of competitive bidding and the development of new sources of supply will aid in obtaining advantageous prices.

Organization

The responsibility for purchasing should be centralized even though the volume of buying may not be large enough to warrant a full-time appointee or a separate staff. Regardless of size of institution, the officer charged with the purchasing function should be responsible to the chief business officer.

Some of the more significant advantages to be gained through centralization of the purchasing function include:

1. A more effective scheduling of the total requirements of the institution, with economies resulting from pooling the requirements of all departments and offices and then purchasing in larger quantities;
2. The development of standard specifications for supplies and equipment;
3. A reduction in administrative costs for purchasing by elimination of multiple purchasing personnel and systems, and by the selection, training, and development of personnel qualified to perform the purchasing operations;
4. The improvement of delivery and service by suppliers through careful selection and uniform and efficient follow-up procedures;
5. An effective and uniform system for inspecting and testing supplies and equipment; and
6. A reduction of inventories through improved control and by the elimination of obsolete and duplicate items.

Specialized purchasing operations may be delegated to personnel outside the central purchasing organization. For example, the procurement of food commodities and supplies often is delegated to the director of the food service; library books, to the members of the library staff; merchandise for resale in the student store, to the manager of the store; insurance, to the institutional insurance officer; and contracts for new construction, to an officer responsible for construction planning or supervision.

Purchasing authority and responsibility should be delegated in writing, and should include any prescribed limits on types of purchases and dollar amounts.

Public Relations and Ethics

Effective purchasing in an educational institution is a cooperative undertaking between buyer and supplier, and between the purchasing staff and other personnel within the institution. The purchasing department must maintain satisfactory relationships with both external suppliers and internal "consumers" in order to fulfill the procurement function properly. Satisfactory relations and effective cooperation between the staff of the purchasing department and the other personnel of the institution will prevail if the procurement functions are performed with understanding and competency. The purchasing staff must be sensitive to problems and needs of departments (and individuals), must try to anticipate where controversies might arise, and must cultivate good public relations.

Suppliers who have made gifts to an institution, or whose officers or representatives are donors or are alumni, or who are located in the same community, occasionally request special considerations. Only if quality, service, and price are identical to those offered by others should the institution consider granting such preference. To grant preference on any other basis is insupportable, since there is no rational way of placing a value on an alleged reason for preference. Furthermore, frequent departure from sound bidding procedures may eliminate competition or place competition on the basis of political pressure or personal contacts rather than on the proper grounds of quality, service, and price.

The purchasing power of an institution should not be used for personal acquisitions for faculty and other staff members unless suppliers are fully aware of the nature of these relationships. Some institutions maintain lists of suppliers offering special consideration to institutional personnel, who then deal directly with each other. Such an arrangement provides a service to faculty and staff members, but avoids possible conflicts of interest and relieves the institution of any problems resulting from the special handling required for purchases of a personal nature.

A code of conduct for the staff members of the purchasing department, defining obligations and ethics, should be published. The following set of principles has been adopted by the National Association of Educational Buyers:

1. To give first consideration to institutional objectives and policies;
2. To obtain the maximum ultimate value for each dollar of expenditure;
3. To cooperate with trade and industrial associations, and governmental and private agencies, engaged in the promotion and development of sound business methods;
4. To demand honesty in sales representation whether offered through the medium of a verbal or written statement, advertisement, or a sample of a product;
5. To decline personal gifts or gratuities which might in any way influence the purchase of materials;
6. To grant all competitive bidders equal consideration; to regard

each transaction on its own merit; to foster and promote fair, ethical, and legal trade practice;

7. To use only by consent the original ideas and designs devised by one vendor for competitive purchasing purposes;
8. To be willing to submit any major controversy to arbitration;
9. To accord a prompt and courteous reception insofar as conditions permit to all who call on legitimate business missions; and
10. To counsel and cooperate with NAEB members and to promote a spirit of unity among them.

Statement of Policies and Procedures

The development and publication of a statement of policies and procedures for the operation of the purchasing function is desirable. The statement should: define the responsibilities of the purchasing department and the delegation of authority within the purchasing organization; establish criteria for the selection of vendors, for the determination of quality, standardization, and other operating policies, and for bidding procedures; and formulate procedures for departments to use in requesting purchases.

Many publicly controlled institutions must employ purchasing procedures prescribed by statutes or governmental regulations. Some states have established central purchasing departments to serve all state agencies, including educational institutions. Because of the unique needs of colleges and universities, such centralized purchasing agencies usually are not effective except for some items where the combined volume purchased by the state agency may effect economies.

The statement of policies and procedures should include provision for regular audits of purchasing operations. Such audits reveal whether proper bidding procedures are being followed, orders are being awarded to the lowest responsible bidders, competitive prices are being obtained, and other procedures and policies are being carried out. Under special conditions, the audit may encompass a review of the ability of bidders to perform.

Functions of the Purchasing Organization

An effective purchasing department will perform the following functions:

1. Prepare, with the cooperation of the using departments, specifications of quality, quantity, and delivery schedules for items to be purchased;
2. Provide using departments with current information on new products, alternative materials, and costs;
3. Encourage competition among vendors through negotiation, competitive bidding, and contract buying;
4. Ensure that purchase orders and contracts contain all necessary conditions, such as warranties, compliance with governmental regulations, shipping instructions, and f.o.b. points;
5. Analyze bids, place purchase orders, and schedule deliveries;
6. Provide for the receipt and inspection of materials ordered, and process all adjustments and claims;
7. Conduct surveys as needed to determine the requirements of the institution for supplies, services, and equipment;
8. Develop standards for equipment and supplies, and encourage the use of these standards throughout the institution;
9. Maintain adequate records and files of requisitions, purchase orders, vendors, catalogues, product information, and prices;
10. Conduct and coordinate research on the supplies used by the institution;
11. Arrange for the disposal of all surplus equipment and supplies, salvage, and scrap; and
12. Advise and assist other departments that have been delegated some purchasing functions.

The purchasing department may also operate a central stores system and maintain an equipment inventory. Other activities of some purchasing departments include: operation of typewriter repair shops, duplicating centers, and photographic departments; control of narcotics licenses and alcohol permits; handling of returnable containers; control of radiological materials; and supervision of vending machines.

Purchasing Procedures

The usual purchasing cycle involves determining needs by the using departments, communicating the needs to the purchasing department, conducting negotiations for purchases, selecting sources of supplies, issuing purchase orders, receiving materials, and establishing such records and files of information as may be appropriate.

Communicating Needs Information about needs of using departments is communicated to the purchasing department by issuance of a requisition on which the requirements are clearly stated. The format and content of requisition forms vary widely among institutions, but, at a minimum, they should provide for adequate description of materials requested; designation of date when needed; designation of account to be charged; approval by appropriate academic officers, such as departmental chairmen, deans, or directors of major academic units; and approval by appropriate business, or budget, officers.

It is desirable to have the requisition form provide space for using departments to indicate any preference for particular vendors, with reasons for such preferences. Such suggestions, while not binding on the purchasing department, often are helpful in finding sources of supply and in evaluating special services which only one vendor may offer.

Determining Quality Determination of suitable quality for the intended purpose must be a cooperative decision of the using department and the purchasing department. The relative technical competence of each group concerning the product to be purchased should determine the degree of its participation in decisions on quality. Determination of the quality of commodities used throughout the institution, such as paper products, office supplies, furniture and office equipment, is primarily the responsibility of the purchasing department; but determining the quality of highly specialized scientific equipment and supplies is primarily the responsibility of the using departments.

Descriptions of quality should conform to recognize standards Nonstandard specifications substantially increase costs, often without increasing quality. Although nonstandard specifications and special restrictions may ensure high quality, they should not eliminate qualified bidders. Whenever possible, it is desirable to define quality in objective terms. Several methods may be used, such as brand names, model or catalogue numbers, standard market grades, performance requirements, conformance to sample, and detailed written specifications and blueprints covering material and design.

If detailed specifications or performance requirements are used, provision must be made for inspection and testing to verify compliance with the specifications. If performance can be accurately and adequately defined and can be precisely measured, performance specifications may be preferable to detailed engineering specifications. Under the latter plan, if the product meets detailed design specifications, the vendor has fulfilled his obligation, whether or not the performance is adequate. If performance specifications are used, the vendor is required to supply a product which will serve the specified purpose, regardless of design.

Determining Quantity   The quantity of products to be ordered is determined by such factors as: amounts needed, availability of quantity discounts, standard shipping units, procurement costs, and costs of keeping the items in inventory. The anticipated need for the items over the next few months to a year can be determined by examining the records of previous purchases and budgetary requests, and by securing the judgment of both the using departments and the purchasing staff.

Source Selection   The materials supplied must be satisfactory to the using departments, but the selection of the source of supply is the responsibility of the purchasing department. Whenever possible, more than one supplier should be considered. Frequently, sources of supply must be developed to fit the needs of the institution, and new suppliers must be informed about the institution and its requirements.

Purchasing department buyers must have acquired a knowledge of marketing and distribution channels for various types of materials, and be capable of selecting the most economical and efficient level for each purchase, giving consideration to educational buying cooperatives.

Determining Price   The circumstances of each purchase will govern the procedures used in determining price and in awarding orders. In an emergency, it may be necessary to place purchase orders without benefit of price negotiation. For items of small dollar value that are purchased infrequently, it may be uneconomical to spend time in negotiation. Various types of commodities for which the volume is either small or irregular, and for which recognized markets and pricing arrangements exist, may not require negotiation. However, where negotiation is omitted, the purchasing officer, or his staff, must know the market, pricing structures, and discount rates to ensure that purchases are made as economically as possible.

Unusual items required for research frequently are available from only a single source, so that competition may not exist. In such cases, the purchasing department is responsible for determining through negotiation, that the price is fair and reasonable, and that all conditions of the sale are understood and acceptable.

Informal quotations may be used to obtain competitive bids when early delivery is required, when specifications are not complete, or when the value of the purchase is nominal. Telephone inquiries and other informal contacts with sales representatives may provide prices quickly on the required items; nevertheless, the request should include as many elements of a formal quotation as are feasible.

Formal quotations call for the preparation of a written bid document, generally known as "Request for Quotation" or "Invitation to Bid." Formal bidding may be either publicly advertised or invited, but in either case the request for quotations or bids must be prepared with great care. Publicly advertised requests for bids involve more technical considerations of the legal aspects of bidding, including detailed clauses regarding time of opening bids and options for rejection. The requests for bids must make clear that the quotations or bids are to be firm prices unless, as circumstances sometimes dictate, cost bids or escalator clauses in the quotations may be desirable.

In selecting bidders, the purchasing department should invite bidders to submit quotations only if it is willing to place the order with them. Unless public bidding regulations require disclosure, it is not desirable to tell unsuccessful bidders the details of the quotations of other bidders, although they should be notified that their bids have not been accepted.

Issuing the Purchase Order A purchase order is a legal document and, when accepted by the vendor, constitutes a contract between buyer and seller. It must therefore, contain all pertinent details of the agreement.

The format and content of purchase orders vary among institutions, as do also the number, distribution, and uses of the copies. The purchase order forms should be prenumbered, identify clearly and completely both the institution and the vendor, describe adequately and specify the quantity of the items being ordered, provide delivery instructions, and show the required delivery date. The order form should show both unit prices and the total price. It should also include other information, such as terms of payment, discounts, f.o.b. points, warranties, insurance requirements, and other items designed to protect the institution from defaults on the part of vendors and negligence and accidents on the part of the carriers. A sufficient number of copies of the purchase order should be prepared to accommodate the needs of the institutions and the vendors.

After an order has been placed by the purchasing department and accepted by a vendor, subsequent changes must be mutually acceptable to buyer and seller. Changes should be specified in writing and copies distributed as were the copies of the original purchase order. This principle applies also to cancellations. When the volume of changes warrants, the development of a change order form will prove advantageous.

The responsibility of the purchasing department does not end with the placing of purchase orders. A follow-up and expediting system is needed to ensure that materials are delivered in time to meet the requirements of the using departments. Delivery dates are indicated on departmental requisitions by using departments, and these must be realistic. Purchase orders include delivery dates as part of the conditions of the order, and procedures must be established to ensure the observance of dates.

Blanket Orders A blanket, or standing, order is a purchase order placed with a supplier for goods or services to be furnished from time to time when requested either by the purchasing department or by a staff member to whom this responsibility has been delegated. Blanket orders are used for routine or repetitive requirements and for small quantities of materials, such as hardware items selected by mechanics as they are needed. They may be preferable to cash purchases, especially if they can be arranged with selected suppliers on predetermined pricing arrangements. Often, they are used to meet certain needs that otherwise would have to be handled on an emergency basis.

Requirements Contracts Requirements contracts usually provide that an institution will purchase all its requirements for specified materials, such as fuel oil, from a given source for a stated period of time. They may be used to obtain advantageous prices by combining the requirements over time from many sources within the institution into one large quotation and contract. The contracts provide flexibility in delivery terms, avoid bulk storage by the institution, and expedite the filling of individual requisitions.

Requirements contracts and blanket orders may provide substantial savings to institutions and improved service to departments. Quotations based on the combined needs of all using departments usually improve the price quoted.

Emergency Procedures Emergencies do arise that make orders for immediate delivery necessary, and procedures should be developed to provide emergency service. Although real emergencies do occur through failure of equipment, needs that cannot be anticipated, and failure of staff members to plan ahead, frequent emergency or confirmation orders may be indicative of poor planning, coordination, and organization.

Low-cost and infrequently used items that require personal selection or that are available only through retail cash sources may be procured economically on a cash purchase basis. Policies and procedures for cash purchases should be established and made known to all staff members. Authorization may be given for petty cash funds or for direct reimbursement of staff members upon presentation of proper documentation. Limits on dollar amounts and other regulating criteria must be clearly stated to ensure that this method is used only when it is economical and appropriate.

Receiving Procedures Central receiving stations or warehouses offer advantages, but also entail disadvantages. Central receiving, at a limited number of locations on a campus, facilitates use of a uniform receiving system and inspection for visible damage to containers; it also reduces chances that materials will be delivered to the wrong place or get lost on campus.

Central receiving entails additional space and additional expenditures for personnel and trucking services. It may cause delays in delivery to using departments because of additional handling and delays in the inspection of contents for verification of quantity and for concealed damage. Unpacking all material at central receiving points may prove unsatisfactory, since it creates repacking costs. Furthermore, the receiving staff members usually are not qualified to inspect items for compliance with specifications. Whether the receiving system is centralized or decentralized, the using department is responsible for prompt inspection and reporting on the condition of items that do not adhere to specifications.

Other Functions Related to the Purchasing Department

Central Stores Colleges and universities should consider establishing central stores for office, physical plant, and laboratory supplies and equipment, and for nonperishable food items. The advantages and extent of stores must be weighed against increased costs for space, facilities, and staff.

Central stores reduce delivery time on stocked items, and may offer savings through quantity buying. They help facilitate standardization, permit a reduction in using department inventories, and reduce the number of small purchase orders. Central stock control also helps reduce losses from obsolescence and deterioration of stocked materials, supplies, and commodities.

On the other hand, contracts that provide for direct shipment from vendors to using departments at prices based on over-all volume may produce delivered prices that are competitive with, or less than, the cost of handling such items through central storerooms. An urban institution, with its greater access to sources of supply, may find less need for extensive storeroom operations than one at a distance from suppliers.

Records must be maintained to disclose the costs of stores operations and the amount of service rendered. Two partial measures of efficiency are turn-over rates and cost of operations as a percentage of total value of materials issued from stores to using departments.

Restocking for central stores should be controlled by a minimum-maximum inventory system, using repeating requisitions, standard order quantities, and standardized terminology and specifications.

Sales of Materials   Control of sales of surplus or discarded and unused equipment and materials is the responsibility of the purchasing department. Responsibility for negotiating and arranging for the sale of some items may be delegated to individual departments, but final responsibility for favorable prices and proper control of cash and charge sales rests with the purchasing department.

New Construction   Contracts for construction and for remodeling often are not the responsibility of the purchasing department. In such instances, the purchasing department may cooperate in the advertising, receiving, and analysis of bids, and in the review and award of contracts and modifications thereof.

The purchasing department is, however, responsible for procuring furniture, furnishings, and equipment for new buildings. This task requires close cooperation with those who are to use the facility, the architects, and the physical plant officers. To be effective, the department needs to participate in the early stages of planning the building and assist in the review of preliminary plans. The furniture, furnishings, and equipment to be acquired must be planned in detail, and the purchasing department should assist in preparing both budget estimates for these items and schedules for their ordering and delivery.

Standardization   The purchasing department should develop and encourage the use of standard specifications for items used in performing the same functions in the various divisions of the institution. Standardization facilitates quantity purchasing, interchangeability in the use of equipment, and reduction in service and inventory costs.

Research and Testing A continuing program of research and testing generally is considered a responsibility of the purchasing department. Testing may be performed in shops, laboratories, and other locations, but under the direction of the purchasing department. Research activities include studies of sources of supply, adequacy of specifications, analyses of commodities in relation to specifications, analyses of substitute materials, and forecasts of market trends.

The purchasing department should maintain a catalogue file that is as extensive as is practicable and files of specialized sources of information such as governmental publications, technical handbooks, and other books and magazines to aid in carrying out the purchasing function. Much helpful information is available from national research laboratories and governmental agencies.

13

Auxiliary Enterprises, Organized Activities, and Service Departments

Wɪᴛʜɪɴ many institutions there are three classifications of service activities that charge for the services they render and for whose effective management direct comparisons of revenues and expenditures are necessary.

An *auxiliary enterprise* is an entity that exists to furnish a service to students, faculty, or staff, and that charges at a rate directly related, but not necessarily equal, to the cost of the service. The general public may be served incidentally by some auxiliary enterprises.

An *organized activity related to an educational department* is an entity that exists to provide an instructional or laboratory experience for students and that incidentally creates goods or services that may be sold. In the course of providing the incidental goods or services, expenditures are incurred in addition to those necessary solely for the educational benefit of the students.

A *service department* is an entity that provides to the various divisions of an institution services that might be purchased from commercial sources, but that, for reasons of convenience, cost, or control, are more effectively provided through a unit of the institution. Charges are determined by the costs.

Examples of auxiliary enterprises are residence halls, food services, student stores, and rental housing. Typical of organized activities are demonstration schools, college theaters, hotels operated in connection with instruction of students in the institutional administration curriculum, and stores that sell the products of experimental farms. Service departments include central duplicating services, motor pools, stenographic pools, and instrument-making, glass-blowing, and machine shops.

The classification of some activities among the three categories may vary from institution to institution, reflecting differences in the purposes for which they exist. For instance, at institutions where gate receipts are sizable, intercollegiate athletics should be classified as an auxiliary enterprise; where gate receipts are negligible and the athletic program is primarily intended for student participation rather than spectator entertainment, intercollegiate athletics may be classified as an organized activity; where there are no gate receipts, it should be a separately identified section of the budget for the department of physical education. Another example of variation in classification is the central duplicating service, which usually is a service department, but might be classified as an organized activity if it is operated as a practical laboratory for students majoring in printing technology.

Irrespective of classification, each activity within these three categories should have its own budget and accounting to identify all operating costs and revenues. In addition to direct costs for salaries and wages, supplies, equipment, and other expenditures, the indirect costs—such as those for administration, plant operation, and maintenance—should be apportioned to each service activity. Only through cost accounting is it possible to establish appropriate rate schedules, identify subsidies if any, and compare costs with commercial costs.

Budgets for auxiliary enterprises and service departments should be prepared under the supervision of the chief business officer. Budgets for organized activities, while prepared by the cognizant academic division, should be developed in consultation with the chief business officer or his representative. Financial and business policies of the institution as a whole should be followed in the management of the service activities, and the disposition of any net income should be determined by institutional policy. Inasmuch as the primary objectives of these service activities may change over time, they should be reviewed periodically to determine whether they are properly classified.

Auxiliary Enterprises

Auxiliary enterprises are related to the educational objectives of colleges and universities and contribute significantly to the achievement of those objectives. The specific functions to be performed by each auxiliary enterprise should be defined by those responsible for determining institutional policy. In determining management policies, both the extent of the activity's contribution to educational and other objectives and the extent to which it can be self-supporting should be evaluated.

The chief business officer and the academic and student personnel officers must work in cooperation for the effective operation of auxiliary enterprises. Responsibility for selecting directors should be shared jointly by these administrative officers. A director should, however, be administratively responsible to only one person. The relationship of directors to the officers of central administration will vary with the type of enterprise, and may vary among institutions, depending on institutional philosophy and organization. The directors of enterprises that are primarily business, financial, or service in character should be responsible to the chief business officer, and directors of enterprises that are primarily educational in character may be responsible to the academic administrative officer. Although a director may be responsible to an academic or student personnel officer, the chief business officer should be responsible for the usual functions of business management such as budget control; receipt, custody, and disbursement of revenues; accounting and financial reporting; procurement of supplies, equipment, and services; and operation and maintenance of the physical plant.

If auxiliary enterprises receive a subsidy, the accounting records and reports should disclose the amount and source. Similarly, if revenues exceed expenditures after provision for reserves and any debt service, the amount of excess and its disposition should also be disclosed.

In developing policies for the program and management of an auxiliary enterprise, the advice and cooperation of representatives of the institutional community to be served should be sought.

STATEMENTS OF AUXILIARY ENTERPRISES

The operations of auxiliary enterprises should be shown in the operating statements separately from the educational and general operations, and should be supported by detailed schedules of revenues and expenditures for each enterprise. Such statements are essential for internal use to ascertain the degree of self-support attained and to provide the basis for the exercise of controls. Separate balance sheets may be prepared but need not be published.

All revenues and expenditures of the enterprises should be entered in the accounts and included in the financial statements. Expenditures should include an allocation of general administrative, general institutional, and physical plant expenses. Routine repairs to buildings, all equipment repairs, and minor equipment replacements should be entered as operating expenditures.

It is desirable to provide annually out of revenues for major renewals and replacements of equipment, for major repairs to buildings, for additions and improvements to buildings, and for additional furniture and equipment. These provisions should consist of fixed annual charges entered as expenditures of the respective enterprises and the transfer of current funds cash or other assets to the plant funds subgroup Funds for Renewals and Replacements. Expenditures for replacements of equipment and for major repairs to buildings are then reported in a Statement of Changes in Fund Balances, rather than as expenditures of the auxiliary enterprises.

Provision out of revenues for the replacement of buildings used for auxiliary enterprises will depend on the institution's financial policies. If the policy is to accrue funds for replacement, fixed annual charges should be entered as expenditures of the given enterprise, and cash or other liquid assets should be transferred to the Funds for Renewals and Replacements subgroup of the plant funds (see Appendix D, "Depreciation and Renewal and Replacement of Plant Assets").

RESIDENCE HALLS

The management of residence halls has both business and educational aspects. Close cooperation between student personnel and business officers is especially important in the development of budgets and of provisions for counseling and other student services.

The type, number, and frequency of operating reports needed will vary with local factors. Some of the more significant periodic reports to be prepared for the administrative offices concerned include: reports on occupancy; expenditures for repairs, custodial services, and utilities; and expenses for counseling, student government activities, and other educational and student personnel programs.

OTHER HOUSING FACILITIES

Many institutions own and operate housing facilities for married students, graduate students, and faculty and staff members. Their management falls within the purview of the chief business officer, although the assignment of space, development of social programs, and establishment of regulations may be the responsibility of a student personnel or other administrative officer.

FOOD SERVICES

The primary function of the food services is to provide food that meets the institution's standards for quality, quantity, and cost. Management includes responsibility for all food-serving areas and activities including dining halls, lunch rooms, cafeterias, tea rooms, soda and snack bars, and catering services for conferences, meetings, student activities, public functions, and other events. Management of vending machines dispensing food products may lie with the food services or may, with other vending machines, be assigned elsewhere.

Because the operation is primarily businesslike in character, the director should be responsible to the chief business officer.

Food services may be procured from contract caterers or management services. Contract food service has both advantages and disadvantages, and an institution should determine whether its interests will be served better under a contract arrangement than by operating its own food service. If contract service is engaged, the contracts should be written with the institution's interest paramount and with institutional authorities in full control over food standards, prices, other significant administrative and management matters, and all policies related to the program.

Effective management requires frequent reports on operations, including one that shows the distribution of expenditures—expressed as percentages of sales—for various objects, such as food products, labor, and other significant categories. Also needed are reports of numbers of students served, numbers of meals served, and cost per meal served.

COLLEGE UNIONS

The union is an integral part of the institution's educational program, and its administrative organization should be coordinated with the established academic, business, and general institutional procedures. It generally encompasses a program for the community life of the institution, including a general cultural-social-recreational program, experience in group leadership for students, and numerous services involving both physical facilities and organization and staff to administer the program and services. Typically it provides offices for student organizations, meeting rooms, lounges, browsing libraries, music rooms, art exhibition areas, craft shops, an auditorium or theater, facilities for dances, receptions, banquets, and other events for students, faculty, alumni, conferees, campus visitors, and guests.

Since unions vary widely in their constituents, functions and purposes, facilities and programs, and organization and administration, each institution must determine the areas of responsibility to be assumed by the director and then assign staff and line relationships accordingly. If the majority of the responsibilities are student-oriented, then the director should report to the dean of students or other student personnel officer. When the activities are various in character, the director should, perhaps, come within the jurisdiction of another administrative officer under the president. In any event, the business affairs should be carried on in conformity with the business practices and procedures of the institution.

It is common practice for an institution to provide for an advisory board body, representing the components of the university community concerned with the union, to assist in developing the program and establishing policies and procedures for use of the building.

For accounting purposes, if the union is financed primarily from general funds, it should be classified under student services. If the union is financed primarily by its revenue-producing activities—space rentals, billiard rooms, bowling lanes, guest rooms, sales and information desks, food service, student stores, barbershops, and the like—it should be classified as an auxiliary enterprise.

Student stores

Student stores are operated by colleges and universities primarily to provide a convenient service to students, faculty, and staff members and thus are to be considered an essential educational service. In performing this function, student stores should stock textbooks, instruments, supplies, and materials required by students in their educational programs. Laboratory manuals, syllabi, and similar teaching aids prepared by members of the faculty and staff should be sold through the student store; for ethical and business reasons, direct sales of such items to students by academic departments or members of the faculty should not be permitted.

The student store is primarily a business operation and requires specialized and sound financial administration. The manager should be responsible to the chief business officer. Reports should include analyses of sales by major categories of stock, data on cost of goods sold, gross profits expressed as percentages of gross sales, and rates of inventory turnover.

In order for the student store to serve the student body and faculty adequately, the manager must be informed of registration estimates and statistics, courses of studies, and required books and instructional materials. He should be notified when a change is to be made to ensure that new books and supplies will be available when needed and to avoid financial loss from stocking discontinued items.

A student store may be organized and operated as a cooperative enterprise, the annual surplus being returned to the members of the organization in the form of cash dividends or credits on future purchases. In most cases its management should be subject to institutional supervision and authority.

INTERCOLLEGIATE ATHLETICS

The intercollegiate athletic program should be classified as an auxiliary enterprise when revenues are significant. If the program is considered a part of instruction, it may be classified either as an organized activity or as a separately identified part of the budget and financial operation of the department of physical education.

Responsibility for proposing policies relating to intercollegiate athletics may be delegated by the chief executive officer of the institution to an athletic board or committee. Whatever the administrative organization, however, intercollegiate athletics should be subject to institutional authority.

The responsibilities of the chief business officer for the financial and business management of the athletic program are identical to those he has for all other activities of the institution. These include budget control; receipt, custody, and disbursement of revenues; procurement; accounting, auditing, and financial reporting; and the operation and maintenance of physical facilities. Institutional policy should determine the use of income resulting from intercollegiate athletics.

UNIVERSITY PRESSES

A university press serves as a publishing outlet for the work of its own and other faculty, in order to make important publications available to scholars and the public, even though many such works have narrow markets. A university press is related more closely to the educational and teaching functions than it is to the business, financial, and service functions. Therefore, the director of the press should be responsible to the chief academic officer.

The organization required for effective administration will be governed by the general institutional policies, the objectives sought, and the financial resources available for its support. Whatever the organization, the enterprise should be managed on the basis of educational policies established by the institution.

VENDING MACHINES

The operation of vending machines and concessions should be under institutional control. Responsibility may be assigned to the manager of the student store, the purchasing department, the director of food services, or other representatives of the chief business officer. All agreements with concessionaires and arrangements for management of vending machines should be under his control. Revenues from vending operations are general institutional revenues and should not be allocated automatically to the support of any one division, department, or activity.

OTHER AUXILIARY ENTERPRISES

Other auxiliary enterprises frequently found include faculty clubs, laundries, and parking facilities. Whatever the auxiliary enterprise, its organization, management, and control should conform to the guidelines for administration set out in this chapter.

Organized Activities Related to Educational Departments

Organized activities—laboratory schools and medical school hospitals may be examples—complement the work of educational departments by providing program support for instruction and research. If an activity is conducted primarily for other than educational purposes, it should not be classified under this title. Organized activities may provide by-products or services that are available, for a charge, to students, faculty, and staff members, or to the general public.

Because they are closely related to instruction and research, their administration should conform to the academic lines of control. The chief business officer's responsibility is, however, somewhat different from that in the usual instructional and research activities, inasmuch as many organized activities involve more business and finance than do instructional departments.

If an organized activity is relatively small and its supervision is the incidental responsibility of regular instructional or research staff members, it need not be given separate or special accounting treatment. An organized activity whose operations are of major magnitude may be shown in the financial reports separately from other organized activities. Even though its detailed accounting may be decentralized, for purposes of institutional control there should be central recording of revenues and expenditures. A large activity may justify special supervision within the educational department. In the latter case, the chief business officer should be consulted in the selection of the supervisor, and he should devise, establish, and supervise detailed accounting records and special operating reports as the size and character of the activity may warrant.

Hospitals administered in connection with medical schools offer special problems in the classification and reporting of operations. If the purpose of the hospital is primarily to support the clinical years of instruction in the school of medicine, it should be classified as an organized activity. If, however, the hospital is managed by the institution primarily as a service to the public or to governmental bodies or agencies, it should be reported under "Extension and Public Services." Frequently, hospitals are shown as a major item of both revenues and expenditures in the category "Educational and General."

The successful operation of organized activities requires a high degree of cooperation and understanding between the chief business officer and academic officers. The primary objectives must remain professional instruction and the training of students in research activities. When an activity ceases to serve these objectives, it should be reclassified.

Efficient management and internal control require detailed statements of revenues and expenditures. Usually, however, the institutional operating statements and financial report need show only gross amounts. The statements should conform to standard accounting practices, and forms recommended by specialized industrial and professional organizations may be adapted to fit the needs of colleges and universities.

Service Departments

Service departments are units created to provide services that might be purchased from commercial sources, but are more economically and conveniently provided, and can be better controlled, by the institution. Examples are: scientific apparatus repair shops, glass-blowing shops, instrument-making shops, statistical and tabulating departments, addressograph and mailing services, secretarial pools, duplicating departments, office machine repair shops, laundries, photographic departments, printing shops, travel bureaus, and audio-visual services.

Management and operation are usually the responsibility of the chief business officer although some service departments, such as a computer center or a glass-blowing shop, may be under the direction of an academic officer or a departmental chairman.

The rates charged by a service department should reflect all operating costs, including salaries, wages, staff benefits, costs of materials and supplies, operation and maintenance of the physical facilities occupied or a "rent" charge in lieu thereof, provision for the renewal and replacement of equipment, provision for debt service, and a share of general administrative and institutional expense.

Part 2

Principles of Accounting and Reporting

14

Principles and Procedures of Accounting and Financial Reporting

Accounting in colleges and universities is the means by which financial data are made available to the controlling bodies, executive officers responsible for efficient administration, and the public. The institutions, whether publicly or privately controlled, are in the nature of public trusts. Thus, the inherent obligations for stewardship and accountability necessitate a system of accounts and reports that will ensure full disclosure of the results of their operations and of their financial position.

The development of the accounting system should be governed by the form and character that the financial data need take in order to promote effective administration. However, certain principles of classification and presentation of accounting data as well as a standard terminology for institutions of higher education have come to be accepted, and colleges and universities should maintain their accounts and present their financial reports accordingly. Conformance facilitates internal administration, public understanding, and comparisons with other institutions. Since service, rather than profit, is the primary objective of educational institutions, the principles for accounting differ from those of commercial enterprises. In commercial accounting, the emphasis is on determining net profit and net worth. In institutional accounting, although these financial objectives do not exist, a knowledge of costs is essential for decision-making purposes and for effective management and control.

The financial resources of educational institutions come from (1) revenues that may be used for general institutional operations; (2) unrestricted gifts and bequests; (3) gifts, bequests, grants, and governmental appropriations that may be used only for specified purposes; (4) gifts, grants, and bequests that must be kept intact and invested, the income only being available for expenditure or use in accordance with the terms of the instruments of gift or grant; and (5) proceeds from borrowings. The financial records and reports of colleges and universities must, therefore, deal not only with current funds revenues and expenditures, but also with the receipt and disbursement of funds whose use is restricted and with accounts for the principal or balances of funds. The accounts should be arranged and classified so that funds having like characteristics and restrictions will be reported in appropriate fund groups.

Government agencies that establish requirements for accounting and reporting by colleges and universities should consider carefully the effect such requirements may have on institutional financial records and reports. Even though some colleges and universities are instrumentalities of governments, their activities are vastly different from those of state agencies such as highway departments and welfare agencies; consequently, their system of accounts and reports must be specifically adapted to the functions, purposes, and objectives of educational institutions. The accounts of publicly controlled colleges and universities may be coordinated with the accounting system of the controlling unit of government, but they should correspond to those of other educational institutions. In no other way can the accounts serve fully the purposes they should serve, or report the financial facts of the institutions adequately and properly.

The principles presented here are applicable to all institutions of higher education, both publicly and privately controlled. The purpose here and in the following chapters is to present methods of reporting financial data, but not to give detailed instructions regarding accounting forms and systems. The recommendations presuppose the presence of competent accounting personnel and a system of bookkeeping adequate to record, classify, and summarize all financial transactions, and to produce reports of operations and fund transactions and of assets, liabilities, and balances by fund group. The financial reports should summarize and be consistent with the information produced in the accounting records.

To meet the requirements of financial accounting and reporting for colleges and universities, the following basic principles are recognized:

1. *The accounts should be classified in balanced fund groups in the books of account and in the financial reports.*

In accounting and reporting for educational institutions, a fund is an accounting entity involving assets, liabilities, revenues and expenditures, receipts and disbursements, and a balance. A fund is established to carry on specific activities or attain certain objectives in the operation of an institution, either at the discretion of the governing board or in accordance with regulations, restrictions, or limitations imposed by sources outside the institution. In order to ensure observance of limitations and restrictions placed on use, a separate account must be maintained for the balance of each fund, and must reflect the results of its transactions or operations. For reporting purposes, funds subject to similar restrictions, or available for like purposes, should be assigned to a fund group, and each fund group should be treated as a separately balanced entity. The usual fund groups are:

Current Funds
Loan Funds
Endowment and Similar Funds
Annuity and Life Income Funds
Plant Funds
Agency Funds

2. *All financial transactions should be recorded and reported by fund group.*

The transactions within the various fund groups should be kept separate and not intermingled. Those receipts that are specified by donors, governmental agencies, or other outside sources to be added to loan, endowment, annuity and life income, or plant funds should be recorded directly in the accounts of the appropriate fund group. In like manner, disbursements of such funds should also be recorded in the accounts of the respective fund groups. Funds restricted to use for operating purposes and all funds unrestricted by donors should be recorded as additions to the Current Funds group.

The Balance Sheet of an institution is a listing of the assets, liabilities, and fund balances of the separately balanced fund groups. The changes in fund balances from one Balance Sheet to the next should be presented in the respective Statement of Changes in Fund Balances. The revenues and expenditures of only the Current Funds group should be reported in the Statement of Current Funds Revenues, Expenditures, and Transfers.

3. *The Current Funds group consists of funds available for current operations, including those for restricted as well as those for unrestricted purposes.*

In the Current Funds group, the balances of unrestricted funds and of restricted funds must appear separately, even though the assets may be combined. If the institution reports the receipt of unrestricted gifts and bequests in the Statement of Changes in Fund Balances—Unrestricted Current Funds, these gifts and bequests must appear as a separate subdivision of the balances. See Principal 14. Funds applicable to the operations of auxiliary enterprises may also be reported separately.

4. *The Loan Funds group consists of funds which are loanable to students, faculty, and staff.*

Funds that are to be invested and only the income used for loans are endowment funds, and should be included in that fund group. Their income should be transferred periodically to the Loan Funds group.

The identity of various types of loan funds should be shown separately in the accounts and reports. Examples are: appropriations from governments to be used for loans to students, loan funds which may be refundable to donors under various conditions, and unrestricted current funds designated by action of the governing board to be used as loan funds.

Receipts of the Loan Funds group and the granting and repayment of loans are not transactions of the Current Funds group and should not be included in the Statement of Current Funds Revenues, Expenditures, and Transfers.

5. *The Endowment and Similar Funds group includes those funds whose principal is nonexpendable as of the date of reporting and is invested, or is available for investment, for the purpose of producing income.*

The following types of funds are included in this group; (*a*) *endowment funds:* funds which donors have stipulated, as a condition of gift, that the principal is to be maintained inviolate and in perpetuity, with only the income from the investments available to be expended; (*b*) *term endowment funds:* funds which donors or other outside agencies, by the terms of the instruments of gift, have provided are to be released from inviolability to permit all or part of them to be expended upon the happening of a particular event or the passage of a stated period of time; and (*c*) *quasi-endowment funds:* funds which the governing board of an institution, rather than a donor or other outside agency, has determined are to be retained and invested. The term *funds functioning as endowment* may also be used to designate this type of fund.

Gifts, bequests, contributions, grants, and other receipts of funds in this group, and their transfers, charges, and other forms of reductions of principal or balances should be presented in the Statement of Changes in Fund Balances—Endowment and Similar Funds; they should not be reported in the Statement of Current Funds Revenues, Expenditures, and Transfers.

a) The total of each of the subgroups of funds should be identified separately in the accounts and in the equity section of the balance sheet.

b) The funds may be classified further to show those for which the income is unrestricted in use, and those for which the income is restricted by donors to specific uses.

c) The funds in the Endowment and Similar Funds group may be pooled for effective investment management unless prohibited either by statute or by the terms of the instruments of gift. It is preferable not to merge assets of Annuity and Life Income Funds, unloaned balances of Loan Funds, and unexpended balances of Current, Plant, and Agency Funds groups with Endowment and Similar Funds in the investment pool.

d) If the assets of the funds in this group are pooled for investment purposes, only one control account need be maintained to reflect book values for each class of investments in the pool. For report purposes, the assets may be shown together in appropriate classes of investments, whether or not the investments are pooled.

e) The operation of an investment pool necessitates adopting procedures that will provide for the equitable distribution of income and the assignment of capital appreciation to all funds participating in the pool. The market-value method is preferable to the book-value method in the operation of investment pools.

f) In the event other funds are admitted for investment purposes to the endowment pool, special attention must be given to the accounting arrangements for admittance to and withdrawal from the pool to preclude crediting such funds with investment income and realized, or unrealized, net gains properly attributable to the permanently invested funds.

g) Pooled investment income should be distributed to the income accounts of the participating funds without consideration of the gain or loss account, in order to prevent dilution of the proper share of the various funds in the aggregate investment income of the pool.

h) Realized gains and losses on investment transactions affect the principal of the invested funds either (1) by increasing or decreasing the individual fund balances or (2) by retaining as an undistributed accumulation the balances that are proportionately applicable to each fund. Such capital gains and losses are not operating revenues and expenditures, and should not be treated differently from the amounts representing the original fund balances. They are subject to the same restrictions and limitations on investment, expenditure, and disposition as the funds from which they arose. *In some instances, realized gains and losses may be attributable to income as a matter of law, for example, when such treatment is required by a specific instrument of gift.*

i) Investments purchased for the funds in this group should be recorded in the accounts and reported at cost. Gifts of securities and other donated assets should be recorded and reported at their market value or at an expertly appraised value as of the date of the gift.

j) The book value of investments should not be changed to reflect fluctuations in market prices. However, market values, based on appropriate periodic review of the investments, should be disclosed in the balance sheet by means of a footnote or other reference.

k) In order to maintain unimpaired the principal of the funds in this group, provisions should be made for the depreciation of real properties which are the investment of funds in this group and for the amortization of premiums on securities purchases. Provision may also be made for the accumulation of discounts.

l) Endowment and term endowment funds should not be invested in institutional property.

m) Endowment and term endowment funds should not be advanced for the use of other funds or fund groups.

n) The principal of endowment and term endowment funds must not be hypothecated, and their investments must not be pledged for any purpose.

6. *Funds held in trust by others should not be reported as belonging to an institution.*

Funds held in trust by others are those that are not actually in the possession, nor under the control, of a college or university, but are held and administered by outside fiscal agents, with the institution deriving the benefit of their income. Where such funds are material in amount they should be indicated on the balance sheet by a footnote or other reference.

Income from such funds should be identified in the Statement of Current Funds Revenues, Expenditures, and Transfers. If the funds are established under irrevocable trusts, the income may be included as Endowment Income, with notation of the amount, or it may be reported as a separate item of revenues immediately following Endowment Income. If the funds are established under revocable trusts, the income should be reported under Gifts, or Gifts Applied, with notation of the amount.

7. *The Annuity and Life Income Funds group includes those funds acquired by an institution subject to annuity contracts, living trust agreements, or gifts and bequests reserving life income to one or more beneficiaries.*

The accounts for this fund group include those for the balances of the funds as well as those that reflect receipts and disbursements. Earnings from the investments of these funds and payments to annuitants and beneficiaries should not be reported in the Statement of Current Funds Revenues, Expenditures, and Transfers, but, rather, in the Statement of Changes in Fund Balances—Annuity and Life Income Funds.

8. *The Plant Funds group consists of funds to be used for the construction, rehabilitation, and acquisition of physical properties for institutional purposes; funds already expended for plant properties; funds*

set aside for the renewal and replacement thereof; and funds accumu-
lated for the retirement of indebtedness thereon.

Physical properties used for institutional purposes consist of land, buildings, improvements other than buildings, and equipment. Properties which are the investment of endowment funds should not be included here, but should be reported in the Endowment Funds group. Physical properties should be carried in the accounts at cost until disposed of. Gifts of physical properties should be recorded at appraised value as of the date of the gift.

The source of the funds expended for institutional plant assets may be shown in the equity section of the balance sheet, under such titles as "Governmental appropriations," "Gifts," and "Current funds."

9. *The necessity for providing for renewals and replacements of the physical plant facilities and other real properties of an institution depends upon the class of property under consideration and the financial program of the institution.*

Except for real properties that are the investment of endowment funds, depreciation accounting as found in commercial and business organizations does not apply to colleges and universities. If the financial program of an institution is such that current funds revenues are set aside for the renewal, replacement, or expansion of educational plant facilities, the allocation of such revenues should be shown in the Statement of Current Funds Revenues, Expenditures, and Transfers as a transfer to plant funds. The amount transferred should be added to the balance of funds for renewals and replacements in the Plant Funds group, and cash or other liquid assets should be transferred to the plant funds.

Depreciation accounting should be followed in accounting for real properties that are the investment of endowment funds. Funded reserves for the amount of the depreciation, carried in the Endowment Funds section of the accounts, should be established from the income of the properties or from other sources. For a discussion of the theory and practice of depreciation accounting in colleges and universities, see Appendix D, "Depreciation and Renewal and Replacement of Plant Assets."

10. *The Agency Funds group consists of funds in the custody of the institution but not belonging to it.*

Colleges and universities often serve as depositories or fiscal agents for student organizations, faculty committees, or for other groups connected with the institutions. Receipts and disbursements of agency funds do not constitute current funds revenues and expenditures and should not be included in the current funds operating statements. Such transactions should be shown in the Statement of Changes in Fund Balances—Agency Funds.

11. *Interfund borrowings of a temporary nature should be reported as assets of the fund group making the advances and as liabilities of the fund groups receiving the advances.*

If money is loaned or advanced temporarily by one fund group to another, that fact should be set forth in the financial records and reports by showing the amount advanced as an asset of the fund group making the advance and as a liability of the fund group receiving it. The purpose of this principle is to ensure that interfund borrowings are disclosed in the financial statements. In particular, advances to plant funds from current funds should not be reflected as an asset of current funds unless there is reasonable expectation that such advances will be repaid within a short period of time. When expectation of repayment does not appear likely, the amount advanced should be accounted for and reported as a permanent transfer from current to plant funds.

12. *All funds restricted by the donor or granting agency at the time of receipt with regard to the purpose for which they may be expended should be recorded as additions to the fund balances of the appropriate fund group.*

Each fund and all restricted receipts from it must be recorded in the proper fund group and subgroup as determined by the restrictions placed on them by the donor or other outside agency. This measure is essential to ensure the proper use of the resources in accordance with the limitations imposed by the donor or grantor. Restrictions or designations by the governing board on unrestricted institutional funds must be recognized in the accounts and reports in a manner that will maintain a distinction between internally designated funds and externally restricted funds, since the governing board can reverse its decision on the former, but cannot lift the conditions of the latter, short of legal action.

In the case of grants or bequests that require matching funds from institutional sources, the allocations of institutional funds represent commitments of governing boards that cannot be reversed. They should be identified on the balance sheet, in the accounting records, and in the financial reports.

13. *Unrestricted current funds, exclusive of unrestricted gifts and bequests, regardless of source, must be reported as revenues in total in the year received or accrued, in the Statement of Current Funds Revenues, Expenditures, and Transfers.*

Unrestricted revenues are those revenues whose use is not subject to restrictions imposed by payors and that may, therefore, be used for any institutional purpose selected by the governing board. Major items of unrestricted revenues include tuition and fees, governmental appropriations for operations, unrestricted endowment income, indirect cost allowances, income from temporary investment of current funds, sales and services of educational departments, and the income of auxiliary enterprises.

14. *All unrestricted gifts and bequests must be reported initially in the year in which received, in one statement, either the Statement of Current Funds Revenues, Expenditures, and Transfers, or the Statement of Changes in Fund Balances—Unrestricted Current Funds. Whichever method is employed must be used consistently from year to year.*

The financial report should reflect in one place the total received during the year from unrestricted gifts and bequests. It should disclose how these resources were applied, and the extent to which they may remain unapplied at the close of the fiscal period.

If institutional policy is to apply all unrestricted gifts and bequests to the support of current operations, the total should be reported as current funds revenues in the Statement of Current Funds Revenues, Expenditures, and Transfers under the title "Gifts."

If institutional policy is to hold unrestricted gifts and bequests for later application or to transfer them as additions to plant, quasi-endowment, or loan funds, the receipt and application of all such gifts must be reported in the Statement of Changes in Fund Balances—Unrestricted Current Funds—Gifts. Any portion of such resources applied to current operations of the year in which received should appear as a deduction on the Statement of Changes in Fund Balances—Unrestricted Current Funds—Gifts and as unrestricted revenues in the Statement of Current Funds Revenues, Expenditures, and Transfers under the title "Gifts Applied."

15. *Restricted current funds must be reported as revenues only to the extent expended during the year.*

Restricted current funds are those resources received for restricted operating purposes, the related expenditures of which may extend beyond the fiscal year in which received. Such items do not constitute current funds revenues until the terms of the gift or grant have been met and the moneys expended in accordance therewith. Furthermore, unexpended balances of restricted gifts and grants sometimes are returnable to grantors. The amount to be reported as revenues in any fiscal period, therefore, should be limited to the amount which has been expended in that period in accordance with the terms of the gift or grant.

16. *Transfers and allocations of unrestricted current funds must be reported in the Statement of Changes in Fund Balances—Unrestricted Current Funds, with the limited exception specified below.*

The governing board has the authority to assign unrestricted funds to fund groups other than current funds, and may subsequently reverse or modify such actions. In addition, unrestricted current funds may be set aside for use in future fiscal years, for operating purposes; such allocations remain as a part of the accumulated balance of current funds —unrestricted until used. As indicated in Principle 12, all such internal actions, and the balances of such internally established transfers or allocations, must be identified and distinguished from externally restricted funds.

The specific exception may occur where the clearly stated intention of the governing board is that a portion of unrestricted revenues of the current fiscal year shall be transferred to another fund group. This transfer may be reported as a deduction in the Transfers section of the Statement of Current Funds Revenues, Expenditures, and Transfers. However, the reverse of such a transfer (for example, the return to unrestricted current funds of amounts previously transferred from revenues) may not be handled in this manner but must follow the general principle and be reflected only on the Statement of Changes in Fund Balances—Unrestricted Current Funds.

17. *Earnings from endowment funds investments should be reported as income from such funds only to the extent that they are distributed to endowment income accounts.*

Investment income is distributed to the income accounts of the funds participating in an investment pool on the basis of the number of shares held by each fund, adjusted for shares held for less than a year. Income stabilization reserves frequently are established for the purpose of ensuring the regularity of relatively fixed amounts of endowment funds income from year to year. The method of establishing such reserves and of providing additions to them will also influence the distribution of endowment funds income.

Under one method, provisions for the income stabilization reserve are made from the pooled income account, the balance of the earnings being distributed to the income accounts of the participating funds as described. Under another method, pooled investment income is distributed to the income accounts of the participating funds before amounts have been set aside for the income stabilization reserve. The amount reported as unrestricted revenues from endowment income in the Statement of Current Funds Revenues, Expenditures, and Transfers should be the total distributed from the pool for the unrestricted endowment funds. Amounts to be added to the income stabilization reserve should be reported under the major category Transfers in the Statement of Current Funds Revenues, Expenditures, and Transfers.

Earnings from the investments of endowment funds whose income is restricted to specific purposes should be reported as additions to the balances of the appropriate fund groups or subgroups. If such earnings are restricted to current operating purposes, the amounts reported as current funds revenues should be only those amounts expended during the fiscal period.

18. *The accounting system should be maintained and financial reports presented on the accrual basis.*

Current funds revenues should be reported when they become due. Expenditures should include charges for materials received and services rendered even though payments for them may not be made until a subsequent fiscal period. The degree of materiality of items, however, may indicate that it is neither necessary nor desirable to accrue all revenues and pro rate all expenditures.

19. *Revenues and expenditures of auxiliary enterprises should be shown separately from other institutional operations.*

The financial operations of auxiliary enterprises should be reported separately in the Statement of Current Funds Revenues, Expenditures, and Transfers. Accounts should be maintained and reports presented on the accrual basis.

Expenditures should include all direct operating costs, charges for the operation and maintenance of the physical plant used by the enterprises, appropriate shares of general administrative and institutional expenditures, and, if applicable, charges for debt service on the physical facilities in which the auxiliary enterprises are located. Any provision made out of revenues of the enterprises for the renewal and replacement of their plant properties should also be included.

20. *Budgets covering all operations of the institution should be prepared and adopted each fiscal year.*

The annual operating budget should cover all current funds revenues and expenditures, and should be adopted well in advance of the fiscal period.

There should be an effective system of control in accordance with the approved budget. Accounts for budgetary control may be incorporated in the general accounting system or they may be maintained separately. An effective budgetary control system should provide for adequate recognition of commitments, or encumbrances, either in the general accounting system or through other records.

Budgets for organized research projects, other sponsored programs, and plant expansion and improvement projects should also be prepared and adopted. An effective means of controlling expenditures in these budget areas should be used, although the methods adopted may differ from those for the annual operating budget.

21. *Provision should be made for internal control and audit. In addition, there should be an annual audit by independent accountants.*

Independent audits should be performed in accordance with generally accepted auditing standards.

22. *A comprehensive financial report should be prepared for submission annually to the chief executive officer of the institution and to the governing board.*

In the interest of full and fair disclosure, an institution's annual report must include, at a minimum, a Balance Sheet, a Statement of Changes in Fund Balances of the respective fund groups and subgroups, and a Statement of Current Funds Revenues, Expenditures, and Transfers. A more detailed report may be issued for limited circulation. Illustrative forms for use in financial reporting are included in this volume as Appendix B.

15

Budgets and
Budgetary Accounting

Bυdgets for colleges and universities are determined by the educational program, the need for supporting services, and the limits of resources. They should be expressed in terms of estimates of support required for approved programs and in terms of resources available for such support. The development of the budget of a college or university is the concern of the major administrative officers as well as the faculty and staff members responsible for carrying out the programs and functions of the institution.

Long-Range Academic and Financial Planning

Colleges and universities should prepare long-range academic plans to assist in meeting the objectives of the institution. Plant development and financial plans should also be prepared on a long-range basis to implement the academic plan. Long-range plans may encompass a period of from five to ten years, or more. Planning is more detailed for the earliest programs and years, and more general for later years.

The long-range plans should include every significant aspect of the educational program and supporting services. Projections should be made of numbers of students, their quality, levels of instruction, and curricular choices. Changes in curriculum and methods of instruction must be considered, as must also expansion of research and public services. Faculty salaries, work loads, student-faculty ratios, staffing patterns, class size, and use of space must be determined for the present and estimated for the future. The need for supporting services (such as general administration) and requirements for physical facilities are dependent upon the academic plan, and all must receive adequate attention in the comprehensive long-range plans.

The budgetary process is used to promote the optimum allocation of resources to the academic program and requires imagination, insight, and creative effort on the part of the chief business officer. In some instances, elaborate techniques, commonly referred to as "program budgeting," have emerged. The value of program budgeting depends upon the establishment of meaningful relationships between projected program and resources, and is enhanced by integration with the accounting system to meet the evolving requirements.

The chief business officer is responsible for estimating costs and developing a long-range financial plan to support the academic program. This process should be carried on in cooperation with the appropriate academic officers. The plan should include estimates of added costs arising from expansion, improvements, and new program provisions, as well as those for increases in salaries and general rises in price levels.

In developing long-range plans, both academic and business officers should consult the studies produced by their institutional research offices. Those offices not only accumulate data basic to long-range plans, but they also engage in continuing analyses and research that are helpful both in the establishment of objectives and in periodic review and modification of plans.

Planning and Developing the Annual Operating Budget

The annual budget should be coordinated with the long-range academic and financial plans. It, however, is specific and detailed and presents the plan to finance the approved academic program and supporting services for a fiscal year. The annual budget is determined largely by the academic program, but it must be formulated within the limits of the resources available. The president, the chief academic officer, and the chief business officer all have responsibilities for its planning and development. The faculty is responsible for developing the departmental-level budget. The governing board is responsible for major policies and for final approval of the comprehensive budget.

Responsibility of the president

Before the organizational and budget units begin preparation of their expenditures estimates, the president should confer with his administrative officers to review the academic plans and establish preliminary estimates of revenues. After budget requests have been submitted and while they are being reviewed, further conferences will likely be desirable. Finally, the president must approve the academic and financial plans and submit the annual operating budget to the governing board.

Responsibility of the faculty and academic officers

The faculty performs the teaching, research, and many of the public service functions of the institution. Therefore, it should be consulted in preparing annual budgets for academic programs. Deans, departmental chairmen, and other academic officers are responsible for achieving the objectives of their divisions, schools, colleges, and departments; they, therefore, should present and justify their budgets to the administrative officers, who must make the recommendations and decisions for the institution as a whole. Academic officers should be thoroughly familiar with the long-range academic plans and should participate in modifying plans when budgetary considerations so require.

Responsibility of the chief business officer

The chief business officer should assist in planning and developing the annual budget for the academic programs, and assume responsibility for nonacademic operations such as the physical plant, many of the auxiliary enterprises, the service departments, and all aspects of business and financial management. He should also coordinate the review and analysis of the budgets of administrative offices and general institutional activities. The annual budgets for all instructional activities must be consistent with the financial plan of the institution, and the plan itself must be kept up to date by periodic review.

Preparation and Adoption of the Annual Budget

As each annual budget is planned, specific policies may need delineation to ensure that the budget elements are developed within the framework of the long-range plan. A statement of the policies, together with a letter of instruction from the president, should be sent as a guide to each person responsible for preparing the budget of an organizational unit. Usually, the department is the budgetary unit, and one person should be made responsible for conducting its affairs within the budget allocation.

The president, or an administrative officer who represents him in these matters, should discuss budget requests with the dean, departmental chairman, or head of the budgetary unit concerned. Thus, while final authority on budget recommendations to the governing board is vested in the president, ample opportunity is given departmental chairmen to explain their requests and to learn, before board action, what the president's recommendations will be. The chief academic officer and business officer should be present at all significant budget conferences.

TYPES OF BUDGETS

The annual current funds budget should be prepared and adopted well in advance of the fiscal period and should include all anticipated operating revenues, expenditures, transfers, and allocations. The anticipated revenues and expenditures should be applied to all areas of operations and activities for the educational and general functions, student aid, and the auxiliary enterprises, including anticipated uses of current funds revenues for purposes other than current operations.

Budgets for restricted current funds should also be included, even though their timing may or may not correspond to the fiscal year. The amounts of anticipated expenditures from restricted funds during the fiscal year should be shown so that the total current operations will be disclosed in the annual budget.

Budgets for construction projects, plant expansion programs, plant improvements, and other plant funds activities should be prepared, but should not be reflected in the current funds annual budget.

ESTIMATING CURRENT FUNDS REVENUES AND EXPENDITURES

Estimates of revenues and expenditures must recognize simultaneously the academic programs and supporting services, and the financing of both. The limit of the programs and services to be provided during a fiscal period will be determined by the resources available. If the resources are insufficient to accomplish the objectives of the long-range plan, the base of support must be broadened or the plan modified.

The compilation of estimates of revenues is the responsibility of the business officer. For many of the revenue items, the estimates should be based upon information supplied by other administrative officials. For example, the anticipated revenues from tuition and fees generally are based on estimated enrollment data prepared by the registrar or the director of admissions. These estimates should take into account general economic conditions, trends of enrollment both within the institution and in similar institutions, attrition rates, and other factors.

The estimate of income from investments requires thorough study. Income from each item in the portfolio should be projected, giving due consideration to economic trends, dividend records of stocks held, and the effect of any anticipated changes in the portfolio. The investment officer or the investment counselor should help in preparing the estimates of income from investments. The amount of investment income budgeted may reflect a predetermined distribution rate rather than the amount actually earned on each separate investment.

Estimates of revenues from gifts and grants should take into consideration past experience, plans for appeals for funds, and alumni activities.

Because of the increasing significance of research grants and contracts, separate estimates should be made of the revenues and expenditures related to such agreements. The magnitude of these projects has an important impact on all other operating areas, such as plant space, personnel, and position control. Budgets for research operations should be integrated with the regular budget but adjusted during the year as new projects are undertaken and others are terminated. The budgets for research grants and contracts should be brought into the regular budget, not for control purposes in the same way as for the unrestricted current funds budget, but for a comprehensive view of the total operating activities.

Estimates of revenues from auxiliary enterprises should be based on enrollments and on past experience in the operation of such units. Revenues should be estimated on a gross basis, including the value of allowances for such items as room and board furnished counselors and other emoluments to staff members employed in the various enterprises. The director or manager of each auxiliary enterprise should assist the business officer in preparing these estimates.

Estimates of revenues from other sources should be based on past experience adjusted for probable future conditions. Estimates of prior year's balances that may be available for rebudgeting and estimates of balances of quasi-endowment, term endowment, and other funds that might be transferred to current funds for operating purposes should be considered in the preparation of the estimates of total unrestricted current funds revenues.

In estimating expenditures, the general policies established in the long-range plan and the specific policies and instructions of the president for the annual budget being developed will serve as guides to departmental chairmen and others in preparing their budget requests. Among such policies are plans for expansion, improvement of existing programs, and the development of new educational programs and projects. Consideration must be given to the effect of salary and promotion policies, vacations, sabbatical leaves, and other staff benefits. Guidelines, such as student-faculty ratios, class size, teaching loads, and staffing patterns may be helpful, but the use of rigid formulae should be avoided.

Provisions should be made in the annual operating budget for contingencies and emergencies. The amounts provided in contingency accounts will depend upon available resources, past experience, and the extent of economic and other uncertainties at the time the budget is prepared. Responsibility and authority for contingency funds generally should not be assigned to departmental chairmen, but may be given to deans and directors.

BUDGET FORMS

The form, content, and arrangement of items in the budget request forms will vary according to the needs of institutions. In general, the forms will be most useful if they follow the pattern of the budget itself and if the account classifications correspond with those in the accounting records and in the internal and annual financial reports.

Budget request forms and final budgets usually reflect the three major object classifications—personal services (salaries and wages), supplies and expense, and equipment. Supporting schedules prepared in the development of the budget may assign amounts within the major classifications for subordinate object categories. For example, personal services might be subdivided in the supporting schedules into separate amounts for faculty and professional salaries, nonprofessional staff salaries, technicians' wages, and casual or temporary wages. Objects such as travel, telephone and communications, and printing, among others, might be detailed in the supporting schedules for the major classifications of supplies and expense. Such subordinate categories are used for management information, with budget controls applying only to the major object classifications.

The budget forms should include columns for comparative figures for at least the preceding fiscal period, the current year, and the budget year. Before the forms are distributed to departmental chairmen and others, the historical figures, supplied by the business office, should be inserted. The forms should also provide space for amounts recommended at each level of review.

The budget request forms for personal services should include more detailed information than do other expenditure items. Each individual position and its incumbent, if known, should be listed, and the term of service, whether academic year, twelve months, or part time, should be clearly shown. This information may be used, after the budget has received final approval, to establish payroll authorizations for making payments. In addition, personnel records showing all faculty and other staff members by name, rank, tenure status, age, and salary for the past several years should be available as budget requests are reviewed at various levels.

Departmental budget requests should be tabulated in summary form to show both the changes in amounts from the budget of the current year and the comparisons with actual expenditures of previous years. These summary reports enable the president to review departmental budget requests with a minimum of effort.

PRESENTATION AND ADOPTION OF THE BUDGET

The form of the various budget analyses prepared for the consideration of the governing board, as well as the amount of detail included in them, will be governed by the needs of the individual institution. Inasmuch as the governing board has the ultimate responsibility for the budget, the members must have sufficient information to permit them to discharge this responsibility. However, the board should leave as many details as possible to the judgment of the president, and should concentrate its efforts on major policies.

The presentation to the board should include a comparison of the proposed budget with budgets of preceding years; explanation of major changes; descriptions of programs added or eliminated; and salary and wage policies. In addition, the board should be informed of the extent to which the budget permits the fulfillment of long-range plans.

When the budget has been approved by the governing board, the business office should send each head of a budgetary unit a copy of his budget. Copies of the approved budget, or excerpts from it, should be sent to the appropriate administrative offices and divisions of the business office. The approved budget constitutes the authority to establish budgetary accounts, the payroll, position control and staffing patterns, and administrative and managerial operating programs.

Budgetary Control and Accounting

BUDGETARY CONTROL

One of the essential elements of budgeting is the establishment of effective budget control. Without good control, the value of a budget is seriously decreased regardless of how accurately or how carefully it has been prepared. One of the main purposes of budgetary control is to ensure that expenditures will not exceed allocations. The adoption of a budget does not guarantee realization of the estimated revenues. The business officer must maintain records that will compare actual revenues with budget estimates, and he should report major variations in budget operations to the president. If it is apparent that the estimated revenues will not be realized, the budget should be formally amended.

Budget control starts with those responsible for each budgetary unit. There is often a mistaken and unfortunate idea that budget control is the sole responsibility of some central agency such as the business office. The chief business officer has responsibility for over-all budget control, including responsibility to call attention to major departures from budget estimates and to take appropriate follow-up action.

The departmental chairman, however, has the first and primary responsibility for control of expenditures within his budgetary unit. He must see that the appointment of staff members and the salaries involved in his unit do not exceed the budget allocations therefor. He must restrict expenditures for supplies and equipment to the amounts allocated for these purposes. He must plan the expenditures for his unit so that the allocations will last through the entire fiscal year. Unless departmental chairmen take these responsibilities seriously, an institution may be in financial difficulty, even though adequate controls are maintained in the central business office. Once the budget has been approved, the educational and financial pattern should not deviate from it without the approval of higher authority.

Reports comparing actual results with budget projections should be prepared and sent to individual budget units at least monthly. These reports should be made available as early as possible after the end of the period covered. Summary reports should be prepared monthly and distributed to the appropriate administrative officers for review and any needed action.

Budgetary accounting

Since the budget is of vital importance in the operation and administration of an educational institution, many institutions make the recording of budgetary control accounts an integral part of the accounting system. This procedure brings under accounting control the records relating to revenues not yet realized and to unexpended balances of allocations.

After the budget has been approved by the governing board, the total estimated revenues for the year are charged in the general ledger to an account for Estimated Revenues, or Unrealized Revenues, and the total estimated expenditures and allocations are credited to an account for Estimated Expenditures, or Budget Allocations for Expenditures. The excess of estimated revenues over estimated expenditures is credited to an account that represents the free and unassigned balance of unrestricted current funds available for future expenditure or allocation. The title "Unallocated Revenues" is suggested for this account; other possible titles are "Unassigned Balance," or "Unallocated Balance," or "Unrestricted Current Funds."

Current funds revenues as received or accrued are credited to the Unrealized Revenues account. Actual expenditures are charged to the Estimated Expenditures account. Subsidiary accounts are maintained in which details of (1) estimated and realized unrestricted current funds revenues and (2) estimated and actual unrestricted current funds expenditures are recorded.

At the close of the fiscal period, any balances remaining in the Unrealized Revenues account, in the Estimated Expenditures account, and in the Unallocated Revenues account are closed into the Unallocated Balance of Unrestricted Current Funds account.

As a part of the budget system, provision must be made for outstanding obligations. There are a number of methods for handling these, any one of which is acceptable as long as it is a part of a total budgetary system that provides for proper control points. These range from a highly detailed, central encumbrance system which is kept as a part of the formal accounting records, to a decentralized, informal memorandum record of commitments kept by each budgetary unit. The method selected should provide effective control and useful information, but should not be inflexible or unreasonably expensive.

In the accounting and budgetary control system there may be records which should be kept locally, that is, at the point of use. In these cases the local records should correlate with, and not duplicate, centrally kept summary records.

Budget Revisions

The budget consists of a series of estimates, many of which are prepared months in advance of the fiscal period to which they relate. Since conditions change with the passage of time, there should be continuous review of the data on which the budget estimates were based. Periodic revisions should be made in order that the budget may always represent an up-to-date estimate of realizable revenues and a realistic plan for expenditures.

Responsibility, authority, and procedures for budget revisions should be a matter of written policy adopted and approved by the governing board of the institution. Whatever policy is adopted should allow the greatest degree of flexibility at each level of authority consistent with the maintenance of proper administrative responsibility.

Revised estimates of revenues should be initiated by the same officers responsible for the original estimates, and should be subjected to the same general procedures of review before they are approved and recorded in the books of account.

Requests for increased expenditure allocations are usually initiated at the departmental level and reviewed by the respective deans before being submitted to the president. If the amounts are within the total of the contingent account, or accounts, in the approved budget, or are covered by increases in anticipated revenues, the president usually has authority to approve such requests. However, if the amounts involved are large enough to change the anticipated net results of the original budget, the governing board should give formal approval before the increased expenditures are authorized.

Financial Reports

T HE financial report of a college or university is a summary of financial information covering the operation of the institution for a period of time and showing its financial position at the end of that period.

Colleges and universities are the recipients of a variety of kinds of revenues: those that may be expended for general institutional operations; gifts, appropriations, endowment funds income, and other revenues that must be expended only for restricted current purposes; and funds that must be kept intact and invested, with only the income available for expenditure. Educational institutions function as owners, operators, and trustees. Their financial reports, therefore, must deal not only with revenues and expenditures of current funds, but also with receipts and disbursements of other fund groups and with the principal and balances of funds.

Annual Financial Reports

The preparation of the annual financial report is the responsibility of the chief business officer. The report must include three primary statements:

The Balance Sheet
Statement of Changes in Fund Balances by fund groups
The Statement of Current Funds Revenues, Expenditures, and
    Transfers

The financial report may also include other schedules that supplement and amplify the basic exhibits. Accepted principles and standards of accounting and financial reporting for colleges and universities should be followed.

Annual Report for Public Distribution

Colleges and universities, whether publicly or privately controlled, are dependent upon public understanding and support; consequently, it is desirable for an institution to publish an annual financial report. The extent of distribution should be sufficient to ensure that representatives of the public and members of groups responsible for its support are adequately informed of its financial affairs.

The financial report should present fairly the essentials of the institution's operations for the period covered and its financial condition at the close of the period. Although excessive detail is to be avoided, the disclosure of resources and their utilization must be adequate to permit general understanding. The Balance Sheet is a presentation of the condition of each fund group as shown by the assets, liabilities, and fund balances at the end of the fiscal period. The fund balances are the result of the accumulated transactions during the year on the balances of the previous year. It is just as essential, therefore, to report the changes that have occurred in each of the fund balances since the date of the previous report as it is to show the condition of each fund group as of the closing date of the report.

A multicolumnar format can be used for both the Balance Sheet and the Statement of Changes in Fund Balances to combine information on all fund groups into one statement. In such presentations, like assets and liabilities and the various fund balances should not be combined in a "Total" column.

The auditor's opinion should be included in the published annual financial report. In publicly controlled institutions, if the requirement is that the services of state, municipal, or other designated auditors be used, and if a delay occurs in the performance of the audit, the financial report should be published with a note explaining why the auditor's opinion is omitted.

A commentary on the financial operations and condition of the institution is desirable. The material should be an interpretation of the financial statement and should be referenced so that the reader can relate the comments to the exhibits and schedules in the report. Charts, graphs, and other illustrative material may be used.

It is desirable that the financial report of each separately incorporated unit, such as university press or intercollegiate athletics, be appended to the institutional financial report.

Annual Reports for Internal Use

A report more detailed than the published report should be prepared in permanent form for use by financial and academic administrative officers, for whom it can constitute a valuable reference. In this report the financial information should be arranged by major accounting subdivisions and should provide details to support the figures in the exhibits of the published financial report. A table of contents and an index are useful adjuncts.

In addition to the annual published report and the detailed internal report, other supporting schedules should be prepared for those responsible for carrying out specific functions, for example, the director of auxiliary enterprises, the director of a fund-raising program, the supervisor of construction projects, the investment manager, and the directors of research programs and activities.

Interim Reports for Internal Use

The number, frequency, and content of reports for internal use will vary among institutions. Small institutions generally require few such reports because of the relative simplicity of their organization. Complex large universities likely will require a wide variety of interim reports on the phases of their financial and business administration.

Many of the reports for internal use disclose in financial terms the progress of the institution at appropriate intervals. For example, every college and university will find it useful to prepare a monthly budget report. The budget report should include (1) comparisons of budget estimates with actual results for all major categories of current funds, revenues and expenditures, and (2) allocations, encumbrances, expenditures, and unencumbered balances of all budgeted units and areas. Budget reports for their respective areas should be furnished to all directors of budgetary units, such as deans, departmental chairmen, managers, and directors.

At the departmental level, budget reports should be sufficiently detailed to provide comparison of actual performance with estimates for each budgeted item within the budget unit. Budget reports for management and control at other levels should be summarized by major organizational units and budget areas, and should identify those areas in which actual performance varies markedly from budget estimates. In this manner attention can be focused on troublesome budget operations that represent exceptions.

Other progress reports for management should be prepared at regular intervals. Examples are reports concerning the operations of restricted current funds, sponsored research projects, gifts received, construction projects, inventories, and cash flow. Frequently, reports are prepared to show trends in financial operations by means of historical data combined with projections. Such reports are especially valuable when important changes in operations are being considered.

Internal reports on special projects or areas of administration should be prepared as needed. Such reports may evaluate the impact of fund sources on the institution's activities; compare revenues from tuition and fees paid by students residing within the state with those paid by out-of-state students; analyze procurement and contracting procedures to ascertain whether sufficient safeguards are maintained; or propose the indirect cost rates for sponsored research programs.

Periodic reports, usually monthly, on earnings from the investments of all endowment funds should be prepared and transmitted to the manager of the investment portfolio, to the investment committee of the governing board, and to other committees and administrative officers of the institution.

Operating reports, on an accrual basis, should be prepared at least monthly for each auxiliary enterprise. Reports for some, such as food service and the student store, may be wanted at more frequent intervals.

Periodic reports of gifts received should be prepared and transmitted to the chief executive officer, to the governing board, and to other administrative officers responsible for fund-raising activities.

The chief business officer should provide those internal reports that are needed and most effective; he should be alert to the needs of his governing board, its committees, and other administrative officers, and furnish them with reports that will contribute to effective management. And he should discontinue any internal reports that do not facilitate administration or lead to management decisions.

Integration of Reports with the Accounting System

There is continual need in the business office to examine new operations and activities. In order for financial reports to serve their purposes most effectively, they must be planned and scheduled as a regular part of accounting activities, rather than result from frequent emergency requests. The business office must be adequately staffed to prepare the annual report and needed interim reports.

17

The Balance Sheet

THE purpose of the Balance Sheet is to present a concise statement of the financial condition of an institution and of the financial resources for which it is responsible at a specified date.

General Considerations

In accounting and financial reporting for colleges and universities a fund is an accounting entity involving assets, liabilities, and fund balances, established for the purpose of carrying on specific activities or attaining certain objectives. Some funds may be used for any institutional purpose whereas others must be used in accordance with special regulations, restrictions, limitations, or designations.

The fund balance of each fund held by an institution should be represented by an account in the general ledger or in subsidiary ledgers with control through summary accounts in the general ledger. The accounts for assets, liabilities, revenues and expenditures, receipts and disbursements, and fund balances of all funds should be so classified that those that have like characteristics and are available for use for common purposes will be set forth, respectively, in separately balanced fund groups.

The following groups of funds are those most commonly found in educational institutions:

Current Funds
Loan Funds
Endowment and Similar Funds
Annuity and Life Income Funds

Plant Funds
Agency Funds

An understanding of the manner in which the financial resources made available to colleges and universities must be used and the characteristics of the various fund groups will, with few exceptions, enable financial officers to classify all funds in the groups suggested. Within some of the major groups, subgroups may be desirable, and these may, or may not, be separately balanced. For example, the Current Funds group consists of unrestricted current funds and restricted current funds. In the Annuity and Life Income Funds group, the balances of the two types of funds should be shown separately; and the plant funds may be divided between (*a*) unexpended plant funds and (*b*) funds expended for plant assets and reported in the Investment in Plant subgroup. In some institutions, other fund groups may be necessary; however, the six major groups listed above will meet the needs of the majority of colleges and universities for adequate and clear financial reporting.

The identity of individual funds must be maintained at all times in subsidiary records, and the identity of the different fund groups must be maintained on the Balance Sheet and in all supporting statements.

The order of presenting the fund groups in the Balance Sheet is not of major importance, although to promote reasonable uniformity among the financial reports of institutions, the sequence presented in this volume is recommended.

If an institution prepares separate balance sheets for any of its administrative units, for example, a separately financed college or a branch on a separate campus, such balance sheets should follow the form recommended in this chapter. In such cases a combined balance sheet by fund groups should be prepared to show the financial condition of the entire institution.

The Balance Sheet is a summary statement. However, sound principles of reporting, even on summary statements, require disclosure of essential details. For example, the cash, receivables, investments, and other assets of the various fund groups should be separately identified and reported.

The Balance Sheet usually is presented as illustrated in Form 1 (in Appendix B). As an alternative, it may be presented in a multicolumnar form, illustrated in alternative Form 2, where a separate column is used for each fund group and major subgroup. In the latter form, like assets and liabilities and the various fund balances should not be combined in a "Total" column.

Regardless of the form used, the Balance Sheet must disclose all interfund borrowings as of the date of the report.

Current Funds

Included in this group are funds available for general operating purposes, those restricted by donors or other outside agencies for specific operating purposes, and those designated by governing boards for future operating purposes. Current Funds include the following categories:

1. Unrestricted Current Funds These are funds that have been earned by or appropriated to an institution free of any restrictions imposed by outside agencies.

2. Restricted Current Funds Such funds have been acquired by, or appropriated by, or contributed to an institution subject to restrictions imposed by outside sources that specify the manner in which the funds are to be used in current operations.

A third section of Current Funds may be established to report the funds related to auxiliary enterprises.

ASSETS OF CURRENT FUNDS

The items usually included as assets of current funds, and explanations of the captions used, are as follows:

Cash includes cash on hand, petty cash, and cash in banks.

Investments includes securities purchased out of current funds or received as assets of current funds. The investments should be valued at cost if purchased or at their expertly appraised value in the case of gifts. The basis of valuation and the market values should be revealed in the report by footnote or other means.

Accounts Receivable includes the usual types of such receivables. Governmental appropriations and advances that are subject to release by a governmental officer for institutional use should be shown here, and not under Cash. Items of major importance should be set out separately. Unpaid student accounts should appear here. Accounts receivable should be shown at face value less an allowance for doubtful accounts.

Notes Receivable includes the usual types of such receivables. They should be shown at face value less an allowance for doubtful notes. Student loan funds notes are not included here but are recorded in the Loan Funds group.

Inventories includes merchandise for sale and supplies and stocks in stores. Examples of the latter are office supplies, fuel, building supplies, and goods not yet charged as expense but carried in stock in general storerooms for future requisition or sale. Items that have been charged as expense should not reappear as inventory, even though they may be on hand in departmental storerooms or offices. Merchandise for sale includes such items as inventories of student stores, university presses, and food service. Other inventory accounts may be established for military uniforms, gymnasium and athletic supplies, merchandise handled through vending machines, and similar items. Inventories of salable and consumable merchandise may be segregated from other inventory accounts, if desired.

Prepaid Expenses and Deferred Charges includes that portion of operating expenditures that is properly chargeable to a period subsequent to the date of the Balance Sheet.

Due from Other Funds represents the amounts of current funds loaned temporarily to other fund groups, as for example, current funds loaned to the Plant Funds group. Permanent transfers from current funds to other fund groups would not appear as assets of this group inasmuch as they will never be repaid to the Current Funds group.

LIABILITIES OF CURRENT FUNDS

The liabilities usually included under Current Funds and explanations of the captions used are as follows:

Accounts Payable and Accrued Expenses represents liabilities for goods received and other expenses incurred for which disbursements have not been made as of the date of the report. Payrolls due and unpaid are included here. Amounts deducted from payrolls and not yet forwarded to proper agencies, such as income taxes withheld, social security taxes, and retirement annuity premiums may be shown here, or they may be shown in the Agency Funds group.

Notes Payable represents liabilities for outstanding notes covering borrowings for current operations. This category does not include any form of indebtedness on the physical plant; such indebtedness should be reported as liabilities of the Plant Funds group.

Deposits includes receipts for various purposes which an institution may be required to repay in whole or in part. They include deposits for breakage, room rental contracts, keys, library books, and reservations for admission to the institution or to the residence halls.

Deferred Revenues includes payments made to the institution in advance for services to be rendered in a subsequent period. Examples are tuition, fees, and room rentals paid in advance.

Provision for Encumbrances appears on the Balance Sheet among the liabilities when it is the practice of an institution to record commitments in the form of purchase orders as current expenditures. If it is the practice of an institution not to record purchase orders as current expenditures, a provision for encumbrances, or commitments, representing outstanding purchase orders for goods or services not yet delivered or received is reported as an allocated portion of the unrestricted current funds balance.

Due Other Funds includes amounts that have been borrowed temporarily from other fund groups and will be repaid.

FUND BALANCES OF CURRENT FUNDS

The balances of Current Funds includes those for unrestricted funds, restricted funds, and, where appropriate, unrestricted gifts. These balances should be shown separately in the equity section of the Balance Sheet, whether or not the assets are combined. The balance of Auxiliary Enterprises funds may also be reported as a separate item.

1. *The Unrestricted Current Funds balance* represents the net accumulation over the years of the excess of current funds revenues over current funds expenditures and transfers. It is available for future operating purposes or any other use determined by the governing board. If any portion is allocated, such amounts may be disclosed in the Balance Sheet or the Statement of Changes in Fund Balances—Unrestricted Current Funds (see Forms 4, 14, and 35). If expenditures and transfers have exceeded revenues over the years, the debit balance should be shown as a deduction in the equity section of the Balance Sheet.

2. *The Unrestricted Gifts balance* represents the net unexpended balances of funds received as unrestricted gifts and bequests whose use has been or will be designated by the governing board.

3. *The Restricted Current Funds balances* are the unexpended balances of funds restricted by donors or other outside agencies to specific

operating purposes. They originate from income on restricted endowment funds, gifts whose donors have placed limitations on their use, and grants from private or governmental sources for research, training, and other sponsored programs. Since restricted current funds are reported as current revenues only to the extent expended during the year, funds thus received but not expended as of the date of the report must be disclosed.

The *endowment income stabilization reserve* should also be included here if amounts added to it each year are withheld from the earnings of investment pools before such earnings are distributed among the participating funds.

4. *The Auxiliary Enterprises Funds balance* title, if used, represents the unexpended balance applicable to such activities, available for future use in connection with the auxiliary enterprises.

Loan Funds

The Loan Funds group includes all funds available for personal loans. Generally such funds are for student loans only; however, if faculty and staff loan funds are available, they may be included in this group, but should be identified separately. Endowed loan funds—endowment funds that are to be invested and only their income used for loans—should be included in the Endowment and Similar Funds group, and their income should be transferred periodically to the loan funds.

ASSETS, LIABILITIES, AND FUND BALANCES OF LOAN FUNDS

The assets of Loan Funds commonly include cash, notes receivable for loans granted, and perhaps temporary investments of cash on hand. Notes receivable should be recorded at face value, less allowance for doubtful notes, if appropriate. Temporary investments should be recorded at cost or, in the case of gifts of securities, at expertly appraised values; the basis of valuation and the market values should be disclosed in the report.

The equity section of the Balance Sheet or the Statement of Changes in Fund Balances—Loan Funds should show separately the balances of government advances for loan funds, institutional funds required to supplement such advances, other refundable loan funds, and funds available for loans to faculty and staff. Unrestricted current funds designated by the governing board to function as loan funds should be identified separately, since action of the governing board at some future date may require that the funds be returned to the Current Funds group or transferred to other fund groups.

Endowment and Similar Funds

The funds included in this group are of three major types: endowment, term endowment, and quasi-endowment funds.

1. Endowment Funds   An endowment fund is one which a donor or other agency has stipulated, as a condition of gift, that the principal is to be maintained inviolate and in perpetuity, and that only the income from the investments of the fund may be expended.

2. Term Endowment Funds   A term endowment fund is one which a donor or other outside agency, by the terms of the instrument of gift, has provided is to be released from inviolability to permit all or part of it to be expended upon the happening of a particular event or the passage of a stated period of time. When such conditions have been met, and upon appropriate action of the governing board, term endowment funds should be reported in the appropriate fund groups, depending on the new uses to which the funds are to be put.

3. Quasi-endowment Funds   A quasi-endowment fund is one which the governing board of an institution, rather than a donor or other outside agency, has determined is to be retained and invested. The term *funds functioning as endowment* may also be used to designate such funds. The governing board has the power to decide at any time to expend such resources and may authorize their transfer to other fund groups.

The identity of the three subgroups of funds described here should be clearly differentiated in the equity section of the Balance Sheet in the Endowment and Similar Funds group and in the Statement of Changes in Fund Balances—Endowment and Similar Funds.

Annuity and life income funds may be included as a separately identified category in this fund group unless they are of major magnitude, in which case they should be reported in a separate fund group.

ASSETS OF ENDOWMENT AND SIMILAR FUNDS

The assets of the funds in this group comprise cash and investments. Investments include securities, real estate, and any investment in institutional plant. They exclude funds held in trust by others (discussed below).

Securities include bonds, notes, preferred stocks, common stocks, and mortgage notes. The total amount invested in each category may be shown either on the Balance Sheet or in supporting schedules, regardless of whether the funds were pooled for investment purposes.

Real Estate includes real property in which endowment funds are invested for the purpose of producing income. Such properties may be acquired by gift, purchase, or foreclosure of mortgage notes.

If any funds included in this group are invested in institutional plant, the amount should appear in this group as a separate type of investment.

Securities and real estate purchased as investments of the funds in this group should be reported at cost. Investments donated for this fund group should be recorded at market value or at expertly appraised value as of the date of the gift or the date of acquiring financial control of the asset. These values should not be changed to reflect changes in market values. Figures reflecting market values of investments, while essential in the management of investment portfolios, should be maintained in memorandum records rather than in the primary accounting records. The basis of valuation and the market values of the investments should be revealed in the financial report by a footnote or other means.

Provisions should be made for the depreciation of real estate improvements, and, when amounts are material, for the amortization of premiums and the accumulation of discounts on securities.

Pledges, including subscriptions, subscription notes, and estate notes, are not ordinarily recorded but may be included here if they reflect fairly financial resources available to an institution. In considering whether a pledge can be deemed a resource of an institution and therefore reflected in its financial statements, the following basic factors should be considered: (1) The pledge must be collectible, not only from the legal standpoint, but from the financial ability of the pledger to pay the amount of his pledge and the willingness of the institution to enforce collection by legal means, if necessary. (2) The pledge must be in writing, with amount definitely stated and a date or dates of payment specified. (3) Confirmation of the existence and the amount of the pledge must be possible by direct correspondence with the pledger or his legal representative. Under these rules, contingent bequests would not qualify for inclusion whereas legally enforceable claims against the estate of a benefactor could be considered an available resource.

LIABILITIES AND FUND BALANCES OF ENDOWMENT AND SIMILAR FUNDS

The liabilities of the funds in this group consist of any form of indebtedness against the assets, such as mortgages payable on real estate investments. Equity accounts include those for the balances of the funds in this group, for gains and losses on investment transactions, and for share adjustments. The accounts for the balances of the funds should identify respectively the total of endowment funds, of term endowment funds, and of quasi-endowment funds. If investment pool gains and losses are accumulated, an additional equity account should be included for Net Adjusted Gains and Losses.

All three types of funds in this group may be further subdivided according to the manner in which the income from their investments may or must be used.

FUNDS HELD IN TRUST BY OTHERS

A college or university, or a group of institutions, may be the beneficiaries of trust funds held and administered by an outside fiscal agent. Since such trust funds are not the property of the institution and are not under its sole ownership and management, they should not be reported as funds belonging to it. They should be indicated, however, in the financial report by a notation or footnote. The value at which such funds are noted will depend to some extent on the availability of full and reliable information from the agency administering the funds. If accurate information is available from the external trustees, the values reported by them may be used; if this information is not known or is not available, the income from the funds may be cited. The valuation of such funds may also depend upon the extent to which an institution benefits from the trust. If an institution is the sole beneficiary, it may include the total value of the trust in its notation; if it receives only a portion of the income from the trust, it should include only an appropriate portion of the total value of the trust fund.

The term *Funds Held in Trust by Others* does not include funds under the control of an institution but administered by a trust company or other custodian as the agent of the institution.

Annuity and Life Income Funds

Annuity funds are those funds acquired by an institution subject to an agreement whereby assets—cash, securities, or other productive investments—are donated to a college or university on condition that the institution pay periodically to the donor or other designated individuals, a stipulated amount, called an "annuity," which payments are to cease at the time of death of the annuitant or at some other specified time. *Life income funds* are similar to annuity funds, except that an institution is required to pay to the donor or other designated individuals only the income earned by the assets of the funds after deduction of appropriate management expenses. The terms "annuity" and "life income" funds are limited to those funds possessing assets that produce income to satisfy all or a portion of the annuity or life income requirements.

Assets, liabilities, and fund balances of Annuity and Life Income Funds

The assets of the funds in this group consist of cash, securities, and other types of investments. Their valuation should be determined and reported in the same manner as the assets of Endowment and Similar Funds.

The liabilities consist of indebtedness against the fund assets. The balance of the funds should be shown in the equity section of the Balance Sheet, the total of the balances of annuity funds being shown separately from the total of the balances of life income funds. This separation may be reflected in the Statement of Changes in Fund Balances—Annuity and Life Income Funds.

If the assets of these funds are pooled, an account for accumulated gains and losses on investment transactions should be shown in the equity section of the Balance Sheet. If there is unexpended income at the date of the report, it should be reported as a liability on the Balance Sheet.

Plant Funds

Plant funds consist of funds to be used for the acquisition of physical properties for institutional purposes, but unexpected at the date of the report; funds expended for, and thus invested in, institutional properties; funds set aside for the renewal and replacement of institutional properties; and funds set aside for debt service charges and for the retirement of indebtedness on institutional properties. The term does not include real properties that are the investment of endowment and similar funds, since such properties are reported in the fund group Endowment and Similar Funds.

The usual sources of plant funds are gifts, grants, bequests, and other forms of contributions designated by donors for plant purposes; appropriations of governmental bodies for capital, or building, purposes; proceeds of loans from governmental agencies, banks, insurance companies, and other financial institutions; and special or designated student fees. Plant funds may also come from other funds already in the possession of an institution that the governing board authorizes to be used for plant purposes, such as current funds, quasi-endowment funds, term endowment funds (upon the expiration of the time, or the achievement of the event, specified in the terms of the original gift), or annuity and life income funds (also, upon the termination of the conditions of the original gift). When the use of such funds for plant purposes represents a permanent change in the existing designated uses of the funds, this fact should be recognized as a transfer of funds. Cash or other assets should be transferred from the fund group providing the resources to the Plant Funds group.

Institutions sometimes advance on a temporary basis—that is, loan for what is expected to be a short period of time—current funds or funds of other groups for plant purposes. Such temporary advances, or short-term loans, should be made only upon authorization of the governing board. The authorization should stipulate the period of the advances and should provide definite schedules of repayments. The advances should be accounted for as assets of the fund group making the advance and as liabilities of the Plant Funds group. If it is later determined that the loans cannot, or will not, be repaid by the plant funds, that fact should be recognized and the governing board should authorize a permanent transfer of the funds.

The accounts for plant funds may be classified and reported in four separately balanced subgroups: unexpended plant funds, funds for the renewals and replacements of plant assets, funds for the retirement of indebtedness on institutional plant properties, and funds invested in institutional plant assets (see Form 1). In an alternative method they may be reported in two separately balanced subgroups: unexpended plant funds, and funds invested in institutional plant assets (see Form 2).

ASSETS OF PLANT FUNDS

The assets of *Unexpended Plant Funds* subgroup include cash, investments, and receivables. If building projects are in the process of construction, temporary accounts for such projects may be included here, the balance in the accounts being transferred to the Investment in Plant subgroup at the end of each fiscal period or when each construction project is completed.

The assets of the *Funds for Renewals and Replacements* and for *Retirement of Indebtedness* consist of cash, investments, receivables, and funds on deposit with others. These may be reported with similar items in the Unexpended Plant Funds subgroup if separately balanced subgroups are not shown.

The assets of the *Investment in Plant* subgroup consist of land, buildings, improvements other than buildings, and equipment. Accounts for building projects in process of construction are also included here to record the amounts transferred from the temporary construction accounts in the Unexpended Plant Funds subgroup.

Plant assets should be recorded in the accounts at original cost. Gifts of plant assets should be recorded at expertly appraised values. The basis of valuation of plant assets should be disclosed in the report by footnote or other means, and the assets should be carried in the accounts at these values until disposed of. Depreciation accounting on the educational plant and on auxiliary enterprises facilities is not applicable. (The reason for this policy is discussed at some length in Appendix D, "Depreciation and Renewal and Replacement of Plant Assets.")

If endowment funds have been invested in institutional plant, the book value of that property should be reported as an asset in the Plant Funds group, and the amount of investment should appear as a liability in the Plant Funds group. An equivalent amount will appear as an investment asset in the Endowment Fund group.

LIABILITIES AND FUND BALANCES OF PLANT FUNDS

The liabilities of the Unexpended Plant Funds subgroup consist of payables; evidences of bonds, notes, or mortgages payable; and temporary advances from other funds for plant purposes. The balances of

Unexpended Plant Funds, of Funds for Renewals and Replacements, and of Funds for the Retirement of Indebtedness should be shown separately as liabilities in the Balance Sheet, whether or not the assets are combined. Any allocations by a governing board of unrestricted current funds to plant funds should be identified separately as unexpended plant funds until expended for plant assets. The governing board may authorize the transfer, at some future time, of such allocations for other fund group purposes.

The liabilities of the Investment in Plant subgroup consist of payables and evidences of indebtedness (such as bonds, notes, and mortgages payable) for funds borrowed and expended for the acquisition or construction of plant assets. The net investment of institutional funds in plant items should be shown in the equity section of the Balance Sheet in this subgroup. This figure may be divided to show the value of plant assets acquired from gifts and donations, from governmental appropriations, and from current, or other, funds.

Agency Funds

These are funds received by an institution from student organizations, individual students, or faculty members, for which the institution acts as custodian or fiscal agent on behalf of the payor. The assets consist of cash and perhaps receivables and temporary investments.

The liabilities and fund balances include payables and the accounts for the balance of the funds due others. If not reported as payables in the Current Funds group, amounts deducted from payrolls and not yet forwarded to proper agencies, such as income taxes withheld, social security taxes, and retirement annuity premiums, may be shown here.

18

The Statement of Changes
in Fund Balances

The Statement of Changes in Fund Balances shows in summary form the changes that have occurred in the balances of each fund group and subgroup as a result of the transactions during the fiscal period. This is a primary statement, equal in importance to the Balance Sheet and the Statement of Current Funds Revenues, Expenditures, and Transfers. The various parts of the statements show the balance of each fund group and its subgroups at the beginning of the year, additions and deductions during the year, and the balances at the close of the fiscal period covered by the report.

Reports of fund balances generally are presented individually for each fund group and subgroup shown on the Balance Sheet, as illustrated in Forms 4–13 in Appendix B. A multicolumnar form (Alternate Form 14) may be used, in which each fund group and subgroup is shown in a separate column. Such presentation must disclose interfund borrowings as of the date of the report. The additions and deductions of all the different groups must not be combined in a "Total" column.

Current Funds

Current funds include several subgroups. The changes in balances of the subgroups may be presented in a multicolumnar form, in which separate columns are used for unrestricted funds, restricted funds, and, if appropriate, unrestricted gifts and bequests, and auxiliary enterprises funds. A Total column may be used to combine the transactions and balances of all subgroups in the Current Funds group.

[183]

UNRESTRICTED CURRENT FUNDS

A statement of changes during the year in unrestricted current funds, consisting primarily of the net result of current operations, is illustrated in Form 4. Additions include the excess of revenues over expenditures and transfers as disclosed in the Statement of Current Funds Revenues, Expenditures, and Transfers (Form 3), and any adjustments and credits to be added to the balance of unrestricted current funds.

Deductions include the excess of expenditures and transfers over revenues, if that situation exists, transfers of unrestricted current funds to other fund groups, and any adjustments and charges qualifying as deductions from the balance of unrestricted current funds.

The allocated and unallocated balances as of the end of the fiscal year should be shown on the Statement of Changes in Fund Balances —Unrestricted Current Funds.

UNRESTRICTED GIFTS

The changes during the year in the balances of these funds are reported in the statement illustrated in Form 35, Statement of Changes in Fund Balances—Unrestricted Current Funds—Gifts. Additions include all gifts and bequests received to which donors have not attached restrictions. The balance represents amounts of unrestricted gifts and bequests which, by action of the governing board, have been designated for specific operating purposes or are being held for future designation. Deductions consist of transfers to current funds revenues of the amounts expended during the fiscal period and the amounts transferred to loan funds, plant funds, and quasi-endowment funds.

If an institution elects to report as current funds revenues all unrestricted gifts and bequests immediately upon receipt, this statement is not necessary. It should be noted also that if the governing board decides upon the latter method, all unrestricted gifts and bequests must be so reported; none may be added directly to plant, loan, or quasi-endowment funds. The basis of reporting unrestricted gifts and bequests may appear as an explanatory comment in the financial report.

RESTRICTED CURRENT FUNDS

The changes during the year in the balances of restricted current funds are presented in the statement illustrated in Form 5.

Additions should be identified by the source of the receipts, that is, gifts restricted by donors for specific operating purposes and for student aid, income from restricted endowment and quasi-endowment funds, and receipts from outside organizations and agencies sponsoring research projects under grants, contracts, and similar agreements.

Deductions include the amount of restricted current funds expended during the fiscal period. Returns to donors or granting agencies should also be reported as deductions in this statement.

Loan Funds

The total balance of loan funds shown on the Balance Sheet is supported by a statement illustrated in Form 6.

Additions during the year include gifts, bequests, and governmental advances designated by donors or outside agencies to be used for lending purposes; interest on loan notes; income from restricted endowment funds; and earnings on any temporary investments of loan funds. Transfers to loan funds from other fund groups, such as the transfer of institutional funds required under the terms of governmental appropriations for student loan funds, and designations by governing boards of unrestricted current funds to be used for loan funds should also be included here.

Deductions include the amount of notes written off because of uncollectibility and any transfers from loan funds to other fund groups. When permitted by the terms of loan funds, costs of collecting notes and other administrative costs may be charged against specific loan funds. When this is done, such charges should be shown as deductions in the statement of fund balances.

Endowment and Similar Funds

In this statement (Form 7), the totals of endowment funds, term endowment funds, and quasi-endowment funds must be identified separately. A multicolumnar form may be used, with separate columns for each subgroup and totals for the entire group.

Additions include gifts and bequests, transfers from other fund groups, income added to principal, and net realized gains on investment transactions. Deductions include any net realized losses on investment transactions, share adjustments on withdrawals, and transfers to other fund groups.

Annuity and Life Income Funds

The changes in this group of funds are shown in a statement illustrated in Form 8. Annuity funds should be separately identified from life income funds.

Additions include the value of assets received under any new agreements during the year, additions to existing agreements, income earned during the year, and net realized gains on investment transactions. Deductions include payments to annuitants and beneficiaries, transfers to other fund groups upon the termination of any annuity agreements, and any other charges against the balances of the funds.

Plant Funds

Appropriate statements should be prepared to show the changes during the year in each of the subsections of the Plant Funds group.

Unexpended Plant Funds (Form 9)

Additions include donations from private sources restricted for plant uses; building, or capital, appropriations of governmental bodies; proceeds from bond issues, mortgages, and other forms of borrowings for plant purposes; special student fees for building purposes; income from temporary investments of unexpended plant funds; net realized gains on the transactions of such investments; and transfers from other fund groups. Unrestricted current funds designated by action of the governing board to be used for plant purposes should be included here, any unexpended balance of such funds being clearly identified.

Deductions include disbursements during the year for plant facilities and any net realized losses on the transactions of temporary investments of plant funds. The disbursements for plant facilities may be divided to show separately the total amounts disbursed for land, for buildings, for improvements other than buildings, and for equipment.

Funds for Renewals and Replacements (Form 10)

Additions consist chiefly of transfers from Current or other fund groups. Other additions may consist of earnings on the temporary investments of the funds in this subsection and any net realized gains on their sale. Deductions include the disbursement of renewal and replacement funds for the purposes indicated and any net realized losses on investment transactions.

Funds for the Retirement of Indebtedness (Form 11)

Additions include transfers from current funds; transfers of income of auxiliary enterprises pledged under indenture provisions for debt services; transfers from other fund groups authorized by action of the governing board to be used for debt service; and earnings and net gains on any temporary investments of funds in this group. Additions may also include governmental appropriations or gifts specifically designated for debt service.

Deductions include disbursements for principal and interest payments, trustees' service charges, and any other related disbursements in connection with the retirement of indebtedness on institutional plant facilities. Any net realized losses on investment transactions are included here.

Sinking funds and reserves held by trustees outside the institution under provision of indebtedness indentures should be included in this subsection. Required deposits to such accounts represent transfers between asset accounts in this subsection, and are not deductions from the balance of funds for the retirement of indebtedness.

Investment in Plant (Form 12)

Additions include the amounts disbursed from unexpended plant funds; amounts expended from current funds for equipment; the appraised value of equipment, collections, and other plant assets received as gifts; and the amount by which the indebtedness on the institutional plant was reduced during the year.

Deductions represent the book value of plant assets which have been disposed of during the year.

The balance in the Net Investment in Plant account may be detailed to show the source of the funds, that is gifts, governmental appropriations, and current or other funds.

Agency Funds

The changes during the year in the balances of these funds may be shown in a statement illustrated in Form 13. This is a report of stewardship only; it is not a report of institutional transactions. Therefore, it is sufficient to present a summary showing only the total of the balances of all such funds at the beginning of the year, additions and deductions during the year, and the total of the balances at the close of the fiscal period. It is not necessary to report the detailed transactions of each fund in the institutional report, although such reports should be made at least annually to the owners of the funds.

Summary and Detailed Statements

Forms 4–13 are illustrations of statements that summarize the changes that occurred during the fiscal period in the various fund balances. Forms 17–24 illustrate schedules which present the transactions of each fund group in greater detail. Such schedules, as well as many others, may be included or omitted from the published institutional report at the discretion of the institution.

19

The Statement of Current Funds Revenues, Expenditures, and Transfers

The revenues and expenditures for current operations of a college or university during a fiscal period, together with transfers from or to the current operating revenues, are shown in summary in Form 3, Statement of Current Funds Revenues, Expenditures, and Transfers. More detailed presentations are shown in Form 15, Schedule of Current Funds Revenues, and Form 16, Schedule of Current Funds Expenditures. Additions to and deductions from endowment, term endowment, quasi-endowment, loan, annuity, life income, plant, and agency funds are specifically excluded from all three forms.

Current Funds Revenues

Current funds revenues generally are classified in three major categories:

Educational and General
Student Aid
Auxiliary Enterprises

At the discretion of the institution, the categories Educational and General and Student Aid may be merged, with each category being subtotaled.

Institutions may administer activities and programs that provide services to the community, the state, the region, or the nation. Some of

[189]

these will be educational in character and, when they are, should be included in the category Educational and General. Others may be primarily community or public services performed by the institution, and are not essential in meeting the educational objectives of the institution. In the latter cases, the revenues from the activities may be reported in separate major categories, immediately following Student Aid, in the Statement of Current Funds Revenues, Expenditures, and Transfers, and in the Schedule of Current Funds Revenues. Some services of this type are:

Hospitals providing services to the community and the state beyond the educational requirements of the institution's medical school;

Regional research or educational facilities such as a computer center serving several institutions;

Regulatory services such as seed control and the natural resources surveys assigned to some state universities and land-grant colleges;

Contract research centers of major magnitude;

International programs involving service or assistance to foreign countries and educational institutions.

Educational and General

This category includes revenues from unrestricted current funds, revenues from restricted funds to the extent they have been expended during the period covered by the financial report, and, where appropriate, revenues from unrestricted gifts and bequests to the extent applied by the governing board during the period.

Education and General revenues should be classified by sources as follows:

A. Student Tuition and Fees
B. Governmental Appropriations
C. Endowment Income
D. Gifts (*or* Gifts Applied)
E. Sponsored Research
    Governmental
    Nongovernmental
F. Other Separately Budgeted Research
G. Other Sponsored Programs
    Governmental
    Nongovernmental
H. Recovery of Indirect Costs—Sponsored Programs
I. Sales and Services of Educational Departments

J. Organized Activities Related to Educational Departments

K. Other Sources

The sequence of the items in the Statement of Revenues may be determined by the institution; however, to achieve reasonable uniformity among the financial reports of institutions, the above order is recommended.

A. *Student Tuition and Fees* Under this title should be included all tuition and fees assessed against students for educational and general purposes, net after refunds. Charges for room, board, and for other services rendered by auxiliary enterprises are not included here, but, instead, are reported under the category Auxiliary Enterprises.

Tuition and fee remissions or exemptions should be assessed and reported as student fees revenues although it is not intended to effect collection from the students. A corresponding amount, as well as the amount of other student aid granted out of current revenues, should be shown as expenditures under the category Student Aid.

In the subcategory Tuition should be included revenues from charges for all instructional programs, including regular sessions, summer sessions, and off-campus programs when credit is granted for courses.

Revenues from student fees assessed specifically for debt service on institutional plant or for plant expansion purposes should not be included under this title, but should be reported directly as additions to the appropriate subgroup of the plant funds accounts. If a portion of tuition is to be applied to plant funds, the amount should be shown as a transfer to plant funds.

B. *Governmental Appropriations* Included in this title should be all amounts received from or made available by governmental sources out of governmental revenues that are expendable for educational and general purposes. This title also includes funds disbursed for an institution by a governmental treasury on separate institutional vouchers. Any amount entered as revenues but not yet received or drawn against must appear as a receivable on the Balance Sheet. Revenues from governmental agencies for sponsored research or other sponsored programs should not appear here, but should be reported under Sponsored Research or under Other Sponsored Programs.

C. *Endowment Income* This title applies to income from the investments of both unrestricted and restricted endowment, term endowment, and quasi-endowment funds. The amount to be reported as revenues from unrestricted endowment funds should be either (a) the total earned on the investments of those funds during the year of the report or (*b*) the amount distributed from income of an investment pool for unrestricted operating purposes. The amount to be reported as revenues from restricted endowment funds should be the amount of income expended during the year.

If endowment funds investments include real estate, the income should be reported on a net basis after allowing for all costs of managing the properties.

If funds held in trust by others are established under irrevocable trusts, the income therefrom may be reported under Endowment Income with appropriate notation as to the amount, or it may be reported as a separate item immediately following Endowment Income.

D. Gifts (or *Gifts Applied*)   Under this title should be reported the amount of unrestricted gifts and bequests applied as current funds revenues during the fiscal period. If the governing board provides that all unrestricted gifts and bequests are to be applied as current revenues and reported initially in the Statement of Current Funds Revenues, Expenditures, and Transfers, all such funds become revenues automatically upon receipt; in such instances the title "Gifts" will be used.

If funds held in trust by others are established under revocable trusts, the income therefrom should be reported as other unrestricted gifts. If the income is sizable, appropriate notation should be made in the financial report.

E. Sponsored Research   This title includes revenues from governmental agencies or other outside organizations or individuals for specific research projects for which payments will be made in accordance with contracts, grants, or other written agreements. Amounts equal to direct costs expended are transferred from current restricted fund balances and reported as restricted revenues. Amounts equal to allowable indirect costs associated with those direct costs are transferred from current restricted fund balances and reported as unrestricted revenues. If desired, the revenues from governmental sources may be shown separately from those from nongovernmental sources.

F. Other Separately Budgeted Research   Under this title should be reported the gross revenues from all separately organized research divisions that are not financed in the manner described for Sponsored Research activities. Examples are research bureaus and institutes and agriculture and engineering experiment stations. If the revenues produced by such divisions are not material, they may be reported under Sales and Services of Educational Departments.

G. *Other Sponsored Programs* This title includes revenues from all separately budgeted programs, other than research, that are supported by sponsors outside the institution. Examples are training programs, training and instructional institutes, and similar activities, for which payments will be made in accordance with contracts, grants, or other written agreements. The basis for reporting revenue is similar to that for sponsored research.

H. *Recovery of Indirect Costs—Sponsored Programs* This title includes recovery of indirect costs accruing from sponsored research and other sponsored programs. As noted above: Amounts equal to allowable indirect costs associated with the direct costs are transferred from current restricted fund balances and reported as unrestricted revenues.

I. *Sales and Services of Educational Departments* Incidental revenues of educational departments are included here, such revenues being reported by departments. If the departmental activities producing the revenues are conducted primarily for professional training of students, they should be classified as Organized Activities Related to Educational Departments.

J. *Organized Activities Related to Educational Departments* Revenues of organized activities should be reported separately by activities and not merged with incidental revenues reported in Sales and Services of the departments to which they relate, nor with revenues reported under Other Sources.

If the instructional or laboratory experience of students is secondary to service to students and staff, then the activity should be classified and reported under Auxiliary Enterprises. If service to the community or state is paramount, as in the case of some state hospitals operated by state universities, the revenues should be reported under a separate major category.

K. *Other Sources* All items of revenues for educational and general purposes not covered elsewhere should be reported under this title. Important items and those of major magnitude should be listed separately.

STUDENT AID

Under this category may be reported an amount equal to the total amount of restricted funds expended during the fiscal period for scholarships, fellowships, grants-in-aid, and prizes and awards. Amounts should be identified according to Gifts, Endowment Income, and Other Sources.

AUXILIARY ENTERPRISES

The gross revenues of auxiliary enterprises should be reported under this major category.

Revenues from intercollegiate athletics usually are reported here. If an intercollegiate athletics program is operated as an integral part of a department of physical education, its transactions should be reported under Organized Activities Related to Educational Departments. If the program is operated by a separate corporation, the transactions would not be included in the institutional operating statements. However, the financial statements of the separate corporation should be appended to the institutional report or otherwise be referred to in that report.

Similarly, revenues from college unions operated by institutions should be reported here. If a union is operated by a separate corporation, its financial statements should be handled as described for intercollegiate athletics.

The financial transactions of service departments and general storerooms are not reported here. Normally such transactions do not result in revenues to the institution because they are essentially journal entries reflecting interdepartmental transfers (see chapter 20, "Accounting and Reporting Procedures for Fund Groups," pages 200–214).

Current Funds Expenditures

The report of current funds expenditures includes those of both unrestricted and restricted current funds. All items of expenditures are included, such as salaries, wages, and other forms of compensation; consumable supplies and materials, services, and other costs of operations; and expenditures for equipment. They are reported in summary in Form 3, Statement of Current Funds Revenues, Expenditures, and Transfers, and in greater detail in Form 16, Schedule of Current Funds Expenditures.

Current funds expenditures generally are classified in three major categories:

Educational and General
Student Aid
Auxiliary Enterprises

At the discretion of the institution, the categories Educational and General and Student Aid may be merged, with each category being subtotaled.

As noted at the beginning of this chapter (pages 189-90) under "Current Funds Revenues," expenditures for those activities and programs that are conducted primarily as community or public services may be reported under separate major heads immediately following Student Aid in the Statement of Current Funds Revenues, Expenditures, and Transfers and in the Schedule of Current Funds Expenditures.

Within the major categories, current funds expenditures should be classified by function or organizational unit. Although the statement may be expanded or supplemented to show expenditures by object, such classification is subordinate to the classification of expenditures by function and organizational unit.

The form of the Statement of Current Funds Expenditures provides for classification of expenditures for the entire institution. If it is the policy of an institution to charge each college or other educational unit with its proportionate share of general administration, general institutional expense, library, and physical plant expenditures in order to show the extent to which each unit is financially self-sufficient, subsidiary schedules may be prepared for the units. Nevertheless, a Statement of Current Funds Expenditures for the institution as a whole should be presented.

EDUCATIONAL AND GENERAL

Educational and General expenditures should be classified in the following functional categories:

A. Instruction and Departmental Research
B. Organized Activities Related to Educational Departments
C. Sponsored Research
D. Other Separately Budgeted Research
E. Other Sponsored Programs
F. Extension and Public Service
G. Libraries
H. Student Services
I. Operation and Maintenance of Physical Plant
J. General Administration
K. Staff Benefits
L. General Institutional Expenses

The sequence of the items in the expenditure statement may be determined by institution; however, to achieve reasonable uniformity among the financial reports of institutions, the above order is recommended.

A. *Instruction and Departmental Research*   Under this title should be included all expenditures of the departments, colleges, schools, and instructional divisions of the institution. It includes compensation for deans, faculty members, secretaries, technicians, laboratory and other assistants; office expenses; laboratory and instructional expenses; other operating expenses; and expenditures for equipment.

Expenditures incurred for instructional programs for students pursuing regular courses of study leading to collegiate degrees, whether offered off-campus or on-campus under the jurisdiction of an extension department, should be included under this heading. Amounts reported here should include expenditures for research not separately budgeted or financed.

The instructional divisions—schools, colleges, and departments—may be listed in this statement, or their expenditures may be summarized here and the details reported in subsidiary statements. If the administrative organization of the institution does not provide for divisions, schools, or colleges, the departments of instruction should be listed.

Expenditures for museums should be included with expenditures of the departments of instruction which they serve. Museums organized to serve the entire institution may be shown under a separate main heading or under General Institutional Expenses. Museums which are primarily of a public service nature may be reported under Extension and Public Services.

B. *Organized Activities Related to Educational Departments*   This title includes the gross expenditures for the activities listed under the same title in the Statement of Current Funds Revenues. Each activity should be reported separately, and all charges applicable to their operations should be included.

C. *Sponsored Research*   This title includes expenditures for direct costs of research projects in accordance with the terms of grants, contracts, or other agreements, representing restricted current funds expenditures. Amounts equal to indirect cost allowances may be reported as unrestricted current funds expenditures opposite this caption, if desired, in order to equalize, for report purposes, the total revenues and expenditures for Sponsored Research. When this is done, an offsetting deduction should appear in the Statement of Current Funds Expenditures, Unrestricted, following the total for Educational and General.

D. *Other Separately Budgeted Research*   Expenditures for research bureaus and institutes, experiment stations, and similar organizational units should be reported under this title. Some separately budgeted research programs and activities may produce revenues, for example, a bureau of economic research; others may be supported by governmental appropriations, for example, Agriculture Experiment Stations; many other activities, the expenditures of which are reported under this title, produce no revenues, nor do they receive governmental appropriations. Expenditures should be reported here for such activities and for all separately budgeted research programs, regardless of the source of financial support. The title excludes departmental research not separately budgeted or financed, which is reported under Instruction and Departmental Research.

E. *Other Sponsored Programs*   Here should be reported the expenditures for the same activities and programs included under this title in the schedule of revenues. Examples are training programs, training and instructional institutes, and similar activities. If desired, totals may be combined with those of expenditures for sponsored research under a title such as Sponsored Research and Other Sponsored Programs.

F. *Extension and Public Service*   Under this title should be included expenditures of educational and other activities designed primarily to serve the general public. If of major magnitude, individual activities may be reported separately, as described on page 190 of this chapter.

G. *Libraries*   Under this title should be included the total expenditures for separately organized libraries, both general and departmental. The expenditures include those for salaries, wages, other operating expenses, books, subscriptions, continuations, and binding costs.

H. *Student Services*   Expenditures for services to students are included here. Examples are: registrar's office; admissions office; offices of the deans of students, men, and women; guidance and testing programs; health service, unless it is an auxiliary enterprise; the financial aid office; and institutional subsidies to student activities.

I. *Operation and Maintenance of Physical Plant*   This title includes all expenses for salaries, wages, supplies, materials, other similar expenses; expenditures for equipment for the operation and maintenance of the institutional plant; and miscellaneous general services not charged elsewhere. If expenditures are charged directly (prorated) to auxiliary enterprises and organized activities relating to educational departments, they should be excluded or deducted from the total included under this title. Costs of work performed by the physical plant department for organizational units should be charged to those units and not included in the total reported for Operation and Maintenance of Physical Plant.

J. General Administration   Under this title should be included all expenditures of the general executive and administrative offices serving the entire institution. Administrative expenditures chargeable directly (prorated) to auxiliary enterprises or to organized activities related to educational departments should be excluded or deducted from the total included under this title.

K. Staff Benefits   Staff benefit expenditures may be reported here or may be distributed to the accounts to which the salaries and wages of faculty and other staff members are charged. Staff benefits funded directly by governmental or other outside agencies would not be included here; however, where the total figures are material and are determinable, they should be disclosed, either in a footnote or some other manner. Amounts charged directly (prorated) to auxiliary enterprises and to organized activities related to educational departments should be excluded or deducted from the total included under this title.

L. General Institutional Expenses   This title includes other expenditures for the entire institution exclusive of libraries and physical plant operation and maintenance. Wherever possible, such items should be charged as departmental and office expenses, although practices will vary among institutions because of budget and other managerial policies.

If any expenses of this group are charged directly (prorated) to auxiliary enterprises or to organized activities relating to educational departments, they should be excluded or deducted from the total of General Institutional Expenses.

Student Aid

In this category should be reported expenditures for all forms of student aid granted from current funds. Expenditures from both unrestricted and restricted current funds are included here, the amount expended from restricted current funds being shown, also, as revenues for Student Aid. Aid to students in the forms of remission of tuition and fees and of exemption from the payment of such charges should be reported under this heading as expenditures of unrestricted current funds. However, remissions of tuition and fees granted because of faculty or other staff status or connection of students should be reported as Staff Benefits, not as Student Aid.

The expense of scholarships where service is required of students receiving such payments should not be reported here, but should be shown as expenses of the departments or organizational units to which the service is rendered.

AUXILIARY ENTERPRISES

This category includes the gross expenditures of the enterprises indicated. Physical plant charges, general institutional expenses, administrative charges, and other indirect costs should be included. In the Schedule of Current Funds Expenditures (Form 16), operation of each auxiliary enterprise should be reported separately.

The Transfer Section—Current Funds, Revenues, Expenditures, and Transfers

Transfers to a fund group other than Unrestricted Current Funds may be reported in the Statement of Current Funds Revenues, Expenditures, and Transfers if they constitute assignment by the governing board of a portion of unrestricted current fund revenues. Examples of such transfers from revenue are additions to student loan funds, plant funds, and quasi-endowment funds and also transfers used for debt service and for renewal and replacement of plant assets.

If it is the policy of an institution to report all unrestricted gifts and bequests initially in the Statement of Changes in Fund Balances, applying a portion as revenue, it would be appropriate to report only transfers used for debt service and for renewal and replacement of plant assets on the institution's Statement of Current Funds Revenues, Expenditures, and Transfers.

20

Accounting and Reporting Procedures for Fund Groups

Current Funds

Current funds are those resources of an institution which are available for operating purposes. They include funds restricted by donors or other outside agencies for specific operating purposes and unrestricted funds including gifts and bequests designated by governing boards for operating purposes.

"Operating purposes" are those activities engaged in by colleges and universities in achieving the primary objectives for which they are established: instruction, research, and public service. The term also includes the supporting services necessary to achieve the primary objectives.

Unrestricted Current Funds

Funds which have been earned by, or appropriated or contributed to, a college or university free from any restrictions imposed by donors, payors, or outside agencies as to their use are unrestricted current funds. Although such funds generally are used for operating purposes, they may be designated by governing boards for other institutional uses.

Basis of Reporting Unrestricted current funds revenues and expenditures should be accounted for on the accrual basis. Because one of the primary purposes of accounting and reporting in colleges and universities is to provide financial information to meet the needs of management, the total operating revenues and expenditures must be accumulated accurately and consistently from year to year and be disclosed in the reports. Revenues should be reported when they become due, and expenditures should include charges for materials received and services rendered even though payments for them may not be made until a subsequent fiscal period.

However, unlike accounting and reporting for commercial enterprises, it is more important that the financial statements of a college or university disclose clearly the institution's stewardship of the resources and property entrusted to it than it is to determine net profits and net worth. Therefore, it may not be necessary to accrue all revenues or to prorate all expenditures. For example, most institutions do not accrue income from investments nor allocate to subsequent fiscal periods the cost of insurance premiums. When the revenues to be received are related directly to costs already incurred, the amounts should be accrued and reported as revenues and as receivables.

Interdepartmental Transactions Such transactions should not be accounted for and reported as current funds revenues and expenditures since to do so would inflate the total operating figures for the institution. Certain transactions, however, should be reflected in the operating statements, such as:

1. Materials produced by a departmental activity and sold to other departments or to auxiliary enterprises; for example, the sale of milk by the dairy department to the dining halls. This transaction should be treated as revenues of the organized activity related to the dairy department and as expenditures of the food services.

2. Sales and services of auxiliary enterprises to other departments; for example, catering by the food service department for student or faculty groups, for receptions, and for the entertainment of institutional guests; and the sales to offices and instructional departments by the student store. Such transactions should be treated as revenues of the respective auxiliary enterprises and as expenditures of the offices, departments, or organizations receiving the services or materials.

Examples of interdepartmental transactions that should not be reported as institutional revenues and expenditures are:

1. Sales and services of central stores and of service departments. The transactions of such units should be handled on a revolving fund

basis. Costs of materials and expenditures for personal services should be charged to the appropriate units, and credits for the services and materials furnished to using departments of the institution should be credited to the appropriate units. If a subsidy from institutional funds is authorized for the support of a central store or service department, the amount of such subsidy should be reported as an expense of the institution. If an excess of credits over charges of a service department or central store is treated as revenue of the institution, such amounts should be reported as revenues in the institutional reports. The value of services and materials obtained from service departments and central stores by offices and departments of the institution must be accounted for and reported as expenditures of those departments, just as if they had been obtained from sources outside the institution.

2. Transfers of supplies or equipment from one department to another, such as laboratory materials of the chemistry department transferred to the biology department. Such transactions should be treated as reductions in expenditures of the department transferring the materials, and as expenditures of the department receiving them.

Reporting for Auxiliary Enterprises   The operations of auxiliary enterprises should be accounted for and reported separately from other current funds. The accounts for such activities should be maintained on the accrual basis, and their gross revenues and expenditures should be included in the institutional Statement of Current Funds Revenues, Expenditures, and Transfers. If any auxiliary enterprises are operated as separate corporations, for example, intercollegiate athletics, college unions, or university presses, their reports should be appended to the institutional financial report or otherwise referred to in that report.

Reporting for Branches, Colleges, and Divisions   If an institution desires to maintain separate accounts for branches, colleges, and divisions, and show the revenues and expenditures of such units separately in its published report, subsidiary schedules should be prepared for each such unit. Control accounts for the units should be maintained in the primary accounting records, and the Statement of Current Funds Revenues, Expenditures, and Transfers should present the aggregate transactions for the entire institution. A columnar form of report may be used showing this information both for each of the units and for the institution as a whole.

Reporting in Institutions Operated by Religious Groups   The administration of colleges and universities conducted by religious organizations or orders does not differ greatly from that in other educational institutions. Sometimes the business and financial operations of the educational institution and of the affiliated or sponsoring organizations are carried out under the supervision of one officer, with the financial transactions of both entities being recorded in one office. In such cases, the accounts of the two activities must be carefully segregated.

The chief difference between educational institutions operated by religious groups and other colleges and universities is the compensation of faculty and staff members who also are members of the sponsoring organization. The faculty and staff of these institutions may be composed in large part of members of the affiliated organizations who contribute their services to the educational institution and receive no salary or other type of personal remuneration.

Reporting the estimated value of contributed services in such institutions is desirable in order to facilitate comparison of their financial operations with those of other colleges and universities. The estimated value of contributed services may be included in the financial reports, but must be clearly identified.

The monetary value of contributed services can be determined on the basis of payments to other faculty and staff members having equal qualifications, training, experience, and responsibilities at the institution. If the number of salaried personnel on the campus is too small to provide reliable salary and wage data, reference may be made to other sources for such figures. They may be obtained from neighboring institutions of similar size and comparable objectives and organization; or, they may be obtained from reports of salary schedules and other salary and wage payments published by such organizations as the American Association of University Professors, the U.S. Office of Education, and the National Education Association. These published sources are especially helpful since the data relate to large numbers of institutions and individuals, and are reported by geographical locations, size, control (public or private), and type (liberal arts college, university, professional school, etc.).

Multicolumnar work papers may be used in computing these values, the following items of information being shown for each nonsalaried individual: name, highest academic or professional degree, other professional training, rank or title, number of years of service or experience, teaching hours, work load, duties or other services performed, and the estimated gross value of the contributed services. Other appropriate information may be included at the discretion of the institution.

The estimated value of contributed services should be included in the Statement of Current Funds Revenues, Expenditures, and Transfers, and shown as expenses where the services are performed, for example, administrative offices, instructional departments, library, or auxiliary enterprises. The items should be clearly identified as "Contributed Services" and should not be combined with figures which represent payments of salaries and wages. The value of contributed services should be adequately supported in the books of account and financial records of the institution.

The services of members of religious organizations and other nonsalaried personnel may be handled on a disbursement basis as part of the regular payroll procedures. Checks may be drawn each pay period in favor of the individuals or of the sponsoring organization or group, and the amounts charged to the appropriate accounts where the services are performed. Such charges must be clearly identified as "Contributed Services."

The total estimated value of contributed services reported as current funds expenditures should also be included in the Schedule of Current Funds Revenues and clearly identified as "Estimated Value of Contributed Services of [the sponsoring organization]." In reporting such amounts, however, deduction should be made for any payments by the college or university with respect to maintenance costs and other living or personal expenses which are not ordinarily expenses of educational institutions.

The value of contributed services should not be capitalized and reported in the Endowment Fund group. If, however, it is desirable to reflect the significance of the contributions of nonsalaried faculty and staff members, appropriate notations may be included in the financial reports of the institution.

Reporting Unrestricted Gifts and Bequests All unrestricted gifts and bequests should be reported in total either as revenues in the Statement of Current Funds Revenues, Expenditures, and Transfers or as additions in the Statement of Changes in Fund Balances—Unrestricted Current Funds—Gifts.

If the institution's policy is to apply all unrestricted gifts and bequests to current operating purposes, the total received during the fiscal period should be reported in the Statement of Current Funds

Revenues, Expenditures, and Transfers under the title Gifts. This is the policy most commonly followed by colleges and universities.

If the policy is to report unrestricted gifts and bequests initially in the Statement of Changes in Fund Balances, and to report such resources as revenues only as applied, all unrestricted gifts and bequests should be reported in this manner; none should be reported initially as current funds revenues or as additions to other fund groups or subgroups. The disposition of unrestricted gifts and bequests should be shown in this statement, identifying separately the amounts applied as current funds revenues, and the amounts transferred to loan funds, to plant funds, and to quasi-endowment funds. Under this method the governing board should apply unrestricted gifts and bequests first to current revenues in an amount to equal the excess of expenditures and transfers over other revenues and should avoid the practice of making transfers from current revenues to other fund groups except for plant debt service and renewals and replacements, which are reported in the Transfer section of the Statement of Current Funds, Expenditures, and Transfers, as discussed in the next subsections.

Current Funds Used for Debt Service Interest payments on amounts borrowed for current operations should be accounted for as expense and reported in the category Educational and General under the title General Institutional Expenses in the Statement of Current Funds Revenues, Expenditures, and Transfers. Repayments of principal of such borrowings do not constitute expenses; neither do the proceeds from the borrowings constitute revenues. Such transactions involve only the Balance Sheet accounts, Cash and Notes Payable.

In the case of debt service on funds borrowed for the acquisition or construction of plant facilities, current funds used to meet such debt service charges should be transferred from current funds to the Plant Funds subgroup, Funds for Retirement of Indebtedness. Such transfers should be shown at the end of the Statement of Current Funds Revenues, Expenditures, and Transfers, under the major category Transfers. An alternative method of reporting the transfers is to show them in the Statement of Funds Balances—Unrestricted Current Funds as deductions from the unrestricted current funds balance and as additions to the balance of funds for the retirement of indebtedness (Forms 4 and 11).

If the debt service involves amounts borrowed for auxiliary enterprises plant, the transaction must appear as an expenditure in the operating statements of the appropriate auxiliary enterprises.

In all such transactions, cash or other liquid assets must be transferred from current funds to the Plant Funds subgroup, Funds for Retirement of Indebtedness.

Current Funds Used for Renewal and Replacement of Plant Assets Any amounts of current funds revenues set aside for the renewal and replacement of educational plant assets should be shown in the Statement of Current Funds Revenues, Expenditures, and Transfers under the major category Transfers. Amounts provided from the revenues of auxiliary enterprises for the renewal and replacement of auxiliary enterprise plant assets should be included in the statements of expenditures for the respective enterprise.

Provisions for renewals and replacements made from previously accumulated current funds should be shown as deductions from the unrestricted current funds balances.

In both cases, cash or other liquid assets must be transferred from current funds to the Plant Funds subgroup, Funds for Renewals and Replacements.

Current Funds Set Aside for Operating Purposes A governing board may use two methods to set aside portions of unrestricted funds for future operating purposes.

The first method applies when a governing board allocates unrestricted current funds for specific operating purposes. In effect, this results in allocating portions of the accumulated excess of current funds revenues over current funds expenditures, and may be shown on the Balance Sheet or the Statement of Changes in Fund Balances as Unrestricted Current Funds Balances—Allocated. When expenditures are subsequently incurred for the stated purposes, they are reported on the budget accounts for the appropriate departments or organizational units in the Statement of Current Funds Revenues, Expenditures, and Transfers. In the Statement of Changes in Fund Balances—Unrestricted Current Funds, an amount equal to the total of such expenditures may be restored to the Unallocated portion by deduction from the Allocated portion of the fund (see Form 4).

The second method applies only to unrestricted gifts and bequests. It is applicable only when an institution elects to apply as current funds revenues only a portion of unrestricted gifts and bequests. It is not applicable in institutions that report total unrestricted gifts and bequests as current funds revenues in the year in which received.

Under the second method, unrestricted gifts and bequests may be designated for specific operating purposes. Such designations should be recorded as deductions from the undesignated balance of Unrestricted Gifts and as additions to specific accounts in this section. When expenditures are incurred for the designated purposes, equal amounts should be transferred from the respective account balances to unrestricted current funds revenues in the same manner as that followed in reporting expenditures and revenues for Restricted Current Funds.

Current Funds Used for Other Fund Purposes Unrestricted current funds may also be used for any institutional purposes authorized by the governing board. Such funds may be transferred to quasi-endowment funds; they may be used to establish new loan funds, to meet required supplements to governmental appropriations for loan funds, or to increase existing loan funds; they also may be transferred to plant funds for plant expansion and rehabilitation purposes, or for the retirement of indebtedness.

Transfers of current funds to other fund groups may be reported in the Statement of Current Funds Revenues, Expenditures, and Transfers under the separate section for Transfers, only if the governing board has clearly specified that revenue of the current year is to be the funding source for the transfer. Otherwise, all such transfers must be reported in the respective Statements of Changes in Funds Balances.

RESTRICTED CURRENT FUNDS

Restricted current funds are expendable for operating purposes, but are restricted by donors or other outside agencies as to the specific purposes for which they may be expended. Examples are gifts for scholarships and fellowships or for the purchase of books or equipment; grants from foundations, industries, individuals, and governmental bodies for research projects and other sponsored programs; and income from investments of endowment funds restricted by donors as to its use. Expenditures should be accounted for and reported on the accrual basis.

For reporting purposes, at the close of the fiscal period, or periodically, the expenditures should be analyzed according to the organizational units responsible for the use of the restricted funds, and reported as expenditures of those units, identified as restricted expenditures in the Statement of Current Funds Revenues, Expenditures, and Transfers.

Revenues of restricted current funds should be reported in this statement in an amount equal to the total expenditures of such funds for the year. The amount of revenues should be analyzed according to the sources of funds, such as gifts, grants, governmental appropriations, and endowment income.

In presenting the Statement of Current Funds Revenues, Expenditures, and Transfers, and in all supporting schedules, the use of a multicolumnar form makes it possible to distinguish clearly among the transactions of unrestricted and restricted funds and at the same time to show the total current funds revenues and expenditures for the entire institution during the period of the report.

Loan Funds

Loan funds generally are operated on a revolving fund basis, repayments of loans and interest payments on the notes, if any, remaining in the Loan Funds group for lending to other students. However, the terms of gifts, bequests, and governmental grants may specify other ways in which repayment of notes and interest are to be used. For example, the conditions of a gift may require that loan repayments and interest be added to the principal of the endowment fund, the income from which provides the loan fund. In other cases, only the repayments of loans are to be returned to the endowment funds, any interest payments being retained in the Loan Funds group. Other conditions and stipulations for managing loan funds may prevail, and the provisions of gifts and bequests and the conditions under which loan funds are established should be examined to ensure that all required management, accounting, and reporting stipulations are complied with.

Provisions should be made for an allowance for doubtful notes by charging the required amounts against the balance of the fund from which the loans were made. The allowance should be reported as a deduction from the related notes receivable.

The assets of loan funds may be pooled for lending purposes unless prohibited by restrictions or other requirements in the administration and use of the funds. The identity of each loan fund, however, must be maintained in the accounting records.

Income from any temporary investments of loan funds and net realized gains on the sale of such investments should be credited to the balance of the funds so invested; such receipts do not constitute resources which may be used for operating purposes or for any uses other than loan funds.

Endowment and Similar Funds

The accounting records for Endowment and Similar Funds should include an account for the balance of each fund. This is required even though the assets of some or all of the funds are pooled for investment purposes. If a fund is separately invested, each investment of the fund must be identified. If the assets are pooled they should be accounted for in appropriate classes of investments, such as bonds, preferred stocks, common stocks, mortgage notes, and real estate.

An account for net realized gains and losses on investment transactions should be established for investment pools. The accumulated net gains and losses may be carried as an equity account, or, if desired, may be distributed periodically to the balances of the participating funds. Realized gains and losses on a separately invested fund should be distributed directly to the fund, thus changing the fund balance each time an investment is sold.

Valuation of Investments Each purchased security should be carried in the accounting records and reported at its cost, including commissions, taxes, and other acquisition expenses. A security or other investment received as a gift should be entered at its market value on the date on which the gift is consummated. If the security is listed on an exchange, an appropriate value is the mean of the high and low prices reported for the day. For unlisted securities which appear on regularly published quotation lists, the mean of the bid and asked prices reported for the day should be used. If the donated investment has limited marketability, the accounting records should reflect an estimated market value as established by a qualified, disinterested appraiser. In such instances it is desirable to retain the written appraisal and information to establish the competence of the appraiser.

The cost or appraised value of investments should remain unchanged in the accounting records, except for entries to reflect additions, sales or partial sales, and other similar adjustments. Figures reflecting market values of investments, although essential for the management of the investment portfolio, should be maintained in memorandum records rather than in the primary accounting records.

Principal and Income It is essential to distinguish properly between principal and income, because different limitations may apply to each.

Realized gains and losses on investment transactions are respectively additions to or deductions from the fund balances. They may be reflected in the fund balance accounts at the time they are realized, or they may be retained in an appropriate account as undistributed accumulations applicable proportionately to each fund balance. Such capital gains and losses are not operating income and expense, and should not be treated any differently from the amounts representing the original fund balances. They are subject to the same restrictions and limitations on investment, expenditures, and disposition as are the funds from which they arose.

Stock dividends that are distributed in the same form of securities as the investment holding, should be recorded as additions to the holdings with no change in the total book value. Stock dividends paid either in different classes of stock or in securities of other corporations may constitute either income or distribution of principal, depending upon the relationships of the two securities.

Proceeds from the sale of stock rights and warrants should be recorded as reductions in book values of the investments, not as income. If stock rights are exercised, the amounts expended should be added to the book values of the investments. If stock rights belonging to one fund are exercised by another fund, the value of the rights should be recorded as a sale between the two funds at fair value of the rights.

Premiums and discounts on bonds and other types of fixed-income investments represent adjustments of the rate of return on the investments. Premiums should be amortized and discounts accumulated ratably at the time income is received. Amortization of premiums should be computed to the earliest call date; accumulation of discounts should be computed to the maturity date of the investment.

Reporting Rate of Return on Investments An item of information frequently included in the financial reports of colleges and universities is the rate of return earned during the year on the investments of endowment and other funds. Such rates should be computed on the basis of the market value of the average investment holdings during the year. The rate of return on the investments relates to the assets of the pools, not to the balances of the participating funds.

Real Estate Real estate held as the investment of endowment funds may be purchased, donated, or acquired by foreclosure of mortgages. Expenditures for permanent improvements and special assessments should be capitalized. Expenses for such items as repairs, operations, insurance, taxes, and management fees are chargeable against income. Depreciation should be accounted for on such property to maintain unimpaired the principal of the funds so invested. See Appendix D, "Depreciation and Renewal and Replacement of Plant Assets."

Transfers of Investments Between Funds Investments may be transferred from one fund or fund group to another, but such transfers should have the same formal approval as would purchases from a third party. The value of the investments transferred should be determined as of the date of the transfer. Any profits or losses within each fund group resulting from the transfer should be handled and recorded in the same manner as if the transactions were with outsiders.

Annuity and Life Income Funds

Separate accounts must be maintained for the balance and for the receipts and disbursements of each fund in this group. Income from the investments of the funds and payments to annuitants and beneficiaries should be accounted for and reported here and not as revenues and expenditures of current funds.

In the case of annuity funds, two methods may be followed in accounting for the excess or deficit of investment income over payments to annuitants. In one, the difference is charged or credited annually to the balance of the fund involved; in the other, the accumulated difference is carried in a separate account until the termination of the annuity agreement, at which time the balance in the account is charged against or credited to the balance of the fund.

Gains and losses resulting from investment transactions should be accounted for as follows: (*a*) if the funds are separately invested, the gains should be credited and losses charged directly to the principal of the funds involved; (*b*) if the assets are pooled for investment purposes, a reserve account should be established to which gains should be credited and losses charged, following the methods described elsewhere for endowment pools.

Plant Funds

Unexpended Plant Funds All receipts for plant construction and for other plant or capital purposes should be recorded in the Unexpended

Plant Funds subgroup. Receipts include governmental appropriations for buildings and improvements, gifts for plant purposes, and transfers from other fund groups. These should be credited to the balance of unexpended plant funds. Proceeds from borrowings from outside sources for plant purposes should be recorded in this subgroup, appropriate evidence of the indebtedness in the form of notes, bonds, or mortgages payable being shown as liabilities of this subgroup.

When construction is started and the unexpended plant funds are disbursed, a temporary account should be opened for "Construction in Progress" to which are charged all costs pertaining to the project. For report purposes, this account may be closed at the end of the fiscal period, with the asset value, that is, the cost of construction to the date of the report, being transferred to the Net Investment in Plant subgroup. As an alternative, the temporary account may be maintained in the Unexpended Plant Funds subgroup until the structure is completed, at which time the asset value would be transferred in total to the Net Investment in Plant subgroup.

If the project is financed from borrowed funds, the related liability for indebtedness should be transferred from the Unexpended Plant Funds accounts to the Net Investment in Plant subgroup at the same time the value of the new structure is transferred. If the project is financed from institutional plant funds, the balance of unexpended plant funds would be reduced by the value of the new structure as it is transferred to the Net Investment in Plant subgroup.

Funds for Renewals and Replacements   Provisions made from current funds revenues or from the balance of unrestricted current funds for the renewal and replacement of educational plant assets should be represented by the transfer of appropriate amounts of cash or other liquid assets from current funds to this subgroup of the plant funds. Other receipts or additions include earnings and net gains on the temporary investments of the funds, provisions made out of the revenues of auxiliary enterprises for renewals and replacements, and transfers from other fund groups.

All receipts and transfers for this purpose should be credited to an appropriate account, or accounts, to produce the balance of funds available for renewals and replacements. All disbursements of such funds for the purposes indicated should be charged to the same account or accounts. Neither the receipt nor the disbursement of funds for renewals and replacements of plant assets should be reported in the Statement of Current Funds Revenues, Expenditures, and Transfers.

Funds for Retirement of Indebtedness All funds for debt service charges and for the retirement of indebtedness on educational plant assets should be credited to this subgroup in an account, or accounts, that disclose the balance of funds available for this purpose. Governmental appropriations, special student fees, gifts, and all other receipts clearly identifiable as funds to be used for debt service should be recorded here and not reported as current funds revenues. Any portion of income from the operations of auxiliary enterprises and any other funds designated for debt service purposes should be transferred from other fund groups to this subgroup (see Form 11).

All disbursements for debt service on institutional plant indebtedness should be recorded as transactions of this subgroup and not as current funds expenditures or as disbursements of other fund groups. Also, entries in the account or accounts for the balance of this subgroup should clearly identify the amounts of principal reductions and interest payments. Payments on the principal of indebtedness represent the investment of institutional funds in plant assets, and appropriate adjustments must be made in the account Net Investment in Plant (see Form 12).

The provisions of loan indentures frequently require specific deposits to sinking funds to ensure future interest and principal payments and also may require deposits to reserves to ensure proper upkeep and maintenance of the properties. Such deposits represent transfers between asset accounts in this subgroup, and are not deductions from the balance of funds for the retirement of indebtedness.

Investment in Plant The accounts in this subgroup of the plant funds disclose, in the asset section of the Balance Sheet, the book value of the institutional plant properties. In the liability section are shown the amounts of any funds borrowed for their acquisition or construction, and the institution's equity in the plant assets; that is, the net amount of institutional funds expended for plant assets (see Form 1).

A temporary account may be carried among the assets in this subgroup for construction in progress to which is charged the value of construction transferred from the similar account in the Unexpended Plant Funds subgroup, as previously described. At the end of the fiscal year or when the project is completed, the temporary account should be closed and the value of the plant asset added, as appropriate, either to the account for Buildings or the account for Improvements Other than Buildings.

If the project is financed from borrowed funds, the related liability for the indebtedness is also transferred from the Unexpended Plant Funds subgroup to this subgroup. If the project is financed from institutional plant funds, the credit is to the account for Net Investment in Plant. The balance in this account may be subdivided to show the source of the institutional funds, such as governmental appropriations, gifts, and current or other funds.

The value of the assets in the Net Investment in Plant subgroup is increased during the year through the expenditures of plant funds, as described above, and through gifts of plant assets to the institution (see Form 12).

The Net Investment in Plant account is increased by the additions to the plant assets as just described, and by the liquidation of indebtedness for plant purposes through the disbursement of the funds for the retirement of indebtedness.

Another source of increases to both the asset accounts and the Net Investment in Plant account is the expenditure of current funds through operating budgets for furniture, furnishings, apparatus, office machines, and similar items of equipment. The amount of current funds so expended must be capitalized in the Equipment account and in the Net Investment in Plant account (see Form 24). The book value of equipment disposed of during the year must be removed from the same accounts, as described in chapter 11, "Inventory of Plant Assets," (pages 106–15).

Agency Funds

The responsibilities of a college or university for the management, accounting, and reporting for agency funds are only that of a fiscal agent. The funds are not the property of the institution; therefore reports on the transactions of such funds should be only reports of stewardship to the organizations or agencies of which the agency funds are the property.

21

Internal Control
and Audits

Iɴᴛᴇʀɴᴀʟ control comprises a plant of organization and the methods and procedures adopted by an institution to safeguard its assets, to check accuracy and reliability of its accounting data, to promote operational efficiency, and to encourage adherence to prescribed policies. The existence of a system of internal control serves to reduce errors and to discourage misuse of funds.

The responsiblity of the business office staff should be assigned so that the duties and activities of one person or group are complementary to those of others. No one person should have complete control over all aspects of a financial transaction. For example, no one staff member should prepare bills for students, collect the payments, deposit the cash, and maintain the records of student's accounts receivable; no one person should employ staff members, prepare payrolls, and issue pay checks; and no one person should issue purchase orders, verify the receipt of materials, approve invoices, and issue checks in payment.

Mechanical equipment, such as registers with locked-in counters and lists, check-writing machines, accounting machines with automatic totaling devices, and computers and other electronic data processing equipment can aid in achieving effective internal control. When such equipment is used, the internal control system must be concerned less with the organization of the business office staff, and more with evaluating the programing procedures to ensure adequate checks on the reporting operations and resulting information produced by the mechanical equipment. Effective programing rather than assignment of complementary duties to staff members provides the means of achieving internal control in a mechanized system.

Internal Auditing

Internal auditing is a staff function that serves management by reviewing the accounting, financial, and other operations of the institution. The internal auditor should be under the direction of the chief business officer. His activities should be directed toward the following general objectives: determining that the system of internal control is adequate and that it is functioning; ensuring that institutional policies and procedures are being followed; verifying the existence of assets shown on the books of account and ensuring the maintenance of proper safeguards for their protection; preventing or discovering dishonesty; and determining the reliability and adequacy of the accounting and reporting system and procedures. The internal auditor should report the results of his examinations to the chief business officer and should recommend corrective action where necessary.

To aid the internal auditor in accomplishing these objectives, the chief business officer should establish policies with regard to the objectives and scope of the audit program, develop awareness within the institution of the function of internal auditing, and take action on the findings and recommendations presented to him by the internal auditor.

Staff   The internal auditing function should be directed by an internal auditor responsible to the chief business officer. He should have formal training in the objectives, techniques, and procedures of internal auditing; experience in the field also is desirable. The size of the staff and the amount of time devoted to internal auditing will depend upon the size of the institution, complexity of the operations, and the form of administrative organization. In large institutions internal auditing should be performed by a full-time staff; in small institutions it may be performed by someone who is responsible for other business and financial duties.

To accomplish the objectives of internal auditing, the internal auditor should have a high degree of independence. Insofar as practicable he should not be assigned line responsibilities. To ensure complete objectivity in reviewing and appraising policies and practices, the internal auditor should not be responsible for the development and installation of systems and procedures, preparation of records, routine examination of vouchers, regular reconciliations of bank accounts, or the preparation of financial statements. He should not engage in any activities that he normally would be expected to review and appraise.

Program A formal written program for the internal auditing operations should be prepared to define the extent and frequency of review of the financial and business operations of the institution. The program should list all departments and activities subject to audit. The frequency of internal audits will be determined, in part, by such factors as the nature of the activity, changes in personnel, significant changes in volume of work, the introduction of new or revised procedures, and the adequacy of internal controls. The program should include provision for examinations of cash receipts, cash disbursements, payrolls, construction accounts, maintenance activities, inventories, and investments.

Procedural reviews and audits of specific operating functions should be coordinated in advance with supervisory personnel in the departments to be examined. Surprise internal audits should be performed in certain situations, especially those involving cash, securities, and inventories.

At appropriate intervals, detailed schedules of work should be prepared, indicating the audits to be conducted. Periodically, the record of completed audits should be compared with the work schedule.

Audit Report The audit report should include a description of the activity examined, the period of time covered by the audit, exceptions noted, and recommendations. Detailed descriptions of audit steps performed should be available even though not included in the report. Comments should be confined to important matters; minor points, such as clerical errors, should be brought to the attention of the department being audited at the time of the examination.

The auditor's report should include an opinion on the propriety of the transactions examined, the adequacy of procedures followed, and compliance with institutional policy. Criticisms of unsatisfactory conditions and procedures should be accompanied by recommendations for correction. The audit report should be addressed to the chief business officer, who should determine what further distribution of the report should be made. Copies of all internal audit reports should be made available to the external auditors.

Review of Systems and Procedures The internal audit includes the review of business operations and procedures and the identification of need to improve systems. When extensive procedural changes and the development of systems are contemplated, the internal auditor should review the proposed systems to ensure that they provide for adequate internal control.

Areas of Internal Control

Some of the major areas of internal control are described here. Most institutions will install, in addition, control procedures covering investments, accounts receivable, and student fees.

Cash Receipts   The internal control program should provide for the safeguarding of cash by dividing the duties of business office staff members among those responsible for the billing, receipts, banking, and recording of cash items. The business office should maintain control over cash collected throughout the institution, including cafeterias, dining halls, athletic departments, auditoriums, theaters, college unions, and student stores. Forms, procedures, and reports for the control of cash should have the approval of the business office.

Receipts should be deposited intact and preferably daily. The internal control system should provide for verification that all receipts are deposited in banks, and are properly entered on the accounting records. Bank balances should be reconciled by staff members other than those responsible for collections, recording, and disbursements.

Disbursements   Disbursements should be made only on the basis of several completed steps: an approved requisition, a pre-numbered (or otherwise controlled) purchase order, certification of the receipt of the goods or services requested, comparison of vendor's invoice with the purchase order and requisition, and verification of the computation and footing on the vendor's invoice. All disbursements, except those for small amounts, should be made by institutional checks that are pre-numbered or otherwise controlled. Small items may be paid out of petty cash funds, controlled and accounted for as imprest funds.

Payroll work should be so assigned among the staff that the responsibilities for the functions of employing, computing and checking the payrolls, and issuing checks are divided. When salary checks are distributed to employees through their departments, the internal control system should require the internal auditor, at irregular and unannounced intervals, to distribute salary checks directly to employees or otherwise verify the existence of all individuals named on the payroll. The internal control system should also include means for verifying salary payments deposited directly to individual bank accounts.

Inventories   Inventory systems are required for consumable supplies in central stores, merchandise for resale, and equipment. Inventories of consumable supplies can be controlled through perpetual inventory systems, with summary accounts in the accounting records in the business office. Inventory details should be maintained in the warehouses, stores, and centers where the supplies are located. Withdrawal of supplies and materials from such storerooms should be made only upon submission of properly signed and approved requisitions. The internal audit staff should observe the taking of physical counts of inventories and review the reconciliation of differences between the physical counts and the accounting records. In instances where it is not feasible to maintain perpetual inventories of merchandise for resale, the business office should require frequent physical inventories. (Internal control over the inventory of equipment is discussed in chapter 11, "Inventory of Plant Assets.")

Relationship with External Auditing

A close working relationship should exist between the internal and the external auditors. Effective coordination with the internal audit program will reduce the time required for, and thus the cost of, the external audit. The clear distinction between the internal and the external audit must be recognized. The external auditor performs his service on an independent basis, and his report is directed to the governing board of the institution. The internal auditor, as an employee of the institution, provides management with information about whether the business and financial operations are being conducted in accordance with approved policies and procedures.

External Auditing

The governing board should require an audit by independent certified public accountants who are qualified by training and experience to audit the accounts of educational institutions. The independent audit not only examines the accuracy and integrity of the financial reports, but also brings to the business office, assistance, expert advice, and an independent point of view on accounting and fiscal problems. In some institutions audits are made by representatives of state or local governments. These audits should be as comprehensive as those made by public accounting firms and should be in accordance with generally accepted auditing standards.

The arrangements for the external audit should be in writing. The auditor himself will determine the nature and extent of the review of the financial position and operations required for him to render a sound opinion. He should be furnished copies of the general statutes, articles of incorporation, bylaws, regulations, and pertinent legal opinions. He should have access to the minutes of the governing board and its committees.

The Auditor's Report   The accounting staff of the institution should close the books of account and prepare statements and supporting schedules for the annual financial report. The institution must assume full responsibility for the accuracy of the statements and schedules. The responsibility of the independent public accountant is to examine the statements and schedules and render an opinion on the fairness with which they present the financial condition and operating results of the institution.

When the financial statements reflect material departures from generally accepted accounting principles or when the auditor has been unable to follow generally accepted auditing procedures, he will be required to qualify his opinion. Other qualifications may be required because of limitations placed upon the extent of the examination at the time the external auditor is engaged. Institutions should avoid, whenever possible, imposing such limitations. The auditor's opinion may contain explanatory comments that are not qualifications or exceptions; it is, however, preferable for the institution to make such explanations.

The Auditor's Opinion   The auditor's opinion should follow the standard form recommended by the American Institute of Certified Public Accountants for reporting on financial statements of commercial enterprises. If the institution maintains its accounts in conformity with generally accepted accounting principles for colleges and universities, as set forth in this volume, the certificate or opinion should read substantially as follows:

To the Board of Trustees
X University

We have examined the Balance Sheet of X University as of June 30, 19— and the related Statement of Revenues, Expenditures, and Transfers, and the Statement of Changes in Fund Balances for the year then ended. Our examination was made in accordance with generally accepted auditing standards and accordingly included such tests of the accounting records and such other auditing procedures as we considered necessary in the circumstances.

In our opinion, the accompanying Balance Sheet, the related Statement of Revenues, Expenditures, and Transfers, and the Statement of Changes in Fund Balances present fairly the financial position of X University at June 30, 19—, and the results of its operations for the year then ended, in conformity with generally accepted accounting principles applied on a basis consistent with that of the preceding year.

(Name)

(Date)

Review of the Audit Report The audit report should be reviewed with an appropriate committee of the governing board. The auditor may submit explanatory comments on the operating results and on the financial position of the institution if he believes they will be of value to the governing board or to the administration.

Appendix A

The Chart of Accounts

A SYSTEMATIC classification of accounts is an essential part of an accounting system. The accounts should be developed to be consistent with the organizational structure of the institution, and their form and content should be arranged to be in agreement with the financial reports to be presented.

The arrangement should be formalized in a chart of accounts, and, for ease of identification and reference, each account should be assigned an appropriate symbol or code number. Classification should be according to the fund groups held by the institution, as described in chapter 17, "The Balance Sheet." Within each fund group, the accounts should be listed according to assets, liabilities, and fund balances accounts.

The illustrative chart of accounts for a college or university presented below shows those accounts generally found in the general ledger or carried in subsidiary ledgers with appropriate control accounts in the general ledger. This chart is presented as a guide for institutions in developing their own detailed charts of accounts and to help them set up their accounts in conformity with the principles of accounting and reporting presented in this volume. The system of accounts may be expanded, contracted, or modified to meet the needs of the individual institution and to conform to its organizational structure, but in any case it should incorporate the basic elements common to all educational institutions.

In designing or revising a chart of accounts, the code numbers or symbols assigned to the accounts should progress in a logical order. Because each fund group is carried in the accounting records as a separately balanced group, the accounts in any given group should be assigned a code number that, perhaps by a prefix, identifies that fund group—for example, all accounts related to current funds should be identifiable as such; all accounts for plant funds should be identifiable as such. Similarly, within the major fund groups, consistent code numbers should identify subgroups, assets, liabilities, and fund balances. Other code numbers or symbols can be used to identify sources of revenues and receipts, as well as to identify functions, organizational units, and objects of expenditures and disbursements.

In developing a chart of accounts, it is important to exercise economy in the use of digits and characters for code numbers, to plan a logical arrangement for the chart, and to make ample provision for future expansion of account numbers.

General Ledger Accounts

CURRENT FUNDS—UNRESTRICTED

Asset Accounts

Cash
Petty Cash
Investments
Accounts Receivable—*detailed as needed; for example:*
  Students
  Governmental Appropriations
Allowance for Doubtful Accounts—*credit balance account*
Notes Receivable—*detailed as needed*
Inventories—*detailed as needed; for example:*
  College Store
  Dining Halls
  Central Stores
  Plant Operation and Maintenance Supply Store
Prepaid Expenses and Deferred Charges—*detailed as needed*
Due from Other Funds

Liability and Fund Balances Accounts

Notes Payable
Accounts Payable and Accrued Expenses
Deferred Revenues
Deposits
Reserve for Encumbrances
Due Other Funds
Fund Balances—Allocated—*detailed as needed; for example:*
  Reserve for Computer Use Survey
  Provision for Faculty Self-improvement Program
Fund Balances—Unallocated

If unrestricted gifts are reported in the Statement of Changes in Fund Balances—Unrestricted Current Funds—Gifts, rather than in the State-

General Ledger Accounts (*cont*)

CURRENT FUNDS—UNRESTRICTED (*cont*)

ment of Current Fund Revenues, Expenditures, and Transfers, the Fund Balances section might be as follows:

Fund Balances—Gifts
Fund Balances—Other:
    Allocated—*detailed as needed*
    Unallocated

Operating Accounts—*The following control accounts in the general ledger for actual revenues and expenditures are supported in detail by Current Funds Expenditures and Current Funds Revenues accounts in subsidiary ledgers. If desired, several control accounts may be provided in lieu of single control accounts:*

Revenues Control—*credit account*
Expenditures Control—*debit account*

When budgetary accounts are carried in the general ledger, the following control accounts would appear in the chart of accounts. They are supported in detail by Current Funds Revenue and Current Funds Expenditure accounts in subsidiary ledgers:

Estimated Revenues, *or* Unrealized Revenues
Expenditure Allocations, *or* Budget Allocations for Expenditures
Unassigned Budget Balance, *or* Unallocated Budget Balance

CURRENT FUNDS—RESTRICTED

If the assets of such funds are separated from those of Unrestricted and Designated Current Funds.

Asset Accounts

Cash
Investment
Accounts Receivable—*detailed as needed*
Due from Other Funds

Liability and Fund Balance Accounts

Accounts Payable
Due Other Funds
Provision for Endowment Income Stabilization
Fund Balances—*This is a control account, and is supported by separate*

General Ledger Accounts (*cont*)

CURRENT FUNDS—RESTRICTED (*cont*)

accounts for each restricted current fund. Several control accounts may be provided in the general ledger in lieu of a single control account.

Operating Accounts—*Revenues and expenditures of restricted current funds may be accounted for in the operating accounts for the unrestricted current funds. When this is not done, operating accounts should be provided as follows:*
Restricted Revenues Control—*credit account*
Restricted Expenditures Control—*debit account*

LOAN FUNDS

Asset Accounts

Cash
Investments
Notes Receivable
Allowance for Doubtful Loans—*credit balance account*

Liability and Fund Balances Accounts

Fund Balances—*This is a control account, and is supported by separate accounts for each fund, carried either in the general ledger or in a subsidiary ledger. Separate accounts should be carried for the balances of governmental appropriations for loan funds, other refundable loan funds, loan funds available to faculty and staff members, and loan funds created by action of the governing board through the transfer of unrestricted current funds, or any other funds, to the loan funds group.*

ENDOWMENT AND SIMILAR FUNDS

Asset Accounts

Cash
Investments—*detailed as needed; for example:*
    Bonds
    Preferred Stocks
    Common Stocks
    Mortgage Notes
    Real Estate

General Ledger Accounts (*cont*)

ENDOWMENT AND SIMILAR FUNDS (*cont*)

Reserve for Depreciation—*credit balance account*
Reserve for Amortization of Bond Premiums—*credit balance account*
Reserve for Accumulation of Bond Discounts
Due from Other Funds

Liability and Fund Balances Accounts—The fund balances accounts should be classified as to Endowment, Term Endowment, *and* Quasi-endowment Funds, *even though the investments of the funds may be merged in one or more investment pools.*

Payables—*detailed as needed; for example:*
   Mortgages Payable
   Notes Payable
Due Other Funds
Balances of Endowment Funds
Balances of Term Endowment Funds
Balances of Quasi-endowment Funds

In order to differentiate between the balances of funds for which the income is unrestricted and those for which the income is restricted, the following accounts may be employed:
Balances of Endowment Funds—Unrestricted
Balances of Endowment Funds Restricted—*detailed as needed; for example:*
   Professorships
   Instructional Departments
   Scholarships
   Library
   Loan Funds
   (*Note—The balances of term endowment and quasi-endowment funds may also be identified in this manner.*)

Reserve for Gains and Losses in Investment Transactions—*Separate accounts should be established for each investment pool.*

ANNUITY AND LIFE INCOME FUNDS

If the funds in this section are pooled for investment purposes, accounts for the assets may be classified as shown below for each investment pool. If

General Ledger Accounts (cont)

ANNUITY AND LIFE INCOME FUNDS (cont)

*any funds are separately invested, accounts should be set up for the invest-
ments of such funds.*

Asset Accounts

Cash
Investments—*detailed as needed; for example:*
  Bonds
  Preferred Stocks
  Common Stocks
  Mortgage Notes
  Real Estate
Reserve for Depreciation—*credit balance account*
Due from Other Funds

Liability and Fund Balance Accounts

Payables
Due to Other Funds
Undistributed Income—Annuity Funds
Undistributed Income—Life Income Funds
Reserve for Gains and Losses on Investment Transactions—*This account
would be used if funds are pooled for investment purposes.*
Balances of Annuity Funds
Balances of Life Income Funds—*These control accounts are supported
by separate accounts for each fund. Within the two categories the
accounts may be listed alphabetically by name, or they may be classified
in any other manner at the discretion of the institution.*

Income and Disbursement Accounts

Income from Investments—*credit account; detailed by each agreement*
Disbursements—*debit account; detailed by each agreement*

PLANT FUNDS—UNEXPENDED

Asset Accounts

Cash
Investments
Receivables—*detailed as needed*
Due from Other Funds

General Ledger Accounts (cont)

Plant Funds—Unexpended (cont)

Liability and Fund Balances Accounts
Accounts Payable
Notes Payable
Bonds Payable
Due Other Funds
Fund Balances—*This is a control account, and is supported by individual accounts for separate funds, if they exist, for plant purposes.*

Plant Funds—Funds for Renewals and Replacements

If the assets of such funds are separated from the assets of Unexpended Plant Funds.

Asset Accounts
Cash
Investments

Liability and Fund Balance Accounts
Fund Balances—*This is a control account, and is supported by individual accounts for separate funds, if they exist, set aside for the indicated purpose.*

Plant Funds—Funds for Retirement of Indebtedness

If the assets of such funds are separated from the assets of Unexpended Plant Funds.

Asset Accounts
Cash
Investments

Liability and Fund Balance Accounts
Fund Balances—*This is a control account, and is supported by individual accounts for separate funds, if they exist, set aside for the indicated purpose.*

General Ledger Accounts (*cont*)

PLANT FUNDS—INVESTMENT IN PLANT

Asset Accounts

Land
Buildings
Improvements Other Than Buildings
Equipment
Construction in Progress

Liability and Fund Balance Accounts

Notes Payable
Bonds Payable
Mortgages Payable
Due Other Funds
Net Invested in Plant—*detailed as desired; for example:*
    Net Invested in Plant from Gifts
    Net Invested in Plant from Governmental Appropriations
    Net Invested in Plant from Current (or Other) Funds

AGENCY FUNDS

Asset Accounts

Cash
Investments

Liability and Fund Balance Accounts

Fund Balances—*Accounts for each Agency Fund should be carried either in the general ledger or in subsidiary ledgers.*

Current Funds Revenues Accounts

EDUCATIONAL AND GENERAL

Student Tuition and Fees—separate accounts as needed

Governmental Appropriations—separate accounts as needed

Endowment Income—separate accounts may be established for:
Unrestricted Endowment Income

Current Funds Revenues Accounts (cont)

Educational and General *(cont)*

Restricted Endowment Income
Income from Funds Held in Trust by Others
In addition, endowment income accounts may be established by type of security; for example, bonds, preferred stocks, common stocks, mortgage notes, and real estate.

Gifts—separate accounts may be established for:
Unrestricted Gifts
Restricted Gifts

Estimated Value of Contributed Services—if appropriate

Sponsored Research
Governmental
Nongovernmental

Other Separately Budgeted Research—separate accounts as needed

Other Sponsored Programs
Governmental
Nongovernmental

Recovery of Indirect Costs—Sponsored Programs

Sales and Services of Educational Departments—detailed as needed; for example:
Film Rentals
Publications
Testing Services

Organized Activities Related to Educational Departments—detailed as needed; for example:
Audio-visual Activities—*unless classified as a Service Department*
Dental Clinic
Home Economics Cafeteria
Demonstration School
Speech and Hearing Clinic

Other Sources
Income on temporary investments of current funds
Conference and Workshops

Current Funds Revenues Accounts (cont)

EDUCATIONAL AND GENERAL (cont)

Parking fees and fines—*unless Parking is classified as an Auxiliary Enterprise*

Proceeds from public affairs, such as exhibits and lectures

STUDENT AID

Gifts

Endowment Income

Governmental Appropriations

Other

AUXILIARY ENTERPRISES

Intercollegiate Athletics

Residence Halls

Faculty Housing

Food Services

College Union

Student Store

Additional revenue accounts may be established for sources of sales, types of commodities sold, and cash and interdepartmental sales.

Current Funds Expenditures Accounts

Current funds expenditures accounts should bear identifying codes and symbols that will identify functions, such as Instruction and Departmental Research, General Administration, Student Services; identify organizational units, such as Department of Physics, Controller's Office, Registrar's Office; and identify the object of expenditures, such as Salaries and Wages, Supplies and Expense, Equipment. If desired, interdepartmental purchases, as contrasted with purchases from outside sources, may also be identified by code or symbol. The object coding and symbols should be designed to provide for common usage of the symbols and the objects throughout the entire chart of accounts, although, of course, there will be individual object

Current Funds Expenditures Accounts (*cont*)

codings that will be used only for Instruction, Research, Administration, Plant Operation and Maintenance, and other functions.

EDUCATIONAL AND GENERAL

Instruction and Departmental Research
Accounts by divisions, schools, colleges, and departments of instruction, following the administrative organization of the institution.

Organized Activities Related to Educational Departments
Accounts for each such activity for which revenue accounts have been established.

Sponsored Research
Accounts by individual projects, classified by organizational units.

Other Separately Budgeted Research
Accounts by individual projects, classified by organizational units.

Other Sponsored Programs
Accounts by individual projects, classified by organizational units.

Extension and Public Service
Accounts for each organizational unit in this category, such as:
Agricultural Extension Activities
Continuing Education
Departmental Research Bureaus
Public Lectures and Concerts

Libraries
Accounts for all libraries, both central as well as departmental.

Student Services
Accounts for all organizational units, such as:
Registrar
Dean of Students
Director of Admissions
Financial Aid Officer
Health or Infirmary Services—*unless classified as an Auxiliary Enterprise*

Operation and Maintenance of Physical Plant
Accounts for all organizational units and functions, such as:
Administration
Custodial Services

Current Funds Expenditures Accounts (*cont*)

EDUCATIONAL AND GENERAL (*cont*)

Maintenance of Buildings
Maintenance of Grounds
Utilities
Police and Watchmen
Trucking Services
Fire Protection
Motor Pool and Transportation Services—*unless classified as a Service Department*
Property Insurance

General Administration—*detailed as needed; for example:*
Governing Board
President
Chief Academic Officer
Chief Business Officer
Investment Officer
Legal Counsel

Staff Benefits—*detailed as needed; for example:*
Retirement Contract Premiums
Group Life Insurance Premiums
Health and Medical Insurance Premiums
Workmen's Compensation Insurance

General Institutional Expense—*detailed as needed; for example:*
Alumni Office
Auditing
Catalogues and Bulletins
Commencements
Convocations
Development Office
General Insurance—*other than Property Insurance*
Interest on Current Funds Loans
Legal Fees
Memberships
Publications
Public Relations
Telephone and Telegraph—*unless charged to departmental budgets*

Current Funds Expenditures Accounts (cont)

STUDENT AID

Accounts as needed and desired for undergraduate and graduate scholar-ships, fellowships, grants-in-aid, prizes, and awards.
Tuition remissions—*unless classified as scholarships or fellowships*
Accounts may be set up for instructional divisions and departments, such as:
School of Medicine
Department of Physics

AUXILIARY ENTERPRISES

Accounts as needed and desired for the same enterprises included in the Current Funds Revenues accounts.

SERVICE DEPARTMENTS

Nominal, or Interim, accounts for all organizational units classified in this category. These accounts should be closed out at the end of each fiscal year.

Classification of Expenditures by Object

The object classification of expenditures identifies that which is received in return for the expenditures. Object classification has importance as a tool for internal management, but should be considered complementary to the classification of expenditures by function and organizational unit and should not replace these classifications in the various schedules of current funds expenditures described in this volume. The value of object classification will depend on the usefulness of the information it provides to management, and the classifications may be omitted from published financial reports, or they may be used, to any degree considered desirable by the individual institution. The use of object classifications, and the related identifying codes and symbols, should not be carried to an extreme; the number of categories should be limited to those that will be of genuine value to management.

Three major object classifications are found in most colleges and universities: Salaries and Wages, Supplies and Expenses, and Equipment. Breakdowns of objects within these major categories may be necessary or desirable in some situations.

Salaries and Wages

In the various salary and wage expense accounts, it may be desirable to distinguish between groups of faculty and other staff members, such as full-time and part-time personnel; student and nonstudent workers; and professional, secretarial, clerical, skilled, and nonskilled employees. Appropriate code numbers and symbols within the category for Salaries and Wages will aid in identifying, collecting and summarizing information.

Supplies and Expenses

Because of their general significance to nearly all organizational units within an institution, it may be beneficial to identify significant categories of these expenditures, such as supplies, telephone, travel, and other objects.

Equipment

The following object categories within this classification may prove helpful in the accounting and reporting systems of educational institutions: scientific equipment, laboratory apparatus, office machines and equipment, library books, furniture and furnishings, motor vehicles, machinery and tools of the physical plant division, and, where applicable, livestock.

Appendix B

Illustrative Forms

[237]

Balance Sheet, June 30, 19—

ASSETS

CURRENT FUNDS:

Unrestricted-

Cash	$ 289,400	
Investments, at cost (approximate market $685,000)	686,400	
Accounts receivable, less allowance for doubtful accounts of $5,900	280,400	
Notes receivable, less allowance for doubtful notes of $1,000	86,500	
Inventories, at cost	146,900	
Prepaid expenses and deferred charges	114,900	$ 1,604,500

Restricted-

Cash	$ 187,600	
Investments, at cost (approximate market $110,000)	107,000	
Accounts receivable - principally agencies of the U.S. Government	472,700	767,300

TOTAL CURRENT FUNDS $ 2,371,800

LOAN FUNDS:

Cash	$ 19,900	
Investments, at cost (approximate market $20,000)	19,700	
Notes receivable, less allowance for doubtful notes of $7,700	386,700	

TOTAL LOAN FUNDS $ 426,300

ENDOWMENT AND SIMILAR FUNDS:

Cash	$ 7,900	
Investments, at cost (approximate market $1,910,000)	1,466,000	
(Funds held in trust by others, approximate market value of $78,300, earnings thereon to benefit the University)	—	

TOTAL ENDOWMENT AND SIMILAR FUNDS $ 1,473,900

LIABILITIES AND FUND BALANCES

CURRENT FUNDS:

Unrestricted-

Temporary notes payable to banks	$ 200,000	
Accounts payable and accrued expenses	200,000	
Provision for encumbrances	86,000	
Deposits	112,000	
Deferred revenues	102,100	
Fund balances (Form 4)	904,400	$ 1,604,500

Restricted-

Accounts payable and accrued expenses	$ 170,200	
Provision for endowment income stabilization	12,000	
Fund balances (Form 5)	585,100	767,300

TOTAL CURRENT FUNDS $ 2,371,800

LOAN FUNDS:

Fund balances (Form 6)	$ 426,300	

TOTAL LOAN FUNDS $ 426,300

ENDOWMENT AND SIMILAR FUNDS:

Mortgages payable on real estate	$	27,500
Fund balances (Form 7)-		
Endowment funds	$980,000	
Term endowment funds	340,000	
Quasi-endowment funds	102,000	
Net adjusted gains and losses	24,400	1,446,400

TOTAL ENDOWMENT AND SIMILAR FUNDS $ 1,473,900

[238]

Balance Sheet, June 30, 19—

FORM 1—Continued

ASSETS

ANNUITY AND LIFE INCOME FUNDS:

Cash	$	4,500
Investments, at cost (approximate market $285,000)		223,900
TOTAL ANNUITY AND LIFE INCOME FUNDS		$ 228,400

PLANT FUNDS:

Unexpended Plant Funds-

Cash	$	270,900	
Investments, at cost (approximate market $740,000)		736,200	
Appropriations receivable		300,000	
Accounts receivable		348,100	$ 1,655,200

Funds For Renewals and Replacements-

Cash	$	109,500	
Investments, at cost (approximate market $180,000)		177,700	287,200

Funds For Retirement of Indebtedness-

Cash	$	57,000	
Investments, at cost (approximate market $260,000)		254,800	311,800

Investment in Plant, at cost-

Land	$ 1,025,000		
Buildings	19,755,200		
Improvements other than buildings	922,400		
Equipment	6,631,800		
Construction in progress	1,934,800		30,269,200

TOTAL PLANT FUNDS	$32,523,400

AGENCY FUNDS:

Cash	$	87,300
Investments, at cost (approximate market $70,000)		68,900
TOTAL AGENCY FUNDS		$ 156,200

LIABILITIES AND FUND BALANCES

ANNUITY AND LIFE INCOME FUNDS:

Undistributed income	$	400
Fund balances (Form 8)		228,000
TOTAL ANNUITY AND LIFE INCOME FUNDS		$ 228,400

PLANT FUNDS:

Unexpended Plant Funds-

Accounts payable	$	178,800	
Advances from U.S. Government		260,000	
Temporary notes payable to banks		350,000	
Bonds payable		400,000	
Fund balances (Form 9)		466,400	$ 1,655,200

Funds For Renewals and Replacements- Fund balances (Form 10)	287,200
Funds For Retirement of Indebtedness- Fund balances (Form 11)	311,800

Investment in Plant-

Notes payable	$	310,000	
Bonds payable		3,974,800	
Net investment in plant (Form 12)		25,984,400	30,269,200

TOTAL PLANT FUNDS	$32,523,400

AGENCY FUNDS:

Fund balances (Form 13)	$	156,200
TOTAL AGENCY FUNDS		$ 156,200

Note - Details of the ending fund balances may be shown in the statements of changes in fund balances, as illustrated in these forms, or in the balance sheet.

[239]

Balance Sheet, June 30, 19—

	Current Funds		Loan Funds	Endowment and Similar Funds	Annuity and Life Income Funds	Plant Funds		Agency Funds
	Unrestricted	Restricted				Unexpended	Net investment in plant	
ASSETS:								
Cash	$ 289,400	$187,600	$ 19,900	$ 7,900	$ 4,500	$ 437,400		$ 87,300
Investments, at cost	686,400	107,000	19,700	1,466,000	223,900	1,168,700		68,900
Appropriations receivable						300,000		
Accounts receivable, less allowances for doubtful accounts	280,400	472,700				348,100		
Notes receivable, less allowances for doubtful notes	86,500		386,700					
Inventories, at cost	146,900							
Prepaid expenses and deferred charges	114,900							
Land							$ 1,025,000	
Buildings							19,755,200	
Improvements other than buildings							922,400	
Equipment							6,631,800	
Construction in progress							1,934,800	
	$1,604,500	$767,300	$426,300	$1,473,900	$228,400	$2,254,200	$30,269,200	$156,200
LIABILITIES AND FUND BALANCES:								
Temporary notes and advances payable	$ 200,000					$ 610,000		
Accounts payable and accrued expenses	286,000	$170,200			$ 400	178,800		
Deferred revenues	102,100	12,000						
Deposits	112,000							$156,200
Long-term debt-								
Notes payable				$ 27,500		400,000	$ 310,000	
Bonds payable							3,974,800	
Fund balances-								
U.S. Government grants refundable			$294,200					
Net adjusted gains and losses			32,000	24,400				
Allocated by Governing Board	125,000			102,000				
Restricted		585,100	100,100	1,320,000	228,000	487,600		
Unallocated	779,400					577,800		
Net investment in plant							25,984,400	
	$1,604,500	$767,300	$426,300	$1,473,900	$228,400	$2,254,200	$30,269,200	$156,200

Note - Endowment funds with an approximate market value of $78,300 are held in trust by others for the benefit of the institution.

Statement of Current Funds Revenues, Expenditures, and Transfers
for the Year Ended June 30, 19—

	Total	Unrestricted	Restricted
Revenues (Form 15):			
Educational and General-			
Student Tuition and Fees	$ 964,100	$ 964,100	
Governmental Appropriations	2,688,000	2,326,400	$ 361,600
Endowment Income (including $6,500 received from funds			
held in trust by others)	39,000	12,000	27,000
Gifts	472,700	441,400	31,300
Sponsored Research-			
Governmental	1,008,000		1,008,000
Non-governmental	200,000		200,000
Other Separately Budgeted Research	61,000	61,000	
Other Sponsored Programs-			
Governmental	27,000		27,000
Non-governmental	10,000		10,000
Recovery of Indirect Costs - Sponsored Programs	30,000	30,000	
Sales and Services of Educational Departments	43,200	43,200	
Organized Activities Relating to Educational Departments	59,500	59,500	
Other Sources	28,000	24,900	3,100
Total Educational and General	$5,630,500	$3,962,500	$1,668,000
Student Aid	81,200		81,200
Auxiliary Enterprises	1,153,500	1,153,500	
Total Revenues	$6,865,200	$5,116,000	$1,749,200
Expenditures (Form 16):			
Educational and General-			
Instruction and Departmental Research	$2,282,600	$1,899,500	$ 383,100
Organized Activities Relating to Educational Departments	79,700	79,700	
Sponsored Research	1,208,000		1,208,000
Other Separately Budgeted Research	61,000	61,000	
Other Sponsored Programs	37,000		37,000
Extension and Public Service	27,500	6,400	21,100
Libraries	124,700	105,900	18,800
Student Services	181,800	181,800	
Operation and Maintenance of Physical Plant	417,200	417,200	
General Administration	167,600	167,600	
Staff Benefits	368,100	368,100	
General Institutional Expenses	224,100	224,100	
Total Educational and General	$5,179,300	$3,511,300	$1,668,000
Student Aid	194,400	113,200	81,200
Auxiliary Enterprises (including debt service of $205,800)	1,130,900	1,130,900	
Total Expenditures	$6,504,600	$4,755,400	$1,749,200

Statement of Current Funds Revenues, Expenditures, and Transfers
for the Year Ended June 30, 19—

	Total	Unrestricted	Restricted
Transfers:			
To—			
Loan funds for supplements to U.S. Government grants (Form 6)	$ 4,000	$ 4,000	
Quasi-endowment funds (Form 7)	100,000	100,000	
Plant funds for—			
Additions (Form 9)	150,000	150,000	
Renewals and replacements (Form 10)	43,500	43,500	
Retirement of indebtedness (Form 11)	17,500	17,500	
Total Transfers	$ 315,000	$ 315,000	
Excess of Revenues over Expenditures and Transfers	$ 45,600	$ 45,600	$ —

Statement of Changes in Fund Balances—
Unrestricted Current Funds
for the Year Ended June 30, 19—

	Total	Unallocated	Allocated
Balances, July 1, 19--	$837,800	$732,800	$105,000
Additions-			
Excess of revenues over expenditures and transfers (Form 3)	$ 45,600	$ 45,600	
Expiration of term endowment fund (Form 7)	21,000	21,000	
	$ 66,600	$ 66,600	
Transfers between unallocated and allocated-			
Amounts included in current expenditures on projects for which funds had previously been allocated		$ 40,000	$(40,000)
Allocations for specific future operating purposes		(60,000)	60,000
		$(20,000)	$ 20,000
Balances, June 30, 19-- (Form 1)	$904,400	$779,400	$125,000

Statement of Changes in Fund Balances—
Restricted Current Funds
for the Year Ended June 30, 19—

	Total	Educational and general	Student aid	Auxiliary enterprises
Balances, July 1, 19--	$ 355,164	$ 267,394	$73,350	$14,420
Additions-				
Governmental appropriations	$ 380,000	$ 380,000		
Endowment income	47,136	35,086	$12,050	
Gifts	198,900	130,300	67,400	$ 1,200
Sponsored research	1,351,500	1,351,500		
Other sponsored programs	52,000	52,000		
Other sources	3,100	2,320		780
	$2,032,636	$1,951,206	$79,450	$ 1,980
Deductions-				
Expenditures (Form 3)	$1,749,200	$1,668,000	$81,200	
Indirect cost recoveries on sponsored programs transferred to unrestricted current funds (Form 3)	30,000	30,000		
Refunds to grantors	23,500	23,500		
	$1,802,700	$1,721,500	$81,200	$ -
Balances, June 30, 19-- (Forms 1 and 17)	$ 585,100	$ 497,100	$71,600	$16,400

Statement of Changes in Fund Balances—Loan Funds
for the Year Ended June 30, 19—

Balances, July 1, 19--		$383,180
Additions-		
Gifts		$ 36,400
Endowment income		140
Interest and investment income		4,200
Transfers from current fund (Form 3)		4,000
		$ 44,740
Deductions-		
Uncollectible notes charged off		$ 1,160
Death and teachers' cancellations		460
		$ 1,620
Balances, June 30, 19--		
(Forms 1 and 18):		
U.S. Government grants, refundable	$294,200	
University loan funds-		
Established by donors	100,100	
Established by Governing Board	32,000	$426,300

Statement of Changes in Fund Balances—
Endowment and Similar Funds
for the Year Ended June 30, 19—

	Total	Endowment funds	Term endowment funds	Quasi-endowment funds	Net adjusted gains and losses
Balances, July 1, 19--	$1,313,700	$954,000	$341,000	$ 2,000	$16,700
Additions-					
Gifts	$ 33,000	$ 18,000	$ 15,000		
Income added to principal	3,000	2,000	1,000		
Annuity funds upon death of annuitant (Form 8)	3,000	3,000			
Net gains on sales of securities	14,700	3,000	2,000		$ 9,700
Transfers from current funds (Form 3)	100,000			$100,000	
	$ 153,700	$ 26,000	$ 18,000	$100,000	$ 9,700
Deductions-					
Expiration of term endowment (Form 4)	$ 21,000		$ 19,000		$ 2,000
Balances, June 30, 19-- (Forms 1 and 19)	$1,446,400	$980,000	$340,000	$102,000	$24,400

Statement of Changes in Fund Balances—
Annuity and Life Income Funds
for the Year Ended June 30, 19—

	Total	Annuity funds	Life income funds
Balances, July 1, 19--	$223,300	$86,500	$136,800
Additions-			
Gifts	$ 10,000		$ 10,000
Investment income	11,700	$ 2,300	9,400
	$ 21,700	$ 2,300	$ 19,400
Deductions-			
Transfer to endowment funds upon death of annuitant (Form 7)	$ 3,000	$ 3,000	
Payments to annuitants and beneficiaries	13,000	3,600	$ 9,400
Net losses on sales of securities	1,000	200	800
	$ 17,000	$ 6,800	$ 10,200
Balances, June 30, 19-- (Forms 1 and 20)	$228,000	$82,000	$146,000

Statement of Changes in Fund Balances—
Unexpended Plant Funds
for the Year Ended June 30, 19—

Balances, July 1, 19--		$346,400
Additions-		
Governmental appropriations		$505,000
Investment income		10,000
Transfers from current funds (Form 3)		150,000
Restricted student fees		10,000
Gifts and grants		75,000
		$750,000
Deductions-		
Expenditures for plant facilities (Form 12)		$630,000
Balances, June 30, 19-- (Forms 1 and 21):		
Restricted	$266,000	
Unrestricted	200,400	$466,400

Statement of Changes in Fund Balances— Funds for Renewals and Replacements for the Year Ended June 30, 19—

Balances, July 1, 19--	$314,000
Additions-	
State appropriations	$ 95,000
Investment income	6,700
Net gains on sales of securities	500
Transfers from current funds (Form 3)	43,500
Transfers from auxiliary enterprises	36,100
	$181,800
Deductions-	
Expenditures	$208,600
Balances, June 30, 19-- (Forms 1 and 22)	$287,200

Statement of Changes in Fund Balances— Funds for Retirement of Indebtedness for the Year Ended June 30, 19—

Balances, July 1, 19--	$308,800
Additions-	
Transfers from current funds (Form 3)	$ 17,500
Transfers from auxiliary enterprises	169,700
Investment income	10,300
Accrued interest on sale of bonds	3,000
	$200,500
Deductions-	
Bonds retired	$112,500
Principal repayment on long-term notes payable	15,000
Bond interest paid	60,000
Interest paid on long-term notes payable	5,000
Interest paid on temporary notes payable to banks	5,000
	$197,500
Balances, June 30, 19-- (Forms 1 and 23)	$311,800

[247]

Statement of Changes in Net Investment in Plant
for the Year Ended June 30, 19—

Balances, July 1, 19--	$25,178,900
Additions-	
Amounts expended from-	
Unrestricted current funds	$ 80,000
Unexpended plant funds (Form 9)	630,000
Funds for retirement of indebtedness (Form 11)	127,500
Funds for renewals and replacements	21,400
Gifts in kind (market value at date received)	20,000
	$ 878,900
Deduction-	
Disposals of plant facilities	$ 73,400
Balances, June 30, 19-- (Form 1)	$25,984,400

Statement of Changes in Fund Balances—Agency Funds
for the Year Ended June 30, 19—

Balances, July 1, 19--	$119,500
Additions	$301,100
Deductions	$264,400
Balances, June 30, 19-- (Form 1)	$156,200

Statement of Changes in Fund Balances
for the Year Ended June 30, 19—

	Current Funds		Loan Funds	Endowment and Similar Funds	Annuity and Life Income Funds	Plant Funds		Agency Funds
	Unrestricted	Restricted				Unexpended	Net investment in plant	
Balances, July 1, 19--	$837,800	$ 355,164	$383,180	$1,313,700	$223,300	$ 969,200	$25,178,900	$119,500
Excess of revenues over expenditures and transfers	45,600							
Governmental appropriations		380,000				600,000		
Endowment income		47,136	140					
Gifts and grants		198,900	36,400	33,000	10,000	75,000	20,000	
Sponsored research		1,351,500						
Other sponsored programs		52,000						
Other sources		3,100						36,700
Interest and investment income			4,200		11,700	10,000		
Income added to principal				3,000		27,000		
Accrued interest on sale of bonds						3,000		
Transfers from (to) other funds		(30,000)	4,000	103,000	(3,000)	416,800		
Additions to physical properties from—								
Current funds							80,000	
Unexpended plant funds						(651,400)	651,400	
Gains or (losses) on sales of securities				14,700	(1,000)	500		
Expenditures		(1,749,200)				(187,200)		
Refunds to grantors		(23,500)						
Expiration of term endowment	21,000			(21,000)				
Uncollectible notes charged off			(1,160)					
Death and teachers' cancellations			(460)					
Payments to beneficiaries and annuitants					(13,000)			
Bonds retired						(112,500)	112,500	
Note payments						(15,000)	15,000	
Interest paid						(70,000)		
Disposals of physical properties							(73,400)	
Balances, June 30, 19--	$904,400*	$ 585,100	$426,300	$1,446,400	$228,000	$1,065,400	$25,984,400	$156,200

*The Governing Board has allocated $125,000 of this balance for specific operating purposes.

Note — If the multi-columnar fund balance statement is used, details of the year end fund balances (as illustrated in Forms 4 through 13) should be shown in the balance sheet.

Schedule of Current Funds Revenues
for the Year Ended June 30, 19—

	Total	Unrestricted	Restricted
Educational and General:			
Student Tuition and Fees-			
Tuition	$ 893,600	$ 893,600	
Laboratory	29,600	29,600	
Incidental	15,400	15,400	
Extension division	25,500	25,500	
	$ 964,100	$ 964,100	
Government Appropriations-			
State government	$2,426,100	$2,126,000	$ 300,100
Federal government	261,900	200,400	61,500
	$2,688,000	$2,326,400	$ 361,600
Endowment Income	$ 39,000	$ 12,000	$ 27,000
Gifts-			
Alumni	$ 341,500	$ 332,200	$ 9,300
Churches	31,600	21,600	10,000
Foundations	65,400	60,800	4,600
Industrial	7,400		7,400
Other	26,800	26,800	
	$ 472,700	$ 441,400	$ 31,300
Sponsored Research-			
Federal government agencies	$ 631,000		$ 631,000
State agencies	377,000		377,000
Private sponsors	200,000		200,000
	$1,208,000		$1,208,000
Other Separately Budgeted Research	$ 61,000	$ 61,000	
Other Sponsored Programs-			
State agencies	$ 15,000		$ 15,000
Federal agencies	12,000		12,000
Private sponsors	10,000		10,000
	$ 37,000		$ 37,000
Recovery of Indirect Costs - Sponsored Programs-			
Federal agencies	$ 25,000	$ 25,000	
State agencies	5,000	5,000	
	$ 30,000	$ 30,000	
Sales and Services of Educational Departments-			
College of Education	$ 24,400	$ 24,400	
Engineering testing materials	18,800	18,800	
	$ 43,200	$ 43,200	

Schedule of Current Funds Revenues
for the Year Ended June 30, 19—

	Total	Unrestricted	Restricted
Organized Activities Relating to Educational Departments-			
Television station	$ 24,000	$ 24,000	
Student newspaper	17,800	17,800	
Psychology testing laboratory	17,700	17,700	
	$ 59,500	$ 59,500	
Other Sources-			
Income on temporary investments of current funds	$ 16,200	$ 13,100	$ 3,100
Conference and workshops	7,100	7,100	
Miscellaneous	4,700	4,700	
	$ 28,000	$ 24,900	$ 3,100
Total Educational and General	$5,630,500	$3,962,500	$1,668,000
Student Aid:			
Gifts	$ 50,800		$ 50,800
Endowment income	20,100		20,100
Other sources	10,300		10,300
	$ 81,200		$ 81,200
Auxiliary Enterprises (Forms 25-30):			
Intercollegiate athletics	$ 171,280	$ 171,280	
Residence halls	284,650	284,650	
Faculty housing	13,570	13,570	
Food services	495,970	495,970	
College union	33,400	33,400	
Student store	154,630	154,630	
	$1,153,500	$1,153,500	
Total Revenues (Form 3)	$6,865,200	$5,116,000	$1,749,200

Schedule of Current Funds Expenditures
for the Year Ended June 30, 19—

	Total	Unrestricted	Restricted (Forms 5 and 17)
Educational and General:			
Instruction and departmental research-			
College of Arts and Science	$ 788,600	$ 664,300	$ 124,300
College of Business	381,300	337,300	44,000
College of Education	336,500	290,500	46,000
College of Engineering	605,700	541,900	63,800
Graduate School	170,500	65,500	105,000
	$2,282,600	$1,899,500	$ 383,100
Organized Activities Relating to Educational Departments-			
Television station	$ 35,500	$ 35,500	
Student newspaper	31,500	31,500	
Psychology testing laboratory	12,700	12,700	
	$ 79,700	$ 79,700	
Sponsored Research-			
College of Arts and Science	$ 88,100		$ 88,100
College of Business	20,800		20,800
College of Education	82,400		82,400
College of Engineering	870,200		870,200
Graduate school	146,500		146,500
	$1,208,000		$1,208,000
Other Separately Budgeted Research-			
Bureau of Business Research	$ 40,000	$ 40,000	
Bureau of Governmental Research	21,000	21,000	
	$ 61,000	$ 61,000	
Other Sponsored Programs-			
College of Arts and Science	$ 19,200		$ 19,200
College of Education	17,800		17,800
	$ 37,000		$ 37,000
Extension and Public Service-			
Extension division	$ 21,100		$ 21,100
Conferences and workshops	6,400	$ 6,400	
	$ 27,500	$ 6,400	$ 21,100
Libraries-			
General	$ 97,000	$ 94,700	$ 2,300
Business administration	27,700	11,200	16,500
	$ 124,700	$ 105,900	$ 18,800
Student Services-			
Registrar's office	$ 45,800	$ 45,800	
Dean of students	27,800	27,800	
Student health service	96,200	96,200	
Testing and counseling	12,000	12,000	
	$ 181,800	$ 181,800	
Operation and Maintenance of Physical Plant-			
Administration	$ 19,600	$ 19,600	
Custodial services	57,500	57,500	
Maintenance of buildings	237,900	237,900	
Heating and utility systems	102,300	102,300	
Maintenance of grounds	25,200	25,200	
Equipment and vehicles	9,100	9,100	
Police and watchmen	32,700	32,700	
Property insurance	30,800	30,800	
Expenses allocated to auxiliary enterprises and organized activities	(97,900)	(97,900)	
	$ 417,200	$ 417,200	

Schedule of Current Funds Expenditures
for the Year Ended June 30, 19—

	Total	Unrestricted	Restricted (Forms 5 and 17)
General Administration-			
Governing board	$ 12,900	$ 12,900	
President	39,000	39,000	
Academic vice president	32,000	32,000	
Vice president for business affairs	64,600	64,600	
Counsel	29,900	29,900	
Expenses allocated to auxiliary enterprises and organized activities	(10,800)	(10,800)	
	$ 167,600	$ 167,600	
Staff Benefits-			
Group life and medical insurance	$ 71,200	$ 71,200	
Payroll taxes	94,300	94,300	
Premiums on retirement plan	222,600	222,600	
Expenses allocated to various departments	(20,000)	(20,000)	
	$ 368,100	$ 368,100	
General Institutional Expenses-			
Alumni office	$ 19,200	$ 19,200	
Auditing	10,600	10,600	
Bulletins and catalogues	16,400	16,400	
Commencement	12,100	12,100	
Communications	31,800	31,800	
Convocations	8,600	8,600	
Development office	28,900	28,900	
General insurance	12,600	12,600	
Interest on current funds loans	10,000	10,000	
Memberships	17,900	17,900	
Publications	29,400	29,400	
Public relations	24,100	24,100	
Legal fees	12,500	12,500	
Expenses allocated to auxiliary enterprises and organized activities	(10,000)	(10,000)	
	$ 224,100	$ 224,100	
Total Educational and General	$5,179,300	$3,511,300	$1,668,000
Student Aid:			
Scholarships	$ 122,200	$ 71,400	$ 50,800
Fellowships	51,900	31,800	20,100
Prizes and awards	20,300	10,000	10,300
	$ 194,400	$ 113,200	$ 81,200
Auxiliary Enterprises (Forms 25-30):			
Intercollegiate athletics (including debt service of $52,500)	$ 170,680	$ 170,680	
Residence halls (including debt service of $139,700)	282,670	282,670	
Faculty housing	12,400	12,400	
Food services (including debt service of $10,000)	491,140	491,140	
College union (including debt service of $3,600)	23,750	23,750	
Student store	150,260	150,260	
	$1,130,900	$1,130,900	
Total Expenditures (Form 3)	$6,504,600	$4,755,400	$1,749,200

Schedule of Changes in Fund Balances— Restricted Current Funds for the Year Ended June 30, 19—

	Balances July 1, 19—	Additions			Deductions			Balances June 30, 19—
		Gifts, grants and appropriations	Endowment income	Other	Refunds to grantors	Indirect cost recoveries earned	Expenditures (Form 16)	
Educational and General:								
Instruction and departmental research—								
College of Education								
Teaching Research Institute - methods research	$ 200							$ 200
(Other various funds to be listed alphabetically under each organizational unit)	44,939	$ 331,176	$30,786				$ 383,100	5,301
Total instruction and departmental research	$ 45,139	$ 331,176	$30,786				$ 383,100	$ 5,501
Sponsored research—								
(Various funds to be listed alphabetically under each organization unit)	$ 95,440	$1,351,500			$18,500	$15,000	$1,208,000	$218,940
Total sponsored research	$ 95,440	$1,351,500			$18,500	$15,000	$1,208,000	$218,940
Other sponsored programs—								
(Various funds to be listed alphabetically under each organizational unit)	$ 49,637	$ 52,000			$ 5,000	$15,000	$ 37,000	$ 49,637
Total other sponsored programs	$ 49,637	$ 52,000			$ 5,000	$15,000	$ 37,000	$ 49,637
Extension and public service—								
(Various funds to be listed alphabetically under each organizational unit)	$ 46,719	$ 120,000					$ 21,100	$145,619
Total extension and public service	$ 46,719	$ 120,000					$ 21,100	$145,619
Libraries—								
(Various funds to be listed alphabetically under each organizational unit)	$ 30,459	$ 59,124	$ 4,300	$2,320			$ 18,800	$ 77,403
Total libraries	$ 30,459	$ 59,124	$ 4,300	$2,320			$ 18,800	$ 77,403
Total Educational and General	$267,394	$1,913,800	$35,086	$2,320	$23,500	$30,000	$1,668,000	$497,100
Student Aid:								
Scholarships—								
(Various funds to be listed alphabetically)	$ 44,200	$ 40,000	$11,600				$ 50,800	$ 45,000
Total scholarships	$ 44,200	$ 40,000	$11,600				$ 50,800	$ 45,000
Fellowships—								
(Various funds to be listed alphabetically)	$ 8,100	$ 27,000					$ 20,100	$ 15,000
Total fellowships	$ 8,100	$ 27,000					$ 20,100	$ 15,000
Prizes and awards—								
(Various funds to be listed alphabetically)	$ 21,050	$ 400	$ 450				$ 10,300	$ 11,600
Total prizes and awards	$ 21,050	$ 400	$ 450				$ 10,300	$ 11,600
Total Student Aid	$ 73,350	$ 67,400	$12,050				$ 81,200	$ 71,600
Auxiliary Enterprises:								
Student union—								
A. T. Smith fund	$ 14,420	$ 1,200		$ 780			$ 16,400	$ 16,400
Total Auxiliary Enterprises	$ 14,420	$ 1,200		$ 780			$ 16,400	$ 16,400
Total (Form 5)	$355,164	$1,982,400	$47,136	$3,100	$23,500	$30,000	$1,749,200	$585,100

Schedule of Changes in Fund Balances—Loan Funds
for the Year Ended June 30, 19—

| | Balances July 1, 19-- | Additions | | | | Deductions | | Balances June 30, 19-- | Cash and investments available for loans |
		Gifts and grants	Endowment income	Interest and investment income	Transfers from current funds	Uncollectible notes charged off	Death and teachers' cancellations		
U.S. Government participation loan funds—									
National defense student loan fund	$214,100	$29,890		$2,810		$ 948	$414	$245,438	$21,400
Health professions educational assistance loan fund	42,100	5,868		890		96		48,762	6,600
	$256,200	$35,758		$3,700		$1,044	$414	$294,200	$28,000
Institutional loan funds—									
Matching funds for U.S. Government participation loan funds	$ 27,680			$ 482	$4,000	$ 116	$ 46	$ 32,000	$ 3,500
D. R. Lamb loan fund	27,500	$ 208	$ 17					27,725	2,100
R. G. Piltower loan fund	4,200		18					4,218	1,700
W. A. Spender loan fund	18,400	434	29					18,863	2,200
L. A. Weaver loan fund	31,200			18				31,218	1,750
Yeater & Townsend loan fund	18,000		76					18,076	350
	$126,980	$ 642	$140	$ 500	$4,000	$ 116	$ 46	$132,100	$11,600
Total (Form 6)	$383,180	$36,400	$140	$4,200	$4,000	$1,160	$460	$426,300	$39,600

Schedule of Changes in Fund Balances— Endowment and Similar Funds for the Year Ended June 30, 19—

	Balances July 1, 19—	Gifts	Additions — Income added to principal	Additions — Annuity funds upon death of annuitant	Additions — Net gains on sales of securities	Additions — Transfers from current funds	Deduction — Expiration of term endowment	Balances June 30, 19—
ENDOWMENT FUNDS:								
Income unrestricted-								
(Various funds listed alphabetically)	$ 272,000	$ 5,000		$3,000				$ 280,000
Income restricted-								
Educational and general-								
Instruction and departmental research-								
(Various funds listed alphabetically)	206,000	7,000						213,000
Libraries-								
(Various funds listed alphabetically)	112,000	2,000						114,000
Student aid-								
Scholarships-								
(Various funds listed alphabetically)	346,000	4,000	$ 2,000		$ 3,000			355,000
Loan funds-								
(Various funds listed alphabetically)	18,000							18,000
	$ 954,000	$18,000	$ 2,000	$3,000	$ 3,000			$ 980,000
TERM ENDOWMENT FUNDS:								
Income unrestricted-								
(Various funds listed alphabetically)	$ 195,000						$19,000	$ 176,000
Income restricted-								
Educational and general-								
Instruction and departmental research-								
(Various funds listed alphabetically)	146,000	$15,000	$ 1,000		$ 2,000			164,000
	$ 341,000	$15,000	$ 1,000		$ 2,000		$19,000	$ 340,000
QUASI ENDOWMENT FUNDS:								
Income unrestricted-								
(Various funds listed alphabetically)	$ 2,000							$ 2,000
Income restricted-								
Student aid-								
Fellowships-								
(Various funds listed alphabetically)						$100,000		100,000
	$ 2,000					$100,000		$ 102,000
NET ADJUSTED GAINS AND LOSSES	$ 16,700				$ 9,700		$ 2,000	$ 24,400
Total (Form 7)	$1,313,700	$33,000	$ 3,000	$3,000	$14,700	$100,000	$21,000	$1,446,400

Schedule of Changes in Fund Balances—
Annuity and Life Income Funds
for the Year Ended June 30, 19—

Funds	Eventual purpose	Balances July 1, 19--	Additions		Deductions			Balances June 30, 19--
			Gifts	Investment income	Payments to beneficiaries and annuitants	Transfer on death of annuitant	Net losses on sales of securities	
Annuity funds-								
Richards, L. M.	For operation of plant	$ 4,725		$ 500	$ 200		$ 25	$ 5,000
Jones, P. R.	Unrestricted	29,050		500	1,500		50	28,000
Wilson, A. T.	For unrestricted endowment	3,000				$3,000		
Bender, A. J.	For student aid	5,625		400	400		25	5,600
James, R. T.	For plant additions	44,100		900	1,500		100	43,400
		$ 86,500		$ 2,300	$ 3,600	$3,000	$ 200	$ 82,000
Life income funds-								
Lane, M. H.	Unrestricted	$ 42,350		$ 3,000	$ 3,000		$ 250	$ 42,100
Jackson, P. P.	For unrestricted endowment	27,150		2,000	2,000		150	27,000
Smith, J. O.	Unrestricted	17,700		1,500	1,500		100	17,600
Ziemann, R. F.	For research	49,600	$10,000	2,900	2,900		300	59,300
		$136,800	$10,000	$ 9,400	$ 9,400		$ 800	$146,000
Total (Form 8)		$223,300	$10,000	$11,700	$13,000	$3,000	$1,000	$228,000

[257]

Schedule of Changes in Fund Balances—
Unexpended Plant Funds
for the Year Ended June 30, 19—

	Balances July 1, 19--	Additions					Deductions	Balances June 30, 19--
		Governmental appropriations	Investment income	Transfers from current funds	Restricted student fees	Gifts and grants	Expenditures for plant facilities	
Arts and sciences building	$ 19,900	$ 90,000		$ 7,500		$30,000	$120,000	$ 27,400
Residence halls and food services	240,000		$ 7,000	80,000			110,000	217,000
Chemical research laboratory	10,000	205,000				25,000	66,000	174,000
Expansion of power plant	1,000	38,000					39,000	
Land acquisition				50,000			25,000	25,000
Physical sciences building	65,500	122,000	3,000	12,500		20,000	210,000	13,000
Yeats Hall addition	10,000	50,000					60,000	
Young Memorial addition					$10,000			10,000
Total (Form 9)	$346,400	$505,000	$10,000	$150,000	$10,000	$75,000	$630,000	$466,400

Schedule of Changes in Fund Balances—
Funds for Renewals and Replacements
for the Year Ended June 30, 19—

| | Balances July 1, 19-- | State appropriations | Additions | | | | Deductions | Balances June 30, 19-- |
			Investment income	Net gains on sales of securities	Transfers from current funds	Transfers from auxiliary enterprises	Expenditures	
Administration building	$ 3,000				$ 4,000		$ 6,000	$ 1,000
Residence halls and food services	204,700	$15,000	$3,800	$500		$36,100	76,100	184,000
Mathematics building	13,600		400				12,000	2,000
Observatory	17,400		600		8,000		18,000	8,000
Power plant and general services building	32,000	70,000			17,900		78,900	41,000
Rohr Hall	16,400				2,000		2,400	16,000
Yeats Hall	14,100	10,000	1,900		11,600		9,200	28,400
Young Memorial	12,800						6,000	6,800
Total (Form 10)	$314,000	$95,000	$6,700	$500	$43,500	$36,100	$208,600	$287,200

Schedule of Changes in Fund Balances— Funds for Retirement of Indebtedness for the Year Ended June 30, 19—

	Consolidated housing and cafeteria bonds July 1,19--	Faculty apartments sinking fund bonds January 1,19--	South group residence halls bonds June 1,19--	Recreational facilities notes March 1,19--	Temporary notes payable to banks	Total (Form 11)
Balances, July 1, 19--	$231,300	$57,500		$20,000		$308,800
Additions-						
Transfers from current funds				$15,000	$2,500	$ 17,500
Transfers from auxiliary enterprises	$117,200	$50,000			2,500	169,700
Investment income	7,800	1,900		600		10,300
Accrued interest on sale of bonds			$3,000			3,000
	$125,000	$51,900	$3,000	$15,600	$5,000	$200,500
Deductions-						
Bonds retired	$ 75,000	$37,500				$112,500
Principal repayment on long-term notes payable				$15,000		15,000
Bond interest paid	50,000	10,000				60,000
Interest paid on long-term notes payable				5,000		5,000
Interest paid on temporary notes payable to banks					$5,000	5,000
	$125,000	$47,500		$20,000	$5,000	$197,500
Balances, June 30, 19--	$231,300	$61,900	$3,000	$15,600	$ -	$311,800

Schedule of Changes in Investment in Plant
for the Year Ended June 30, 19—

	Book value July 1, 19--	Additions from		Deductions Disposals of plant facilities	Book value June 30, 19-- (Form 1)
		Institutional funds	Borrowed funds		
Land:					
Campus	$ 800,000	$ 25,000			$ 825,000
Observatory	200,000				200,000
	$ 1,000,000	$ 25,000			$ 1,025,000
Buildings:					
Administration	$ 2,400,000				$ 2,400,000
Residence halls and food services	3,950,000	$150,000	$600,000		4,700,000
Mathematics	1,900,000				1,900,000
Observatory	1,300,000				1,300,000
Power plant and general services	2,050,400	49,600			2,100,000
Rohr Hall	2,300,200				2,300,200
Yeats Hall	2,995,000	60,000			3,055,000
Young Memorial	2,000,000				2,000,000
	$18,895,600	$259,600	$600,000		$19,755,200
Improvements other than buildings:					
Fountains	$ 22,400				$ 22,400
Parking lots	40,000				40,000
Sidewalks	160,000				160,000
Utilities systems	700,000				700,000
	$ 922,400				$ 922,400
Equipment:					
Administration	$ 503,000	$ 48,000		$11,000	$ 540,000
Residence halls and food services	1,851,400	30,000		21,400	1,860,000
Mathematics	380,000	30,000			410,000
Observatory	1,193,000	20,000		13,000	1,200,000
Power plant and general services	1,581,000	35,000		16,000	1,600,000
Rohr Hall	187,200	12,800			200,000
Yeats Hall	268,000				268,000
Young Memorial	138,800	35,000		12,000	161,800
Library books	360,000	32,000			392,000
	$ 6,462,400	$242,800		$73,400	$ 6,631,800
Construction in progress	$ 1,710,800	$224,000			$ 1,934,800
Total investment in plant	$28,991,200	$751,400	$600,000	$73,400	$30,269,200

Schedule of Revenues and Expenditures
for the Year Ended June 30, 19—
Intercollegiate Athletics

Revenues:
  Sports-

Baseball	$ 1,470
Basketball	22,500
Football	120,710
Tennis	530
Track	750
	$145,960

  Other-

Radio and TV rights	$ 23,720
Concessions	1,600
	$ 25,320
Total Revenues (Form 15)	$171,280

Expenditures:
  Administration and general expense-

Administration	$ 13,520
Publicity	3,750
Tickets and ticket sales expense	11,200
General operations and maintenance of plant	6,900
	$ 35,370

  Sports-

Baseball	$ 2,200
Basketball	8,400
Football	61,610
Golf	2,700
Swimming	2,150
Tennis	1,610
Track	4,140
	$ 82,810

Transfers to plant funds for-

Retirement of indebtedness	$ 50,000
Renewals and replacements	2,500
	$ 52,500
Total Expenditures (Form 16)	$170,680
Excess of Revenues over Expenditures and Transfers	$ 600

[262]

Schedule of Revenues and Expenditures
for the Year Ended June 30, 19—
Residence Halls

Revenues:		
Room rentals		$283,200
Miscellaneous		1,450
Total Revenues (Form 15)		$284,650
Expenditures:		
General administration-		
Salaries		$ 12,700
Office supplies		450
Travel		560
Telephone		3,750
Payroll taxes		3,100
Other		440
		$ 21,000
Room service-		
Salaries		$ 18,750
Laundry		9,100
Repairs		1,720
		$ 29,570
Operation and maintenance of plant-		
Custodial salaries		$ 23,530
Supplies		7,910
Heat, light, power, water		48,100
Insurance		4,200
Repairs		7,180
Equipment		1,480
		$ 92,400
Transfers to plant funds for-		
Retirement of indebtedness		$119,700
Renewals and replacements		20,000
		$139,700
Total Expenditures (Form 16)		$282,670
Excess of Revenues over Expenditures		$ 1,980
and Transfers		

Schedule of Revenues and Expenditures
for the Year Ended June 30, 19—
Faculty Housing

Revenues:
Apartment rentals	$13,400
Miscellaneous	170
Total Revenues (Form 15)	$13,570

Expenditures:
General administration-
Salaries	$ 700
Payroll taxes	120
Telephone	20
Office supplies	30
Other	130
	$ 1,000

Operation and maintenance of plant-
Custodial salaries	$ 2,350
Light, power, water, heat	1,200
Insurance	1,850
Repairs	2,210
Equipment	3,790
	$11,400
Total Expenditures (Form 16)	$12,400
Excess of Revenues over Expenditures	$ 1,170

Schedule of Revenues and Expenditures
for the Year Ended June 30, 19—
Food Services

Revenues:
Meal ticket fees	$487,100
Snack bar sales	8,870
Total Revenues (Form 15)	$495,970

Expenditures:
Food purchased	$252,600

Administration and general-
Salaries	$ 56,200
Payroll taxes	14,100
Other	6,220
	$ 76,520

Service expense-
Salaries and wages	$ 78,200
Laundry and uniforms	10,100
Fuel for cooking	8,150
Tableware	4,320
Linens	4,600
	$105,370

Operation and maintenance of plant-
Custodial salaries	$ 10,900
Supplies	3,200
Heat, light, power, water	9,600
Insurance	2,400
Repairs	1,250
Equipment	14,250
Other	5,050
	$ 46,650

Transfers to plant funds for renewals and replacements	$ 10,000
Total Expenditures (Form 16)	$491,140
Excess of Revenues over Expenditures and Transfers	$ 4,830

[265]

Schedule of Revenues and Expenditures
for the Year Ended June 30, 19—
College Union

Revenues:

Student fees	$10,200
Room rentals	2,750
Recreational income	18,200
Other miscellaneous	2,250
Total Revenues (Form 15)	$33,400

Expenditures:

General administrative expenses-

Salaries	$ 3,150
Payroll taxes	780
Office supplies	1,850
Other	1,480
	$ 7,260

Recreational-

Salaries	$ 2,190
Supplies	980
Equipment	2,170
Other	230
	$ 5,570

Operation and maintenance of plant-

Custodial salaries	$ 1,840
Supplies	970
Heat, light, power, water	840
Insurance	370
Equipment	2,100
Repairs	1,200
	$ 7,320

Transfers to plant funds for renewals and replacements	$ 3,600
Total Expenditures (Form 16)	$23,750
Excess of Revenues over Expenditures and Transfers	$ 9,650

Schedule of Revenues and Expenditures
for the Year Ended June 30, 19—
Student Store

Revenues (sales) (Form 15)	$154,630
Expenditures:	
Cost of sales	$123,600
Selling and administrative-	
Administrative salaries	$ 2,800
Salaries and wages	12,750
Payroll taxes	1,180
Freight	1,250
Advertising	1,070
Supplies	870
Other	160
	$ 20,080
Operation and maintenance of plant-	
Custodial salaries	$ 1,600
Supplies	310
Heat, light, power, water	1,950
Insurance	990
Equipment	1,730
	$ 6,580
Total Expenditures (Form 16)	$150,260
Excess of Revenues over Expenditures	$ 4,370

Schedule of Investments by Fund Groups
June 30, 19—

	Current Funds		Loan Funds	Endowment and Similar Funds	Annuity and Life Income Funds	Plant Funds			Agency Funds
	Unrestricted	Restricted				Unexpended	Renewals and replacements	Retirement of indebtedness	
U. S. Treasury notes	$300,000					$220,000	$131,700		
U. S. Treasury bills	239,400	$107,000	$19,700	$ 10,000	$ 10,000	516,200	46,000	$114,800	$68,900
Corporate bonds				437,700	29,100			140,000	
Preferred stocks				241,800	31,200				
Common stocks				593,200	109,900				
Mortgage notes					109,900				
Certificates of deposit	147,000			8,300	10,000				
Savings accounts				27,200	8,800				
Real estate, less accumulated depreciation of $13,200 and $3,100, respectively				147,800	24,900				
Total (Form 1)	$686,400	$107,000	$19,700	$1,466,000	$223,900	$736,200	$177,700	$254,800	$68,900

Schedule of Long-Term Notes and Bonds Payable
for the Year Ended June 30, 19—

	Consolidated housing and food services bonds of May 1, 19--	Faculty apartments sinking fund bonds of June 1, 19--	Recreational facilities notes of June 1, 19--	South group residence halls bonds of March 1, 19--	Total
Balances, July 1, 19--	$2,775,000	$712,300	$325,000		$3,812,300
Additions-					
Issuance of South group residence halls bonds of March 1, 19--				$1,000,000	1,000,000
Deductions-					
Bonds retired and note payments	75,000	37,500	15,000		127,500
Balances, June 30, 19--	$2,700,000	$674,800	$310,000	$1,000,000	$4,684,800
Unexpended plant fund-					
Bonds payable					$ 400,000
Investment in plant-					
Notes payable					310,000
Bonds payable					3,974,800
					$4,684,800

[269]

Balance Sheet, June 30, 19—

ASSETS

CURRENT FUNDS:

Unrestricted-

Cash	$289,400	
Investments, at cost (approximate market $685,000)	686,400	
Accounts receivable, less allowance for doubtful accounts of $5,900	280,400	
Notes receivable, less allowance for doubtful notes of $1,000	86,500	
Inventories, at cost	146,900	
Prepaid expenses and deferred charges	114,900	$1,604,500

Restricted-

Cash	$187,600	
Investments, at cost (approximate market $110,000)	107,000	
Accounts receivable - principally agencies of the U.S. Government	472,700	767,300

TOTAL CURRENT FUNDS $2,371,800

LIABILITIES AND FUND BALANCES

CURRENT FUNDS:

Unrestricted-

Temporary notes payable to banks	$200,000	
Accounts payable and accrued expenses	200,000	
Provision for encumbrances	86,000	
Deposits	112,000	
Deferred revenues	102,100	
Fund balances arising from-		
Gifts (Form 35)	$495,000	
Other (Form 36)	409,400	
	904,400	$1,604,500

Restricted-

Accounts payable and accrued expenses	$170,200	
Provision for endowment income stabilization	12,000	
Fund balances	585,100	767,300

TOTAL CURRENT FUNDS $2,371,800

(LOAN FUNDS, ENDOWMENT AND SIMILAR FUNDS, ANNUITY
AND LIFE INCOME FUNDS, PLANT FUNDS AND AGENCY
FUNDS WOULD BE THE SAME AS ILLUSTRATED IN FORM 1)

[271]

Statement of Current Funds Revenues, Expenditures, and Transfers
for the Year Ended June 30, 19—

	Total	Unrestricted	Restricted
Revenues:			
Educational and General-			
Student Tuition and Fees	$ 964,100	$ 964,100	
Governmental Appropriations	2,688,000	2,326,400	$ 361,600
Endowment Income (including $6,500 received from funds held in trust by others)	39,000	12,000	27,000
Gifts Applied	427,100	395,800	31,300
Sponsored Research-			
Governmental	1,008,000		1,008,000
Non-governmental	200,000		200,000
Other Separately Budgeted Research	61,000	61,000	
Other Sponsored Programs-			
Governmental	27,000		27,000
Non-governmental	10,000		10,000
Recovery of Indirect Costs - Sponsored Programs	30,000	30,000	
Sales and Services of Educational Departments	43,200	43,200	
Organized Activities Relating to Educational Departments	59,500	59,500	
Other Sources	28,000	24,900	3,100
Total Educational and General	$5,584,900	$3,916,900	$1,668,000
Student Aid	81,200		81,200
Auxiliary Enterprises	1,153,500	1,153,500	
Total Revenues	$6,819,600	$5,070,400	$1,749,200
Expenditures:			
Educational and General-			
Instruction and Departmental Research	$2,282,600	$1,899,500	$ 383,100
Organized Activities Relating to Educational Departments	79,700	79,700	
Sponsored Research	1,208,000		1,208,000
Other Separately Budgeted Research	61,000	61,000	
Other Sponsored Programs	37,000		37,000
Extension and Public Service	27,500	6,400	21,100
Libraries	124,700	105,900	18,800
Student Services	181,800	181,800	
Operation and Maintenance of Physical Plant	417,200	417,200	
General Administration	167,600	167,600	
Staff Benefits	368,100	368,100	
General Institutional Expenses	224,100	224,100	
Total Educational and General	$5,179,300	$3,511,300	$1,668,000
Student Aid	194,400	113,200	81,200
Auxiliary Enterprises (including debt service of $205,800)	1,130,900	1,130,900	
Total Expenditures	$6,504,600	$4,755,400	$1,749,200

[272]

Statement of Current Funds Revenues, Expenditures, and Transfers
for the Year Ended June 30, 19—

	Total	Unrestricted	Restricted
Transfers:			
To—			
Loan funds for supplements to U.S. Government grant	$ 4,000	$ 4,000	
Quasi-endowment funds	100,000	100,000	
Plant funds for—			
Additions	150,000	150,000	
Renewals and replacements	43,500	43,500	
Retirement of indebtedness	17,500	17,500	
Total Transfers	$ 315,000	$ 315,000	
Excess of Revenues over Expenditures and Transfers*	$ -	$ -	$ -

*So titled for illustrative purposes only.

[273]

Statement of Changes in Fund Balances—
Unrestricted Current Funds—Gifts
for the Year Ended June 30, 19—

Balances, July 1, 19--	$449,400
Additions-	
Gifts received during the year from-	
Foundations	$ 60,800
Alumni	332,200
Others	26,800
Churches	21,600
	$441,400
Deductions-	
Applied to current revenues for general support	$395,800
Balances, June 30, 19-- (Form 33)	$495,000

Statement of Changes in Fund Balances—
Unrestricted Current Funds—Other
for the Year Ended June 30, 19—

	Total	Unallocated	Allocated
Balances, July 1, 19--	$388,400	$283,400	$105,000
Additions-			
Excess of revenues over expenditures and transfers (Form 34)	$ - *	$ - *	
Expiration of term endowment fund	21,000	21,000	
	$ 21,000	$ 21,000	
Transfers between unallocated and allocated-			
Amounts included in current expenditures on projects for which funds had previously been allocated		$ 40,000	$(40,000)
Allocations for specific future operating purposes		(60,000)	60,000
		$(20,000)	$ 20,000
Balances, June 30, 19-- (Form 33)	$409,400	$284,400	$125,000

*So included for illustrative purposes only.

Appendix C

Terminology

THE definitions presented apply both to terms that are peculiar to college and university business administration and to terms from general accounting practice that take on special meanings in institutional business administration. Usage in this volume follows definitions below.

ACCRUAL BASIS The basis of accounting and reporting under which revenues are reported when they become due, even though they are received in a subsequent fiscal period; likewise, expenditures for the cost of all materials received and services rendered to an institution are reported even though payments for them may not yet have been made as of the date of the financial report. The accrual basis is contrasted with the *cash basis* (*q.v.*) in which items are reported as revenues and expenditures only when cash is received or made available to an institution and when it is disbursed. The terms *revenues* and *expenditures* are used in the accrual basis of accounting and reporting, and the terms *receipts* and *disbursements* in the cash basis.

AGENCY FUNDS Funds received and held by an institution as custodian or fiscal agent for others; funds of student organizations, individual students, or faculty members.

ALLOCATION An authorization to incur obligations and to make expenditures during a stated period of time, for a specified purpose, and not to exceed the amount provided in the authorization. Examples are budget allocations—amounts made available in annual budgets for the operations of budget organizational units and allocations of the balance of unrestricted current funds for working capital, encumbrances, and contingencies.

ALLOCATION ACCOUNT An account for budgetary control, to which is credited the amount authorized to be expended, and to which are charged *expenditures* and *encumbrances*.

ANNUITY A payment made on the basis of an annuity agreement. This term should not be applied to the payment of pensions to retired members of an institutional staff; *retirement allowances* (*q.v.*) or *pensions* should be used to designate such items.

ANNUITY AGREEMENT   An agreement whereby money or other property is made available to an institution on the condition that the institution bind itself to pay periodically to the donor or other designated individuals stipulated amounts, which payments are to terminate at a time specified in the agreement.

ANNUITY FUNDS   Funds acquired by an institution subject to annuity agreements.

APPROPRIATION   An amount received from, or made available by, governmental bodies.

AUDIT   The examination of documents, records, reports, systems of internal control, accounting procedures, and other information to determine the propriety, legality, and mathematical accuracy of transactions; to ascertain whether all transactions have been recorded; and to determine whether transactions are accurately reflected in the accounts and in the financial statements drawn from them in accordance with generally accepted accounting principles.

AUXILIARY ENTERPRISE   An entity which exists to furnish a service to students, faculty, or staff, and which charges a fee that is directly related to, although not necessarily equal to, the cost of the service. The general public may incidentally be served in some auxiliary enterprises. Examples are: residence halls, food services, and student stores.

AUXILIARY ENTERPRISES PLANT   Buildings, equipment, and furniture and furnishings used by or in the revenue-producing auxiliary enterprises. The term includes dormitories, residence halls, dining halls, college unions, parking facilities, university presses, and print shops.

BALANCE OF FUNDS   The excess of assets over liabilities of unrestricted current funds, unrestricted gifts, restricted current funds, loan funds, endowment funds, term endowment funds, quasi-endowment funds, annuity funds, life income funds, unexpended plant funds, funds for retirement of indebtedness, funds for renewals and replacements, and of agency funds.

BALANCE SHEET   A statement showing the financial position of an institution at a given time, disclosing assets, liabilities, and fund balances. In college and university accounting, the balance sheet should set forth the assets, liabilities, and fund balances of each fund group in balanced sections.

BUDGET   A statement of proposed expenditures for a fixed period or for a specific project, or program, and the proposed means of financing the expenditures. When approved by the proper authorities, budgets are authorizations to incur the expenditures and to collect and apply the revenues as set forth therein.

Budgetary Accounts   Accounts which reflect budget operations as distinguished from those which represent actual assets, liabilities, revenues, and expenditures, e.g., *allocations, estimated* (or *unrealized*) *revenues,* and *unallocated revenues* (*qq.v.*).

Cash Basis   The basis of accounting, in contrast with the *accrual basis* (*q.v.*) under which revenues are accounted for only when received in cash, and expenditures are accounted for only when paid.

Commitments   *See* Encumbrances.

Consolidated Investments   *See* Pooled Investments.

Contract Research and Services   *See* Sponsored Research.

Contributed Services   In institutions conducted by religious orders, societies, or similar groups, the estimated monetary value of the services of members of the organization who receive no monetary compensation.

Current   When used in connection with funds, the operating funds as distinguished from other funds; when used in connection with budgets, the present fiscal period as contrasted with past or future periods.

Current Funds   Funds expendable for current operating purposes, either unrestricted or restricted. This term is not synonymous with *current assets* as used in commercial accounting.

Current Funds Expenditures   Expenditures for current operations made from current funds.

Current Funds Revenues   All receipts and accruals of unrestricted current funds and of restricted and designated current funds expended during the current fiscal period.

Current General Funds   *See* Unrestricted Current Funds.

Current Income   *See* Current Funds Revenues.

Current Restricted Funds   *See* Restricted Current Funds.

Debt Service   All payments in connection with funds borrowed by an institution, e.g., principal payments, interest charges, payments to sinking funds to ensure future principal and interest payments, payments to reserves to ensure proper upkeep and maintenance of the facilities, trustees' service charges, legal expenses, and other items related to indebtedness.

Departmental Research Expenditures   Expenditures for research done as a part of regular instructional services and budgeted as *instruction and departmental research* (*q.v.*) rather than separately as research. The term excludes *sponsored research* and *other separately budgeted research.*

Disbursements   Payments in cash. In institutional accounting it refers primarily to deductions from the balances of the funds and all fund groups except the Current Funds group, where the term *expenditures* (*q.v.*) is used.

Educational Plant   Buildings and equipment used primarily for instructional research, and administrative purposes, and for supporting service operations. The term includes classroom buildings, laboratories, lecture halls, libraries, administration buildings, conference centers, gymnasiums, field houses, armories, recreation fields, heating and power plants, warehouses, shops, garages, laboratory apparatus and equipment, furniture, furnishings, equipment, office machines, motor vehicles and machinery of the physical plant department, library books, and livestock.

ENCUMBRANCES   Obligations incurred in the form of orders, contracts, and similar items that will become payable when goods are delivered or services rendered. This term is synonymous with *commitments.*

ENDOWMENT FUNDS   Funds which a donor or other outside agency has stipulated, as a condition of gift, that the principal is to be maintained inviolate and in perpetuity and that only the income from the investments of the fund may be expended.

EQUIPMENT   All movable property that is of a permanent nature. The term excludes items which are consumed or used up in normal operating functions. Distinctions between equipment and operating supplies and materials may be made on the basis of minimum standards for cost of each unit, probable life, material, and size.

ESTIMATED REVENUES   *See* UNREALIZED REVENUES.

EXPENDITURES   The cost of goods delivered or services rendered, whether actually paid or unpaid, for the operation of an institution and for additions to its plant.

EXPENSES   Charges incurred, whether paid or unpaid, for operation, maintenance, and interest and other charges for operating purposes during the current fiscal period. Cf. EXPENDITURES.

EXTENSION AND PUBLIC SERVICES   Educational and other activities designed primarily to serve the general public as contrasted with enrolled students. Examples are correspondence courses, adult study courses, public lectures, radio courses, institutes, workshops, demonstrations, package libraries, radio and television stations, state-wide surveys, agriculture and home economics extension programs.

FELLOWSHIPS   Financial assistance awarded primarily on the basis of academic achievement and vocational and professional objectives. Fellowships generally are awarded to graduate or postgraduate students. Recipients are not required to render service to the institution as a consideration of their awards, nor are they required to repay them. Cf. SCHOLARSHIPS.

FUNCTIONAL CLASSIFICATION   The grouping of expenditure items according to the purpose for which costs are incurred. These include: instruction and departmental research, organized activities related to educational departments, sponsored research, other separately budgeted research, other sponsored programs, extension and public services, libraries, student services, operation and maintenance of the physical plant, general administration, staff benefits, and general institutional expenses. See chapter 19, "Statement of Current Funds Revenues, Expenditures, and Transfers," and Forms 2 and 15.

FUND An accounting entity established for the purpose of carrying on specific activities or attaining certain objectives in accordance with special regulations, restrictions, or limitations. The term includes assets, liabilities, revenues and expenditures, receipts and disbursements, and balances. This is to be contrasted with other usages in which the term refers either to a sum of money or other resources, or to the stewardship or accountability of the institution. In the plural, the term designates a fund group (*q.v.*).

FUND ACCOUNTS All accounts of assets, liabilities, revenues and expenditures (or receipts and disbursements), and balances necessary to set forth the operation and condition of a fund or a fund group.

FUND GROUP A group of funds of similar character, e.g., *current funds, loan funds, endowment and similar funds, annuity funds, life income funds, plant funds,* and *agency funds* (*qq.v.*).

FUNDS FUNCTIONING AS ENDOWMENT *See* QUASI-ENDOWMENT FUNDS.

FUNDS HELD IN TRUST BY OTHERS Funds held and administered, at the direction of the donor, by an outside trustee for the benefit of an institution or institutions.

GENERAL ADMINISTRATION EXPENDITURES Expenditures of the general executive and administrative offices having to do with the administration of the institution as a whole as contrasted with organizational units such as schools, colleges, instructional departments, and the library. Examples are: the governing board, president, vice-presidents, dean of faculties, business officer, and legal counsel.

GENERAL INSTITUTIONAL EXPENSES Expenses of offices and activities which apply to the institution as a whole except those for general administration and student services. Examples are: alumni office, external audit, catalogues, commencement, interest on loans for current operations, and fees for institutional memberships in organizations.

INCOME Restricted to net income, or revenues less expenses, of an operating unit within an institution, e.g., the student store, parking garage, and other auxiliary enterprises. The term also refers to the earnings on investments, e.g., income on investments. Cf. CURRENT FUNDS REVENUES.

INCOME STABILIZATION RESERVE The accumulated amounts set aside, by action of the governing board, from the income on investments to stabilize the amount of such income available for annual use.

INDEPENDENT AUDIT An audit performed by an independent auditor, in contrast to an audit performed by an internal auditor on the institution's staff. In publicly controlled institutions, an independent auditor may be an official of the governmental body controlling the institution but independent of the executive officer of the educational institution. *See* AUDIT.

INSTRUCTION AND DEPARTMENTAL RESEARCH EXPENDITURES Expenditures of instructional departments, including salaries, office expense and equipment, laboratory expense and equipment, and other expenses. The term includes research not separately organized or separately budgeted, but excludes *sponsored research* and *other separately budgeted research* (*qq.v.*).

INTERNAL AUDIT   An audit made on a continuous basis by persons on the staff of the business office. *See* AUDIT and INDEPENDENT AUDIT.

INVESTMENT IN PLANT   A subgroup of the plant funds accounts in which is shown the total carrying, or book, value of all plant properties and facilities except those real properties that are the investment of endowment and similar funds.

LIFE INCOME AGREEMENT   An agreement whereby money or other property is made available to an institution on the condition that the institution bind itself to pay periodically to the donor or other designated individual(s) the income earned by the assets donated to the institution for the lifetime of the donor or of the designated individual(s). If the institution is obligated to pay stipulated amounts rather than only the income actually earned by the assets, the term *annuity agreement* (*q.v.*) should be used.

LIVING TRUST AGREEMENT   *See* LIFE INCOME AGREEMENT.

LOAN FUNDS   Funds to be loaned to students, faculty, or staff. When both principal and interest on the loans granted are loanable, they are included in the Loan Funds group. If only the income from a fund is loanable, the principal is included in the Endowment Funds group, while the cumulative income constitutes the loan fund.

MERGED INVESTMENTS   *See* POOLED INVESTMENTS.

NET INVESTMENT IN PLANT   The equity account in the *Investment in Plant* subgroup of the Plant Funds accounts which shows the amount of institutional funds expended for plant assets, excluding any indebtedness against the assets.

OBJECT CLASSIFICATION   A method of classifying expenditures according to that which is received in return for the expenditures, e.g., personal services, printing and stationery, travel, communications, food, fuel, utilities, repairs, and equipment.

ORGANIZED ACTIVITIES RELATED TO EDUCATIONAL DEPARTMENTS   Entities which exist to provide an instructional or laboratory experience for students and which incidentally create goods or services that may be sold on the campus or to the general public. In the course of providing the incidental goods or services, expenditures are incurred in addition to those necessary solely for the educational benefit of the students.

ORGANIZED RESEARCH   *See* SPONSORED RESEARCH.

OTHER SEPARATELY BUDGETED RESEARCH   Research divisions and activities, such as research bureaus, research institutes, and experiment stations, as distinguished from *sponsored research* (*q.v.*). The term excludes research carried on as part of the regular instructional services which is classified as *instruction and departmental research* (*q.v.*).

OTHER SPONSORED PROGRAMS   Activities, other than research, performed in accordance with the conditions of agreements with governmental agencies or other outside organizations or persons to conduct programs of specified scope. Such agreements may be made on the basis of a cost or fixed-price basis or on the basis of grants accepted by an institution subject to certain terms and conditions. Examples are: training grants, workshops, short courses, other types of special instructional programs, and educational undertakings in foreign countries.

PLANT   The physical property owned by an institution and used for institutional purposes, i.e., land, buildings, improvements other than buildings, and equipment (including library books, collections, and animals). Cf. AUXILIARY ENTERPRISES PLANT. The term does not include real estate properties which are the investment of endowment and similar funds.

POOLED INVESTMENTS   Fund assets pooled or consolidated for investment purposes.

QUASI-ENDOWMENT FUNDS   Funds which the governing board of an institution, rather than a donor or other outside agency, has determined are to be retained and invested. The term *funds functioning as endowment* may also be used to designate funds. The governing board has the right to decide at any time to expend the principal of such funds.

RECEIPTS   Generally, cash received. In institutional accounting it refers primarily to additions to the balances of the funds in all fund groups except the Current Funds group, where the term *revenues (q.v.)* is used.

RENEWAL AND REPLACEMENT FUNDS   Funds specified by external sources or designated by governing boards to be used for the renewal and replacement of institutional plant assets. Reported either in a separately balanced subgroup of the Plant Funds group or in a clearly identified equity account in the Unexpended Plant Funds subgroup of plant funds.

RESTRICTED CURRENT FUNDS   Funds expendable for operating purposes but restricted by an outside agency or person as to use, as distinguished from *unrestricted current funds (q.v.)*, which are available for any current purpose.

RESTRICTED FUNDS   Funds restricted by outside agencies or persons as to use. Such funds are to be contrasted with funds over which the institution has complete control and freedom as to use.

RETIREMENT ALLOWANCES   Sums paid by an institution to employees who have been retired from active service or to their dependents; synonymous with *pensions*.

RETIREMENT OF INDEBTEDNESS FUNDS   Funds specified by external sources or designated by governing boards to be used to meet debt service charges and the retirement of indebtedness on institutional plant assets. Reported either in a separately balanced subgroup of the Plant Funds group or in a clearly identified equity account in the Unexpended Plant Funds subgroup of plant funds.

REVENUES   Revenue results from: the rendering of services and is measured by the charge made therefor to students, sponsors, and others; gains from the sale or exchange of current fund assets; interest and dividends earned on investments; sale of goods; and other increases arising from or for the support of current fund operations, for example, gifts, gifts applied, and appropriations.

Sales and Services of Educational Departments   The incidental income of educational departments resulting from services performed, sales of publications, and similar activities. If such revenues are of major magnitude they may be reported under a separate title identifying the source of revenues.

Scholarships   Financial assistance usually to undergraduate students on the basis of scholastic achievement and financial need. Recipients of scholarships are not required to render service to the institution as a consideration of their awards, nor are they required to repay them. Cf. Fellowships.

Service Department   An entity which provides a service to the various divisions of an institution, which service might be purchased from commercial sources, but which, for reasons of convenience, cost, or control, is more effectively provided through a unit of the institution. Charges to users are determined by the costs of the services rendered.

Sponsored Research   Research activities performed in accordance with the conditions of agreements with governmental agencies or other outside organizations or persons to conduct research of specified scope. Such agreements may be made on a cost or fixed-price basis, or on the basis of gifts or grants accepted by the institution subject to certain terms and conditions. Cf. Other Separately Budgeted Research and Other Sponsored Programs.

Student Tuition and Fees   Matriculation, tuition, laboratory, and other fees, paid by or for students, for educational services. The term does not include fees collected specifically for allocation to student publications, intercollegiate athletics, and similar activities, nor charges for services by the student hospital, college union, residence halls, dining halls, and other auxiliary enterprises. The term also excludes any fees assessed against students for debt service, building funds, or purposes other than educational services.

Surplus   See Unallocated Balance of Unrestricted Current Funds.

Term Endowment Funds   Funds which donors or other outside agencies, by the terms of the instruments of gift, have provided are to be released from inviolability to permit all or parts of them to be expended upon the happening of a particular event or the passage of a stated period of time.

Transfers   The identification of the authorization by a governing board of a specific change in the use of funds, and the moving of their assets, liabilities, and balances from one fund group to another: e.g., unallocated current funds transferred to plant funds; unallocated current funds transferred to loan funds; and, other funds or portions of balances of fund groups transferred to fund groups that encompass the newly authorized uses.

UNALLOCATED BALANCE OF UNRESTRICTED CURRENT FUNDS That part of the balance of unrestricted current funds that has not been set aside for any specific purpose. It is the free and unassigned balance of unrestricted current funds available for allocation to future operating purposes or for other uses as designated by the governing board. Synonymous with the term *surplus* in commercial accounting, which is inappropriate in institutional accounting.

UNALLOCATED REVENUES The title of an account established for budgetary control, to which is credited the excess of the estimated current funds revenues over estimated current funds expenditures as shown by the approved budget. Synonymous with *unassigned balance* and *unallocated budget balance*.

UNEXPENDED PLANT FUNDS Funds specified by external sources or designated by governing boards for the acquisition or construction of physical properties to be used for institutional purposes.

UNREALIZED REVENUES An account set up for budgetary control to which are charged the total estimated current funds revenues as shown by the approved budget, and to which are credited the actual revenues. The term *estimated revenues* may be used for this account.

UNRESTRICTED CURRENT FUNDS Unrestricted operating funds which are available for any current purpose, as distinguished from *restricted current funds* (*qq.v.*).

WORKING CAPITAL The portion of the balance of unrestricted current funds set aside as a reserve against that part of the unrestricted current funds assets that have been utilized to finance receivables, inventories, and similar items and thus are not available for allocation to other uses.

WORKING SCHOLARSHIPS Financial assistance to students requiring the performance of service to the institution as a consideration of the award. Specific types are described by appropriate terms, e.g., *teaching fellowships, graduate assistantships, research fellowships*.

Appendix D

Depreciation and
Renewal and Replacement
of Plant Assets

Purpose of Depreciation Accounting

A review of the purposes of depreciation accounting will reveal that the principles applicable to commercial accounting do not pertain to college and university accounting.

Depreciation accounting in profit-seeking enterprises is the attempt to allocate the cost of a fixed asset having a limited life to each of the accounting periods which benefit from its use. Depreciation accounting is based on the assumption that no cost is incurred at the time the asset is acquired or constructed, but rather that the cost results from use, the passage of time, changes in technology, or exhaustion of the asset. There is a loss in value of the asset, and this loss affects the equity of the owning organization. Depreciation accounting in commercial enterprises is closely related to accounting for profits, taxation, determination of earnings available for distribution as dividends, negotiation of long-term loans, the purchase or sale of a business enterprise, determination of the limitations of capitalization, and the current commercial value of a going concern.

Educational institutions are not profit-seeking enterprises; in almost all instances, neither their income nor their property is subject to tax. Consequently, the primary purposes of depreciation accounting for commercial enterprises are not present in colleges and universities.

The contrast between depreciation accounting in commercial enterprises and in educational institutions may be clarified by emphasizing the stewardship aspects of fund accounting. Through its financial statements a college or university seeks to disclose the funds entrusted to it and the uses made of such funds, by careful segregation into separate fund groups, according to the purposes specified by or inherent in the fund source. Accordingly, funds intended to provide plant facilities for the institution are plant funds and are reported as additions to unexpended plant funds. As the funds are applied to this purpose, they are added to plant investment. The plant accounting cycle is thus completed by virtue of the use or application of plant funds to the plant program which the donor or other fund source specified.

Carrying further the contrast between commercial and educational financing, the college or university counterpart of the profit and loss statement is the Statement of Current Funds Revenues, Expenditures, and Transfers. Revenues flowing in as current income represent funds available for, and in some instances restricted to, current operating purposes. The expenditures reflected in this statement describe the operating purposes to which the available current operating funds have been applied, thus reflecting discharge of the institutional stewardship of entrusted funds. In this context, it would be inappropriate and confusing to purport to show that a portion of operating funds is being diverted from that used to reduce the carrying value, in the plant funds, of plant facilities previously and properly acquired from funds restricted for plant acquisitions. To complete this example, it may be noted that current funds operations ordinarily include the acquisition of normal equipment items, so that reported expenditures include such purchases.

Institutional financial statements may perhaps be better understood if viewed as parallel to commercial statements of source and application of funds, with the college or university presenting separate statements of source and application of funds for plant, for current operations, and for each of the other fund groups.

Depreciation Accounting in Educational Institutions

Although some educational institutions state that they follow the principles of depreciation accounting and include such charges in their statements of current operations, the fact is that they almost invariably are concerned with, and are providing for, the future renewal, replacement, or expansion of their plant assets. This is an erroneous application of the term "depreciation" as generally accepted in commercial enterprises. When this distinction is understood, it is clear that the process in colleges and universities is, in fact, the setting aside of unrestricted current funds for plant purposes by transfers from current funds to plant funds.

The question of accounting for depreciation and for provisions for renewals and replacements of the physical plant assets of colleges and universities is closely related to the types of property held by such institutions. These are: (1) educational plant, including buildings and equipment used primarily for instruction and research, for administrative purposes, and for service operations, such as power plants, shops, and storage facilities; (2) plant used for revenue-producing auxiliary enterprises, such as residence and dining halls; and (3) property that represents the investment of endowment funds.

EDUCATIONAL PLANT

Educational institutions, unlike profit-seeking enterprises, are not expected to obtain the necessary financial resources to replace educational plant assets exclusively from those who are benefiting most directly from their use. Society has recognized the need to make these facilities and services available to those who can benefit from them. Colleges and universities obtain much of their financing for educational facilities from such sources as philanthropy and governmental appropriations, and it is expected that the same sources will continue to provide funds for the renewal, replacement, and expansion of these facilities.

If the financial program of an institution provides for setting aside current funds revenues for the renewal, replacement, and expansion of educational plant assets, the amount of such provision should be reported under Transfers in the Statement of Current Funds Revenues, Expenditures, and Transfers. If previously accumulated current funds are used for this purpose, the provision should be shown as a deduction in the Statement of Changes in Fund Balances—Unrestricted Current Funds. In both cases, an equivalent amount of cash or other liquid assets should be transferred from current funds to the plant funds and reported in the subsection Funds for Renewals and Replacements.

AUXILIARY ENTERPRISE PLANT

The operation of auxiliary enterprises is supplementary to the primary educational functions of a college or university. These activities are similar in some respects to commercial enterprises. Provisions may be made in the budgets of auxiliary enterprises for renewals and replacements. They should, in such instances, be identified as "Provisions for Renewals and Replacements" and reported under this caption in the schedules of current expenditures of the appropriate enterprises. Cash or liquid assets should be transferred from current funds to the plant funds subsection Funds for Renewals and Replacements. This recommended treatment of providing for renewals and replacements should not be confused with depreciation accounting as previously discussed.

ENDOWMENT FUNDS PROPERTIES

Real estate properties, except land, held as the investment of endowment funds must be depreciated in order to give reasonable protection to the principal of the funds so invested, and to reflect properly the net income from such investments.

Funded reserves for the amount of depreciation should be established by the transfer of cash from the income of the properties or, if that income is not sufficient, cash or other liquid assets from other funds.

The accumulated depreciation should be carried in the accounts of the Endowment and Similar Funds group and reported as a deduction from the asset value of the properties.

Summary

1. The principles of depreciation accounting essential to proper accounting and financial reporting in commercial and business organizations do not apply to nonprofit educational institutions.

2. Some colleges and universities employ a procedure to which the term "depreciation accounting" is applied, but which is, in reality, the provision of funds for the future renewal, replacement, or expansion of plant facilities. The distinction between depreciation accounting and the providing for renewal, replacement, and expansion of plant assets should be clearly recognized so that the practices employed by educational institutions and the ensuing transactions can be properly identified, understood, classified, and reported.

3. If the financial program of an educational institution provides for setting aside funds for the renewal, replacement, or expansion of educational plant assets, the process should be recognized as such, and not be considered as depreciation accounting.

If current funds revenues are used in this manner, the provision should be shown at the end of the Statement of Current Funds Revenues, Expenditures, and Transfers as a Transfer to Plant Funds for Renewals and Replacements. If current funds balances from prior periods are used for this purpose, the provision should be shown as a deduction in the Statement of Changes in Fund Balances—Unrestricted Current Funds. Cash or other liquid assets are transferred to plant funds and show in the Funds for Renewals and Replacements subgroup.

4. Depreciation accounting as found in commercial and business organizations is not recommended for auxiliary enterprises plant. If the financial program of an institution provides for setting aside funds from the income of auxiliary enterprises for the replacement of plant facilities and assets, such provisions may be based on equivalent depreciation amounts computed in accordance with general commercial practices; or, they may be based on the anticipated replacement cost of the assets, adjusted in accordance with a recognized price index. Such provisions should be identified as such, and

not as depreciation. The amounts should be shown in the Statement of Changes in Fund Balances—Funds for Renewals and Replacements. Cash or other liquid assets are transferred from current to plant funds.

5. Depreciation concepts and depreciation accounting should be followed in accounting for real properties that are the investments of endowment funds. Funded reserves for the accumulated depreciation charges should be established from the income of the properties, or from other funds, and carried in the accounts for Endowment Funds and Similar Funds. The asset value of properties should be reported net of the amount of such depreciation reserves.

Bibliography

ARNETT, TREVOR. *College and University Finance.* New York: General Education Board, 1922.

AYERS, ARCHIE R., and RUSSELL, JOHN E. *Internal Structure, Organization and Administration of Institutions of Higher Education.* U.S. Office of Education Bulletin 1962, No. 9. Washington: Government Printing Office, 1962.

BABBIDGE, HOMER D., JR., and ROSENZWEIG, R. M. *The Federal Interest in Higher Education.* New York: McGraw-Hill Book Co., 1962.

BAUER, RONALD C. *Cases in College Administration.* New York: Bureau of Publications, Teachers College, Columbia University, 1955.

BELL, BORIS C. *Administration and Operation of the College Union.* Ithaca, N.Y.: Cornell University, 1965.

BLACKWELL, THOMAS E. *College and University Administration.* New York: Center for Applied Research in Education, Inc., 1966.

———. *College Law: A Guide for Administrators.* Washington: American Council on Education, 1961.

BRUMBAUGH, A. J. *State-wide Planning and Coordination of Higher Education.* Atlanta, Ga.: Southern Regional Education Board, 1963.

BURNS, GERALD P. *Administrators in Higher Education.* New York: Harper & Row, 1962.

———. *Trustees in Higher Education.* New York: Independent College Funds of America, 1966.

CADMUS, BRADFORD. *Operational Auditing Handbook.* New York: Institute of Internal Auditors, 1964.

CAFFREY, JOHN G., and MOSMANN, CHARLES J. *Computers on Campus.* Washington: American Council on Education, 1967.

CHAMBERS, M. M. *The Colleges and the Courts, 1962–1966.* Danville, Ill.: Interstate Printers & Publishers, 1967.

———. *The Colleges and the Courts Since 1950.* Danville, Ill.: Interstate Printers & Publishers, 1964.

———. *Financing Higher Education.* New York: Center for Applied Research in Education, 1963.

[291]

CORSON, JOHN J. *The Governance of Colleges and Universities*. New York: McGraw-Hill Book Co., 1960.

CURTI, MERLE, and NASH, RODERICK. *Philanthropy in the Shaping of American Higher Education*. New Brunswick, N.J.: Rutgers University Press, 1965.

CUTLIP, SCOTT M. *Fund Raising in the United States*. New Brunswick, N.J.: Rutgers University Press, 1965.

DE LONG, C. C. *A History of the National Federation of College and University Business Officers Association*. Urbana, Ill.: University of Illinois, 1963.

DICKASON, DONALD E. *A Plan of Position Classification for Colleges and Universities*. Urbana, Ill.: College and University Personnel Association, 1960.

GIBSON, RAYMOND C. *The Challenge of Leadership in Higher Education*. Dubuque, Iowa: William C. Brown Co., 1964.

GLAZE, THOMAS E. *Business Administration for Colleges and Universities*. Baton Rouge, La.: Louisiana State University Press, 1962.

GREENOUGH, WILLIAM C., and KING, FRANCIS P. *Retirement and Insurance Plans in American Colleges*. New York: Columbia University Press, 1959.

HANSON, ABEL A. *Guides to Successful Fund Raising*. New York: Bureau of Publications, Teachers College, Columbia University, 1961.

HARKNESS, CHARLES A. *College Staff Personnel Administration*. Urbana, Ill.: College and University Personnel Association, 1965.

HARRIS, SEYMOUR E. *Higher Education: Resources and Finance*. New York: McGraw-Hill Book Co., 1962.

HENDERSON, ALGO D. *Policies and Practices in Higher Education*. New York: Harper & Bros., 1960.

HOWES, RAYMOND F. (ed.) *Toward Better Preparation of College and University Administrators*. Washington: Association for Higher Education, NEA, 1964.

HUNGATE, THAD L. *Management in Higher Education*. New York: Bureau of Publications, Teachers College, Columbia University, 1964.

INGRAHAM, MARK H. *The Outer Fringe: Faculty Benefits Other Than Annuities and Insurance*. Madison, Wis.: University of Wisconsin Press, 1965.

JOHN PRICE JONES, INC. *American Philanthropy for Higher Education*. New York: John Price Jones, Inc., 1965.

KEEZER, DEXTER M. *Financing Higher Education, 1960–1970*. New York: McGraw-Hill Book Co., 1959.

KNAUTH, E. FREDERIC. *The College Business Manager*. New York: New York University Press, 1955.

KNORR, OWEN A. (ed.) *Long-Range Planning in Higher Education*. Boulder, Colo.: Western Interstate Commission for Higher Education, 1965.

KOHLER, ERIC L. *A Dictionary for Accountants*. 3d. ed. Englewood Cliffs, N.J.: Prentice Hall, 1963.

LEWIS, MARIANA O. *The Foundation Directory*. 3d. ed. New York: Russell Sage Foundation, 1967.

MARTING, ELIZABETH, and FINLEY, ROBERT E. (eds.) *The Financial Manager's Job*. New York: American Management Association, 1964.

MILLER, JAMES L. *State Budgeting for Higher Education*. Ann Arbor, Mich.: Institute of Public Administration, University of Michigan, 1964.

MILLETT, JOHN D. *The Academic Community*. New York: McGraw-Hill Book Co., 1962.

————. *Financing Higher Education in the United States*. New York: Columbia University Press, 1952.

MOREY, LLOYD. *University and College Accounting*. New York: John Wiley & Sons, 1930.

NANCE, PAUL K. *Business Management Practices in Selected Colleges and Universities*. Office of Education Bulletin 1966, No. 12. Washington: Government Printing Office, 1966.

NANCE, PAUL K.; ROBBINS, LESLIE; and CAIN, J. HARVEY. *Guide to College and University Business Management*. Office of Education Bulletin 1965, No. 30. Washington: Government Printing Office, 1965.

NATIONAL ASSOCIATION OF EDUCATIONAL BUYERS. *Purchasing for Educational Institutions*. New York: Bureau of Publications, Teachers College, Columbia University, 1961.

NATIONAL ASSOCIATION OF PHYSICAL PLANT ADMINISTRATORS OF UNIVERSITIES AND COLLEGES. *Fundamentals of Physical Plant Management, Planning, and Construction*. Raleigh, N.C.: The Association, 1966.

NATIONAL COMMITTEE ON THE PREPARATION OF A MANUAL ON COLLEGE AND UNIVERSITY BUSINESS ADMINISTRATION. *College and University Business Administration. Vols. I and II*. Washington: American Council on Education, 1952, 1955.

ORLANS, HAROLD. *The Effects of Federal Programs on Higher Education*. Washington: Brookings Institution, 1962.

POLLARD, JOHN A. *Fund-Raising for Higher Education*. New York: Harper & Bros., 1958.

RIKER, HAROLD C. *College Students Live Here*. New York: Educational Facilities Laboratories, Inc., 1961.

RIVLIN, ALICE M. *Role of the Federal Government in Financing Higher Education*. Washington: Brookings Institution, 1961.

ROURKE, FRANCIS E., and BROOKS, GLENN E. *The Managerial Revolution in Higher Education.* Baltimore, Md.: Johns Hopkins Press, 1966.

RUSSELL, JOHN DALE. *The Finance of Higher Education.* Rev. ed. Chicago, Ill.: University of Chicago Press, 1954.

RUSSELL, JOHN DALE, and DOI, JAMES. *Manual for Studies in Space Utilization in Colleges and Universities.* Athens, Ohio: Ohio University, 1957.

SCHEPS, CLARENCE. *Accounting for Colleges and Universities.* Baton Rouge, La.: Louisiana State University Press, 1949.

STANFORD, EDWARD V. *A Guide to Catholic College Administration.* Westminster, Md.: Newman Press, 1965.

STRICKLAND, STEPHEN (ed.). *Sponsored Research in American Universities and Colleges.* Washington: American Council on Education, 1968.

SWANSON, JOHN E.; ARDEN, WESLEY; and STILL, HOMER E., JR., *Financial Analysis of Current Operations of Colleges and Universities.* Ann Arbor, Mich.: Institute of Public Administration, 1966.

TICKTON, SIDNEY G. *Needed: A Ten Year College Budget.* New York: Fund for the Advancement of Education, 1961.

WELLS, HARRY L. *Higher Education Is Serious Business.* New York: Harper & Bros., 1953.

WILLIAMS, HARRY. *Planning for Effective Resource Allocation in Universities.* Washington: American Council on Education, 1966.

WILSON, LOGAN (ed.). *Emerging Patterns in American Higher Education.* Washington: American Council on Education, 1965.

WOODBURNE, LLOYD S. *Principles of College and University Administration.* Palo Alto, Calif.: Stanford University Press, 1958.

Periodicals

American Education

American School and University

College Management

College and University Business

Educational Record

Higher Education and National Affairs

Institutional Investor

School Management

Index

AMERICAN COUNCIL ON EDUCATION
LOGAN WILSON, *President*

The American Council on Education, founded in 1918, is a *council* of educational organizations and institutions. Its purpose is to advance education and educational methods through comprehensive voluntary and cooperative action on the part of American educational associations, organizations, and institutions.